MASTERS OF MATERIAL CULTURE

W9-BJV-337

Warren E. Roberts was born and raised in Maine. After his college career was interrupted by four years in the U.S. Army ski troops during World War II, he completed his B.A. at Reed College. He then earned his M.A. and Ph.D. degrees from Indiana University, the latter degree being the first Ph.D. in Folklore ever awarded in the United States. His doctoral dissertation was awarded the Chicago Folklore Prize. Since 1949 Dr. Roberts has taught courses in folklore and folklife research at Indiana University, where he is presently Professor of Folklore.

In the 1950s, Dr. Roberts published three books and a number of articles on international aspects of folktale research. After spending a year in Norway as a Fulbright Research Fellow in 1959-60, he began to concentrate on folklife research and material culture, carrying out extensive fieldwork in southern Indiana and expanding the horizons of the department at Indiana University. In this area of study he has published a book on the log buildings of southern Indiana and numerous articles. In addition to being a Fulbright Fellow, Dr. Roberts was also a John Simon Guggenheim Fellow.

Viewpoints on Folklife
Looking at the Overlooked

American Material Culture and Folklife

Simon J. Bronner, Series Editor

Associate Professor of Folklore and American Studies
The Pennsylvania State University at Harrisburg

Other Titles in This Series

Viewpoints on Folklife
Looking at the Overlooked

by
Warren E. Roberts

UMI Research Press

Ann Arbor / London

398.0973
R544v

PACKARD LIBRARY

SEP 0 5 1989

THE COLUMBUS COLLEGE OF ART AND DESIGN

Copyright © 1988
Warren Everett Roberts
All rights reserved

Produced and distributed by
UMI Research Press
an imprint of
University Microfilms, Inc.
Ann Arbor, Michigan 48106

Library of Congress Cataloging in Publication Data

Roberts, Warren E. (Warren Everett), 1924-
   Viewpoints on folklife : looking at the overlooked / by Warren E.
Roberts.
        p. cm.—(American material culture and folklife. Masters
of material culture)
   Includes bibliographies and index.
   ISBN 0-8357-1849-2 (alk. paper)
      1. Folklore—United States.   2. Material culture—United States.
3. United States—Social life and customs.   4. Industries.
Primitive—United States.   I. Title.   II. Series.
GR105.R63   1987
398'.0973—dc19   87-22710
                                                             CIP

British library CIP data is available.

Contents

Tools of the Trades

Overlooked Aspects of Folk Architecture

Foreword

It is safe to say that when the American Folklore Society was founded in 1888, its founders were primarily interested in verbal lore and none of them had been specifically trained as a folklorist. No such discipline existed; instead they were students of literature, anthropologists, and antiquarians whose imaginations allowed them to see and to seriously consider the verbal products of the folk—whoever they were—as ancillary to their major interests and worthy of examination. As a result, those of the founders who had institutional connections were able to incorporate academic courses dealing with the verbal folk arts into their curricula. Although it took over half a century, this led eventually to the establishment of departments primarily devoted to folklore at Indiana University, the University of California at Los Angeles, the University of Texas, the University of Pennsylvania, and still later at the Memorial University at St. John's, Newfoundland.

Indiana University was the first of these institutions to establish an actual degree in the subject of folklore, a Doctor of Philosophy degree (followed shortly thereafter by a Master's degree and a few years later by a Bachelor's degree). The moving force for the establishment of the Department of Folklore at Indiana University was Professor Stith Thompson, himself a direct descendant of the founders of the American Folklore Society, for he had been a student at Harvard University of George Lyman Kittredge who, in turn, had been a student and colleague of Francis James Child, a founder and first president of the Society. An old-style professor of English literature, Thompson's interests were manifold, and he published articles and books on topics ranging from Old and Middle English literature through Shakespeare and some Victorian authors as well as compiled a widely used anthology of world literature and even a composition handbook. But he always had as a central interest the folktale, an interest which first evidenced itself with a study of American Indian folktales and which culminated in the massive and magisterial *Motif-Index of Folk*

Literature and in the definitive book about folktales as a genre: *The Folktale.* It was this scholar who lured Warren Roberts to Indiana University.

When Warren arrived at Indiana University, there was actually only an interdepartmental program chaired by Professor Thompson. Courses in folklore were given in various departments—English (primarily), German, Spanish, French, Anthropology, and in the infant Comparative Literature program. Warren took advantage of these courses and in many ways can be considered to be the person who showed Stith Thompson and the administration of Indiana University that folklore could be an independent area of study. He was, of course, preceded by William Hugh Jansen and Ernest Baughman, accompanied by his close friend Dov Noy, and followed immediately by such scholars as Leonard Roberts and Hiroko Ikeda. But Warren was the first student to receive a Ph.D. in folklore as distinct from a combined degree with some other department in the program.

Although it was most unusual at that time for Indiana University to hire its own products, Warren Roberts was immediately hired by the Department of English where he had been teaching as a graduate student. He continued to teach conventional English courses with an occasional introductory folklore course thrown in, but on Stith Thompson's retirement he was assigned the two-semester graduate seminar on the folktale and it seemed inevitable that he would center his scholarly attention upon the same area as had his mentor, for not only was the folktale seminar a requirement for folklore majors, its was also a very popular course, as much so under Warren Roberts' tutelage as it had been under Thompson's.

But Warren had a hobby: woodworking. He was, and is, especially adept at constructing furniture after antique patterns and especially curious about the methods and tools employed to make such furniture by the cabinetmakers of old. This, when coupled with a Fulbright grant to study in Norway during the academic year 1959–60, changed his scholarly career and also added a new dimension to folklore studies in the United States.

The Scandinavians, especially the Norwegians and the Swedes, have a tradition dating back to the early decades of the nineteenth century of open-air museums which are research and teaching institutions as well as display areas. Though the disciplines taught and employed by the staffs of the open-air museums are not there considered to be a part of folklore even today, they are seen as sister disciplines and there is close cooperation between the open-air museums, folklore departments and institutes, and departments of ethnology. Though officially attached to the Institutt for Folkeminnevidskap in Oslo, Warren became more and more intrigued by the work being done at Bygdøy, Oslo's open-air museum, where he had a close friend whom he met in Bloomington in 1953, Professor Asbjørn Nesheim, the museum's curator of Lapp culture and language. Here Warren saw a way to combine his hobby with his scholarly interests and saw a way to make a significant contribution to the study of folklore. He could apply the techniques and methods employed for the study of verbal lore to the study of material artifacts and the ways in which craftsmen transmitted their skills.

His return to Indiana from Norway in the fall of 1960 came at an opportune time. The concept of folklore was expanding. During the first decades of the twentieth century the verbal lore which was the focus of attention of the founding fathers of the American Folklore Society had been subjected to analysis by the historic-geographic method, a technique descended from the study of medieval manuscripts. It was fruitful, and it greatly enlarged the body of information that existed for folktales, ballads, proverbs, riddles, and the like, but it gave little information about the transmitters of the lore. In the late 1950s and early 1960s, the emphasis shifted from the lore itself to what the lore told about the transmitters and their cultures. This shift greatly expanded the materials felt to be appropriate for study by folklorists. At the same time, the notion of who the folk are expanded far beyond the concepts held by pioneer folklorists to include members of virtually any coherent group. The constant remained tradition, in other words, the informal transmission of information from person to person and generation to generation whether by word of mouth or by demonstration.

The ideas Warren had conceived while in Norway suited this new folkloristic milieu admirably. The craftsmen whose products and methods interested him were highly skilled, not simply the uneducated masses who had been the object of the attention of earlier folklorists. But they did constitute a series of coherent groups. As a consequence, almost immediately upon his return to Indiana, Warren was able to introduce a new course into the curriculum of the Department of Folklore, "Folk Art, Craft, and Architecture," thus expanding the horizons of the department and foreshadowing the direction which folklore studies were to take in the 1970s and 1980s.

In addition to introducing a new subject area into the folklore curriculum, Warren also persuaded the university of the importance of developing an open-air museum. As he points out in the section of this volume entitled "An Autobiographical Note, or How Does One Become a Folklife Researcher?," the next two decades of his life were devoted to searching out appropriate nineteenth-century Indiana buildings for such a museum. Not only did he find many buildings, he physically aided in their disassembly and their movement to university property. This was a labor of love and vision and self-abnegation. Unfortunately, funds ran out, many of the staunchest supporters of the project retired, and the buildings remain in their disassembled state with no immediate prospects for reassembly. But despite the fact that the museum plans are on hold and that the time-consuming labors involved with this search-and-save operation prevented Warren from contributing to scholarly knowledge by immediate publication, the project was a hands-on learning experience that made his teaching invaluable and this present volume possible.

The students, both graduate and undergraduate, whom Warren has introduced to the study of folklife, especially its material culture aspect, have been legion. He now has disciples, most of whose dissertations he directed, teaching or otherwise disseminating information about folklife throughout North America. Some are teaching conventional academic courses often modelled on his; others are employed by state and local folk arts and folklife commissions. Thus Warren's influence has spread far beyond the bounds of conventional folklore departments and to the area of public service and to recognition by people unaware of folklore or folklife as academic disciplines.

Strangely, however, Warren has published articles about folklife and his special interests less frequently in conventional folklore journals than he has in journals published by societies and groups somewhat distant from folklore. Only four of the articles included in this present volume were published in the usual folklore journals; another three were published in a volume devoted to folklore and folklife and in a festschrift for the late Richard M. Dorson; the balance, except for one unpublished article, appeared in nonfolkloristic journals, the bulk in the *Chronicle* of the Early American Industries Association: hardly a journal perused on a regular basis by the average member of the American Folklore Society.

The articles which appeared in the EAIA *Chronicle* deal primarily with material objects, and they range from the very practical "Wood Screws as an Aid to Dating Wooden Artifacts" to the highly speculative "Word Origins and Tools." The former shows that an examination of screws, and by implication other fasteners, used in buildings, cabinets, and tools can be of inestimable value in dating the age of the object in question. The latter is an attempt to explain the spellings, origins, and significance of the words "fillister," "beetle-browed," "try"—as in "try-Plane"—and "dido"—as in "to cut didoes." In this article Warren points out that etymologists could be more exact if they had, in those instances in particular, more knowledge of tools, carpentry, and dialects.

Indeed, Warren's interest in etymology can be traced through many if not all of the articles published in *Viewpoints on Folklife: Looking at the Overlooked.* The most blatant example of course is "Hoosier and Family Names." His justification for a consideration of word- and name-origins as a part of the study of folklife is that, as etymologists and linguists have long recognized, the speakers of any language recreate and respell words and names, even redefine words and names, in accordance with what they believe are their origins and their significance. In addition, of course, many family names and nicknames derive from trades and the products of trades. They are part of the folk perspective and contribute to our understanding of folklife.

Essentially, of course, the etymologies which Warren presents in his articles are folk or popular etymologies, the kind of thing which turns "cole slaw" into "cold slaw," "Westerveldt" into "Westerville," and, to use one of Warren's examples, "filletster" into "fillister." At best, etymology is an inexact science if it can be called a science at all. The study of popular etymology depends as much upon imagination as it does upon a knowledge of linguistics, and it often demands knowledge of dialects and geography. As a consequence, Warren has delved into the work being done by the compilers of linguistic and cultural atlases and has shown in his article "Planemaking in the United States: The Cartography of a Craft" that recognition of the distribution of an artifact and the words and names appropriate to it contributes significantly to our knowledge of folklife.

Indeed, "Planemaking in the United States: The Cartography of a Craft" illustrates the marriage of Warren's original concern with verbal lore as it relates to folktales to verbal lore as it relates to material culture. It also shows the effect of his initial training in the historic-geographic method and the fact that it can be an important tool for the study of folklife. Hints of Warren's basic training in the study of the folktale and the ballad can be found in every article published in this present volume. Underlying all of this, however, is his concern with the transmitters of the lore whether by word of mouth or by demonstration. He clearly shows that a study of material objects can reveal more about ways of life and human relationships than has heretofore been realized, and that to look at the overlooked and to rely upon what one sees rather than upon what one reads is essential if we are to truly understand these relationships.

W. Edson Richmond
Emeritus Professor
English and Folklore
Indiana University
Bloomington, Indiana

Preface

This volume consists of collected essays, mostly articles published between 1971 and the present. A few of the essays have not previously been published. The essays revolve around the theme, "Looking at the Overlooked." I view my research which has been carried out over the years as an attempt—or a series of attempts—to throw light on a broad subject. This broad subject is folklife, a term I and others have used to refer to the way of life of the mass of humanity in Western Europe and the United States prior to the Industrial Revolution which instituted such drastic changes, as well as the ways in which that earlier way of life persisted in fragmented form after the Industrial Revolution.

It is sad but true that the great mass of humanity is simply overlooked when most people write or talk about the past and what life was like then. First of all, Benjamin Franklin correctly observed in 1787, "The great business of the continent [North America] is agriculture. For one artizan [sic] or merchant, I suppose we have at least a hundred farmers."[1] His statistics were reasonably accurate: 95 percent of the population did live on farms and most of those farms were of the small, self-sufficient type. Moreover, the same statistics applied for many years after Franklin made his generalization.

Yet countless writers make the same mistake. They assume that everyone in the past lived in mansions in cities. Witness an article, one of many that could be cited, published in the magazine *Antiques,* a magazine that, over the decades, has been a major spokesman for art historians and those with the art historian's perspective. The article is entitled "Entertaining in America in the Eighteenth Century," and that's all. Note the absence of qualifiers: "in America in the Eighteenth Century." The article is written by Louise Conway Belden, "a research associate at the Henry Francis Dupont Winterthur Museum" and contains statements such as,

> At the end of the century hostesses of moderate means used a single, footed, flat salver or a footed bowl called a *compotier* as a centerpiece. The salver held a cake; the *compotier* a compote of fruit, a dessert cream or fresh fruit. Sometimes hostesses used *compotiers* and salvers in pairs or in fours—in the center of the table or at the corners.[2]

How many of Franklin's hundred farmers is Belden talking about? They and their wives were surely far more familiar with simple pottery than they were with Belden's *compotiers*. And yet Belden, as so many writers have done, simply ignores the fact that she is writing about a tiny and unrepresentative sample of those who lived in America in the pre-industrial era.

It is this error and others equally bad that the proposed reprinted articles will attempt to redress in some small ways. The articles look at the overlooked or notice the neglected. The editor of *Pioneer America,* Milton Newton, Jr., once said of me, "He seems to specialize in pleasantly reexamining old assumptions that may have thrown us off from clear appreciation of historic material culture."[3]

Whether the question be, "Did early builders know so little about wood and were they so careless that they left house logs exposed to the weather to crack and decay?" or be it, "Were people who knew that hundreds of plants were fit to eat but that many more were poisonous unable to recognize that tomatoes were edible?" these essays and others I have written try to demonstrate that our ancestors who were farmers and their families living on small farms and growing, raising, or gathering most of what they needed, were pragmatic, intelligent, hard-working folk who transmitted quantities of knowledge and skills from one generation to the next. The essays try to diminish the misconceptions that our ancestors either were wealthy gentry living in mansions surrounded by servants or were brutish slaves to ignorance and superstition, huddling around tiny fires and staring into the surrounding darkness in hopeless dread.

Historic or traditional material culture is an amazingly wide field, but it is often broken down into folk art, folk crafts, and folk architecture. My essays cover some aspects of each of these three general topics. In most cases the approach can be categorized as broadly functional. That is to say, there is an attempt to understand why artifacts were made the way they were and why things were done the way they were. I have been convinced that such understanding is a first and major step in the study of folklife, the old, traditional way of life of the great mass of people who lived before the Industrial Revolution.

I have received much help with this volume for which I am deeply grateful. Simon Bronner has been most helpful with encouragement and wise editorial advice. Sarah Roberts, Thomas Kirkman, and David Schalliol are responsible for many of the illustrations. My deceased friend, Wallace Sullivan, accompanied me on most field trips and held one end of a measuring tape countless times as we investigated old buildings. Many students and friends have pointed out to me important buildings and artifacts. My family endured many inconveniences over the years when I left for field trips on short notice and returned later than anticipated and many vacation trips have been interrupted to visit inviting buildings and cemeteries. To all these, my grateful thanks.

Notes

1. Cited in *Antiques* (May 1977): 957.

2. *Antiques* (December 1986): 1240.

3. *Pioneer America* 10, no. 2 (December 1978): 4.

Introduction

An Autobiographical Note, or
How Does One Become a Folklife Researcher?

For most people there is a specific event in their lives which, at the time, seems rather unimportant but which, in retrospect, can be seen as pivotal. In my case, the event I now recognize as having decided my career was a class report I made as an undergraduate student. It was in the fall of 1946 and I was a student in a class in American literature taught by Prof. V.L.O. Chittick at Reed College in Portland, Oregon. Prof. Chittick had some interests in American folklore; indeed, he had published a slim volume entitled *Ring-Tailed Roarers*[1] which could be considered as on the fringes of folklore. He proposed a series of topics upon which students in his class could report. The topic "American Folksongs" appealed to me. I asked for and was assigned that topic.

The report I delivered in class was, I know, rather poor, but I read through several books—such as Carl Sandburg's *American Songbag*—and was delighted and intrigued to find that I actually knew some of these songs considered important enough to be granted the imprimatur of being printed in books! As a boy growing up in a small town in Maine I had heard other, older boys singing songs that I had learned; also, my mother loved to sing so I had learned some songs from her.

Reed College had—and still has—the requirement that a senior must write a thesis for the B.A. My fascination with folksongs lead me to approach another professor, William Alderson, who had studied under Bertrand Bronson, a leading ballad scholar of the day. It so happened that Prof. Alderson had recently persuaded the Reed College Library to buy a copy of F. J. Childs' *English and Scottish Popular Ballads*. Hence he suggested that I start reading through the five volumes in ten parts of this work. I did, and eventually produced an acceptable thesis entitled "Comic Elements in the English and Scottish Popular Ballads."

I had decided that I wanted to go on to graduate school so I consulted with Prof. Alderson as to where I might be able to study folklore. He listed the possibilities: Indiana University, the University of California at Berkeley, and the University of North Carolina at Chapel Hill. I wrote letters of inquiry to each of these institutions and received an encouraging reply only from Indiana University, so it was there I applied and was accepted.

Before long at Indiana University it was clear that folktales rather than folksongs were the things upon which to concentrate. The largest number of courses were, of course, taught by Stith Thompson and they all dealt with various aspects of the folktale. Other courses were indeed offered by W. Edson Richmond, George Herzog, and Ermenie Wheeler-Voegelin, but when it came time to write a dissertation, there was no question in my mind that it should be on some aspect of the folktale. With guidance from Stith Thompson I produced a historic-geographic study on a specific tale. The study was awarded the Chicago Folklore Prize for 1954. In a few years I enlarged the material and published it in Germany under the title *The Tale of the Kind and Unkind Girls* (Berlin: Walter de Gruyter & Co., 1958).

I stayed on at Indiana University teaching undergraduate courses in English composition and freshman literature in the English Department, but I also taught undergraduate folklore courses. After a few years, when Stith Thompson retired, I also taught a two-semester graduate seminar entitled "The Folktale."

When the time for my first sabbatical leave approached, I applied for and received a Fulbright Research Award to Norway. I left with my family in the fall of 1959 and spent nearly a full year working in the Norwegian Folklore Archives in Oslo.

I also visited the Norwegian National Folk Museum at Bygdøy near Oslo. These visits had a profound influence on me. It is no exaggeration to say that I went to Norway as a folktale scholar but that I returned to the United States as a folklife researcher, I was fascinated by the way that Norwegian scholars had studied the old way of life of the Norwegian countryside and had preserved buildings and other artifacts in the folk museums. I also believed that American folklorists had done virtually nothing to study and preserve the old way of life of the United States, since I was not fully aware at that time of the work being done by the Pennsylvania Folklife Society. I saw as a mission for myself trying to rectify this situation.

When I returned to Indiana University I continued to teach the same courses as before but in a short time added a graduate course entitled "Folk Art, Craft, and Architecture." After a few years I expanded this course to a two-semester sequence and developed an undergraduate course eventually called "Indiana Folklife." These are the courses I have taught most frequently in recent years.

Upon my return to Bloomington from Norway in 1960 I launched another project. I wanted to develop at Indiana University a folk museum that would represent the traditional ways of life of the rural population of southern Indiana. Most of my time and energy that was left over after teaching went into this museum project. I received encouragement and support from many university officials. Over a period of about fifteen years from the early 1960s to the late 1970s I visited many areas in southern Indiana looking for old buildings that could be acquired and which would be characteristic of the folk architecture of the region. With generous support from the university, I was able to acquire a number of structures: houses, a barn, a church, a country doctor's office, a covered bridge, as well as others. I had them moved to a tract of land on the outskirts of the campus. Unfortunately, the funds needed to establish and maintain the museum have never materialized despite devoted efforts by many people who recognized the potential value of the project; and so, the museum remains an unfulfilled dream.

Even while engaged in working for the museum, teaching was always my main concern. Far less time has been spent on the museum in the past decade and it has probably been a blessing in disguise, for a remarkable number of fine students has been studying at the Folklore Institute. It has been a deep source of gratification and pride that I have played some role in leading some of these students to concentrate their studies in folklife and material culture and have been able to assist them in several ways including helping with their dissertations.

Some, at least, of this autobiographical account is useful as a background for understanding aspects of the articles I have written. It is a truism in folklife research that items can only be properly understood in their cultural context, and something similar holds true for an artifact such as an article. It can be better understood when read within the overall context of the author's experience and development.

The articles on folk architecture included in this collection, for example, have been written as an outgrowth of my work with the proposed folk museum for southern Indiana. In some cases the connection is more direct than in others. "The Whitaker-Waggoner Log House from Morgan County, Indiana," for instance, was written as a result of the many days I spent in the fall of 1966 supervising the disassembling of the house and actually helping with the work. The paper embodying a description of the house was read at a conference held July 26–27, 1968, in Logan, Utah. An abstract of the paper was printed in a monograph published in 1969 and the complete paper was finally printed in 1976. The description of the house and the details of its construction are, of course, the direct consequence of the fact that the building was acquired for the museum and disassembled and moved to the proposed museum site.

But the paper also shows signs of an important theme in all my research and writing. In that article I state: "On the basis of the evidence now at hand, I am persuaded that, in nineteenth-century Indiana when a substantial hewn-log house was built as a permanent home, it was customary practice to cover the outside with siding of some sort, usually clapboards." This statement in much the same form was in the paper as read in 1968. It challenged the then-prevailing notion that log houses when built were not sided, but that siding was always a much later addition. At that time, however, I was taking what I have since come to call a "functional" approach. I tried to explain to myself, at least, why buildings were built the way they were or why the builders followed certain practices. A combination of observations led me to the conclusions that the log houses I had been examining and working with had been covered with exterior siding when first built. Much of the evidence is laid out in the article and need not be repeated here. The prevailing opposite belief was very strong; indeed, I had heard it so often that it took a long time and a great deal of evidence to persuade me to take the opposite view.

Functional explanations such as that the size of rooms in early houses is dependent on the amount of space that can be heated by a single fireplace should be examined first. If, for example, one understands the practical reason why a house is built the way it is, then one is on safer grounds as one speculates about other reasons.

Since that time, therefore, I have tried to examine the evidence, to understand why things were done as they were, and to draw conclusions even though those conclusions may have been in opposition to long-accepted notions. Hence I have written many articles that revolve around the themes of looking at what had previously been overlooked and, as a result, setting the record somewhat straighter insofar as specific items dealing with the folklife and material culture of the past are concerned. The subtitle for these reprinted and newly written essays is, then, *Looking at the Overlooked.*

Another factor also apparent in the Whitaker-Waggoner article is only a variation on the preceding point. When written sources do not agree with evidence derived from authentic artifacts, does one accept the word of the written source or the evidence provided by one's own eyes? In working with old buildings, it seems to me that almost everyone accepts the word of the authors of books on old houses. If a specific old house has narrow floor boards, for example, the restorer is likely to say: "The books agree that old houses had wide floor boards. These narrow boards must be later." So the original narrow boards are taken up and wide boards installed in their place, or they are covered with wide boards. And so in a few years visitors to the house are presented with further "evidence" that all old houses had wide floor boards.

My experience with the Whitaker-Waggoner house together with other similar experiences convinced me that I should examine the artifacts first and draw whatever conclusions I could. Only then would I look at the written sources to see what they had to say on the subject.

Over the years I have come to realize that written records fail the folklife researcher in three important ways.

First, written records are often inadequate and fail to deal with a topic that the folklife researcher is interested in. A simple case in point is census records and their treatment of crafts. The census takers, beginning with the 1850 census, were instructed to record the trade or profession of adults. In the countryside adult males were almost always listed as "farmer" or "farm laborer." (An unmarried son living at home was normally listed as "farm laborer.") To use a simple example, one would assume that in most counties in Indiana there was not a single basketmaker! The typical basketmaker was also a farmer and so he comes to be listed in the census as a farmer. If one has done fieldwork and has found that many farmers made baskets when they did not need to work in the field or otherwise farm, the census figures present no problem. But far too often people writing on crafts forget that these rural craftsmen existed in the countryside because the census largely ignores them.

This problem—the inadequacy of records—is treated especially in "The Folklife Research Approach to Textiles," "Turpin Chairs and the Turpin Family," "Early Tool Inventories—Opportunities and Challenges," and "Planemaking in the United States: The Cartography of a Craft."

Second, written records can be misleading or can be misunderstood without the insights provided by fieldwork. A simple illustration of this may be found in a book devoted to Indiana cabinetmakers. In an early document the book's author found an entry in which a cabinetmaker stated that he had "Dogs for turning." The author includes a print of a canine running inside a big wheel-shaped cage and states: "In this period dogs would have been used as demonstrated in Plate II."[2] Fieldwork shows, however, that in this context, to a craftsman dogs are the metal parts of a lathe. The wooden parts of the lathe would have been made by the craftsman himself.

The problem of written sources which mislead the researcher who has not had the opportunity to do fieldwork is treated in several articles: "Word Origins and Tools," "Early Tool Inventories—Opportunities and Challenges," and "Hoosier and Family Names."

A third problem with written sources is that they can be inaccurate. Every historian knows that this generalization is true, but the historian normally does not depend on fieldwork to correct inaccurate written sources. While I do not want to devote much attention to this point, I once again cite census records. In a trade journal entitled *Stone* published in Chicago in 1891 is an enraged editorial critical of census figures. Under the heading "Indiana Sandstone and the Census," it is stated that the 1890 census shows that 334,000 cubic feet of sandstone was produced in Indiana in 1890 at a profit of $711 while actually there was at least 900,000 cubic feet of sandstone produced with a profit of at least $75,000.[3] In this case the editor of the journal himself did fieldwork. He traveled around the sandstone quarry areas talking to quarrymen and compiling statistics.

An even greater problem with most of those who write about the way in which people used to live is that in ignoring the vast majority of the population, the nontypical 5% of the population is presented as typical. In most parts of the United States, over 90% of the population lived on small, largely self-sufficient farms. They are the people almost completely over-looked in the written records, for it is those who lived in the towns and few cities and the tiny number of wealthy elite about whom information can be found in a variety of written sources. Yet writers on the past and the museums devoted to showing what life in the past was like constantly make the grievous mistake of assuming that all people in the past lived in mansions or in large towns. Anyone can easily find examples of writers who use such phrases as "the typical hostess in Colonial America set her table with . . . ," then proceed to list tableware that the typical hostess, in actuality a farm wife living on a small farm, could not possibly have owned. But because the writer has been able to find some written inventories of wealthy people and has been unable to find or has not even looked for household inventories of the small farmhouses, that writer has fallen into the trap of assuming that the wealthy family is representative of everyone. Or how many museums have invited visitors " . . . to learn what life was like in Colonial America" when the museum shows only the homes and the material possessions of the atypical elite? Surely, a major service that folklife researchers can perform is to constantly point out these and similar mistakes as well as to make available research showing who was typical of the whole population and how they lived.

So much for my personal experiences. A more general view of the development and growth of the field of folklife and material culture must also come from a very personal perspective. In the 1950s I knew in a vague way that some forms of material culture (i.e., folk arts, crafts, and architecture) were considered folklore here in the United States. I knew something of the work of a folklorist, Austin Fife, a true pioneer in folk material culture studies, for he had given a few lectures in Bloomington. I also knew of the publications of the Pennsylvania Folklife Society and its predecessors as well as something about cultural geographers. Yet the impress of Stith Thompson and the other leading folklorists of the day lay so heavy on my mind that I never thought it was really "proper" for a folklorist to include in classes anything on material culture. Nor did I believe that a folklorist could "do research" in material culture; it could be a hobby, perhaps, but not "real research." So much for the effects of graduate school on one reasonably impressionable young mind!

Let me hasten to add that I knew only too well that folklore had to struggle constantly to find a place in the academic sun as a "serious" subject; and add that I blushed inwardly and, perhaps, outwardly when at academic gatherings I had to confess that I was a folklorist; and add further that I had constantly to defend folklore's right to be considered seriously. Consequently, I was afraid of "rocking the boat," of doing anything that had not previously been given the seal of approval as "real folklore" or "real research," and I am afraid I closed my eyes to the possibility that material culture was, or could be, part of folklore and worthy of serious study.

It is for those reasons that my experiences in Norway in 1959–60 were so influential for me. Here were respected scholars carrying out research in traditional material culture and they were continuing a long practice. Here were college courses in folklife and material culture. Here were folk museums carrying out research and presenting their findings to an interested public. I must have said to myself: "If they can do it, so can I!" I returned to Indiana in 1960 a changed person, at least as far as academic matters were concerned.

Because I was aware that folk museums and folklife research went together in Norway, my earliest concerns were to find what similar museums existed in the United States, what their research was like, and what they thought should be included under the rubric "folk arts, crafts, and architecture." As a result, I spent many weeks in the summer of 1961 visiting museums. The first, and for me the most important, was the Farmers' Museum in Cooperstown, New York. It was there that I was able to meet and talk with Louis Jones, a figure of great importance and significance in the field. The factual information I gained there was certainly important, but even more so was the encouragement I received from Louis Jones. Other museums I visited that summer were the Shelburne Museum, Old Sturbridge Village, Mystic Seaport, and the Henry Francis du Pont Winterthur Museum.

Because of my concentration on establishing a folk museum at Indiana University, I made only slight attempts to locate other scholars in other disciplines who had interests in traditional material culture. However, I came into contact with Don Yoder whose work both as scholar and editor had deeply impressed me. Dr. Yoder headed a material culture committee of the American Folklore Society. The committee met during the annual meeings of the society and, under Dr. Yoder's editorship, submitted an annual report which was published in the *Supplement* to the *Journal of American Folklore.* In this way the small number of folklorists interested in the subject kept in touch with one another. It would be fair to say that collecting data was the main activity of the members of the committee.

In retrospect, it probably would have been more effective had the members of this committee tried to establish contacts with scholars interested in material culture in other academic disciplines and held meetings and published a newsletter of some kind, but this sort of enterprise had to wait.

At a meeting of the American Folklore Society in the early 1960s I met Henry Glassie after I had given a paper on the "Lean-To House in Southern Indiana," a paper that showed that a house form now called "the saltbox house" was known in southern Indiana and had probably been brought to the area by mid-nineteenth-century immigrants from New England. I was at once impressed with Dr. Glassie's knowledge and enthusiasm. I also met Dr. Norbert Riedel but had barely begun a correspondence with him when he was killed, I was told, in an automobile accident; a great loss to the study of folklife.

Henry Glassie organized a 1967 conference in Harrisburg, Pennsylvania, which I attended and at which I met many of the scholars studying traditional material culture.

In 1967, too, the Pioneer America Society was founded. I played no part in organizing the society and, indeed, learned of it only later. Within a short time, however, the society began to serve a very important function. It brought together scholars and enthusiasts from a variety of fields who had a common interest—traditional material culture. Examples are local historians such as Henry Douglas, cultural geographers such as Fred B. Kniffen, folklife researchers such as Henry Glassie, architectural historians such as Walter R. Nelson,[4] and others. This was a vital development for the study of traditional material culture. It also was of vast importance for folklife research in that it awakened folklife researchers, or at least this folklife researcher, to the methods and goals of other disciplines dealing with traditional material culture.

Prior to that time I had conceived of folklife research purely in the light of folklore research. And folklore research when I was a graduate student meant the historic-geographic method: collecting, archiving, type and motif indices, and historic-geographic monographs. Hence I felt that folklife researchers should collect by photographing and measuring old houses, should establish house types such as the saltbox type, and should study the distribution of the type as a main step toward discovering the age and origin of that type.

To my knowledge, the first folklife researcher to break out of this mold was Henry Glassie. His doctoral dissertation, published as *Pattern in the Material Folk Culture of the Eastern United States* (1968), was written at the University of Pennsylvania and the influence of Don Yoder is apparent in it. This work's primary claim to acceptability to folklorists as "real research" lies in the emphasis on distribution of cultural items, one of the bases of folklore scholarship. But within a short time Glassie took a new tack. He began trying to explain important information about human beings and about human culture and its development and changes by interpreting traditional material culture. Although it is not by far the first example of this trend, his *Folk Housing in Middle Virginia* (1975) is probably the best example. In this work, for instance, he shows how changes in house form, such as the introduction of the multi-room house with a hallway, mirror changes in society, in this case the slow disintegration of community ties and the growth of individuality. From that day to this, Henry Glassie has been an inspiration to other folklife researchers, and a noticeable change in the field can be observed following his lead.

In this new environment inspired by Glassie's example I likewise began to see that other kinds of research methods and goals were "real research" besides those in the historic-geographic-method mold. My fieldwork had previously lead me to general conclusions that the study of traditional material culture had more to offer than distribution maps. I allowed these conclusions, therefore, to color my published research, no longer fearing that I might be scorned for doing research unworthy of a true scholar. After all, the trail was already blazed!

In this vein, one of the three articles published in 1971 that are included in this book, "Function in Folk Architecture," tries to grapple with some questions besides those addressed in earlier folklore research. Function is a major one. After all, folklorists concerned with tales, songs, riddles, and the like had devoted no attention to functional considerations, having assumed that such genres were entertainment only. Certainly, collectors of folklore paid no attention to function—they seemingly paid little attention to the informants! These generalizations—and they are gross generalizations that ignore many fine points—do not apply to anthropologists, especially of the Malinowski school, but I am generalizing only about scholars who would have considered themselves folklorists first and foremost.

The other two of my articles published in 1971 are shorter introductory essays on fieldwork and on folk crafts. They are purely descriptive and mark no change from folkloristic concerns.

The 1972 article, however, "Folk Architecture in Context: The Folk Museum," marks another attempt to demonstrate that folklore research and folklife research are not identical. This article introduces the notion that context affects cultural items, a notion largely hitherto ignored by folklorists in their research, though admittedly a notion familiar to anthropologists.

The development in my groping after methods and goals appropriate to a new discipline in America continues in "The Whitaker-Waggoner Log House in Morgan County, Indiana " (1976). As previously mentioned, this article was first read as a paper at a 1968 conference held in Logan, Utah. An abstract of the paper was printed in a 1969 publication of the conference papers. These publication facts show that my concerns about the distinctiveness of folklife research were already developing in the late 1960s. At any rate, this research questions long accepted "facts" as to whether pioneer builders in Indiana built log cabins as crudely as the history books state. The investigation of log construction can lead to new conclusions about the state of technology and the cultural practices of an earlier era.

Another article published in 1976, "Some Comments on Log Construction in Scandinavia and the United States," had also been long incubating. It was inspired by a trip to Norway in the summer of 1967, a trip devoted largely to examining log buildings, reading about them in Norwegian publications, and consulting authorities such as Hilmar Stigum, Professor of Folklife at Oslo University and curator of buildings at the Norwegian Folk Museum. The main conclusion is that American log buildings are so different in virtually every way from Scandinavian log buildings that it is highly unlikely the Swedes introduced log construction to the American colonies. Again, the thesis of Swedish origins had been accepted by architectural historians for many years, but folklife research techniques brought this thesis into question. In this case the folklife researcher looks at the artifacts, which can be a long and painstaking process, and draws his conclusions even if the historical records do not support him. Here the written record shows that the Swedes were supposedly the first settlers in this land who came from a country with an ancient and important log construction technology. The log buildings themselves, however, show that it is unlikely that the Swedish influences were that important.

Since 1976 I have tried to concentrate more heavily on folk crafts rather than folk architecture. The principle that the study of artifacts should provide insights into human nature and human culture has always been my guide, but I have emphasized the following approach in studying crafts. I have tried to correct and supplement the record of the past by doing fieldwork and using the results thus obtained in evaluating the written record. Folk architecture largely has been ignored by historical writers of the past with one exception, the "pioneer log cabin." Consequently, folk architecture has not lead such writers to erroneous conclusions about human life and society of the past. With other artifacts, however, it is unfortunately true that art historians and historians in general have used such artifacts and have drawn misleading conclusions from them.

A simple illustration is the generalization repeated in many sources that "people" considered tomatoes to be poisonous and grew them only for decoration until one brave man in the late nineteenth century stood before a crowd and actually ate a tomato. Since he did not immediately drop dead, "people" began eating tomatoes. What sort of conclusions would be drawn from this story about "people"? That these people who grew tomatoes but never dared eat them must have been "superstitious," afraid to experiment, and incapable of instituting any change. If one looks at the evidence, however, it is clear that people in the United States had been eating tomatoes for a long time before the late nineteenth century so that a totally different attitude towards such people results.

I subscribe to the truism that one cannot understand the present nor plan for the future unless one knows the past. I would only add that if one has a distorted picture of the past, one will misunderstand the present and make faulty plans for the future. I am not naive enough to think that the few and insignificant attempts to correct and supplement the record of the past that are published in this book will make much difference. I do feel, however, that I have provided examples of ways in which folklife research methods can be used to achieve a better understanding of the past, and I hope that folklife research will be able to contribute in the future a truer picture of past life. Indeed, I strongly believe that such a contribution should be the main purpose of folklife research.

Most of the essays included in this volume have been published previously. In some of these, changes of various kinds have been made, some of which are extensive, and misprints have been corrected.

Notes

1. *Ring-Tailed Roarers: Tall Tales of the American Frontier* (Caldwell, Idaho: The Caxton Printers, 1941).

2. Betty Lawson Walters, *Furniture Makers of Indiana, 1793 to 1850* Indianapolis: Indiana Historical Society, 1972), p. 16.

3. *Stone*, 4, no. 5 (September 1891): 128–29.

4. These scholars wrote articles published in Volume 1 of *Pioneer America*, the Society's journal.

Viewpoints on Folklife

1

Folklife and Traditional Material Culture: A Credo

Published as part of a symposium, this essay presents my views as to why folklife researchers should concentrate on traditional material culture rather than contemporary material culture or the material culture of the elite.

*   *   *

Material culture studies? Although it makes for a bulky term, the qualifier "traditional" should be inserted in the initial position making it read "traditional material culture studies." I believe we cannot include all material culture in our purview. To do so would include the material culture of the industrial era, for example, such as industrial robots and the Empire State Building. I don't know many who would propose a field trip to the Empire State Building and would set out with tape measure and camera to make floor plans and take photographs.

So, first of all, who are "we" as used above? I suppose when I say "we" and "us" I am referring basically to the readers of *Material Culture*, both actual and potential, a very loose fraternity/sorority who are interested in "old stuff"—buildings, farm implements, baskets, and the like—and who are willing to take the time and effort to study them and write and talk about them.

I will expound shortly on the old truism that we should not study artifacts for their own sake but should study artifacts to gain insights into those people who made and used them. I subscribe fully to this truism. By using the word "traditional" I mean to exclude four areas of material culture even though they can be important. I realize, now that I have reached the age of 60, that there are only so many things that one can reasonably expect to do in one lifetime, and so, with considerable regret, I propose the following limitations.

This article originally appeared in *Material Culture* 17 (1985): 89–95.

First, we cannot really study the material culture of the industrial era, of mainstream America in the twentieth century. In addition to the fact that one needs to be a multi-faceted engineer at the very least to study modern material culture, if one studies the material culture of mainstream America in the twentieth century, one will therefore, according to the truism enunciated above, be studying mainstream American culture. I submit to you that "most of us" do not have the interest, the training, or the tools to study contemporary American popular culture. That is the province of the sociologist who has at least tried to develop the methods and tools to study contemporary society. If the journal *Material Culture* wishes to publish articles on the design of movie palaces in the 1930s, so be it. I feel that such a study belongs in a journal devoted to popular culture or the architecture of the popular culture of twentieth century America.

Next, we cannot really study the material culture of the elite society of the pre-industrial era. We have avoided floor plans and photos of the mansions of the rich and the aristocratic and we have not photographed their paintings, their silverware, or their costume. Leave that subject to the historians, the architectural historians, and the art historians who have prepared countless hundreds of volumes for the coffee tables of America. Let us concentrate on the common people, the "folk" who have been so neglected by the historians, architectural historians, and art historians.

Next, we have not in the past studied the material culture of exotic peoples, tribal peoples, or anthropological peoples. These peoples have, for many decades, been studied by anthropologists who have included all aspects of their culture, including material culture, in their purview.

Finally, it seems to me that "we" should not try to study the material culture of those parts of the world where we cannot do fieldwork. We cannot do meaningful fieldwork if we can't understand the language of those among whom we are working. For most of us, therefore, that means pretty much the United States and Canada. I hope I will not be accused of being ethnocentric. I feel so strongly that one cannot hope to understand a people unless he or she can speak their language flawlessly that I want to restrict my research and fieldwork to the United States and Canada. I would also include the countries from which the people living in the United States and Canada prior to the industrial era came. Obviously, if we want to know the background of German architecture in the United States, for example, we have to know as much as we can about architecture in Germany. I don't flatter myself, however, that I am going to do any meaningful fieldwork in Germany. The best I can hope to do is to get help from German scholars studying their folk architecture. About all I can do is twist Patrick Henry's words and say, "If this be ethnocentrism, then make the most of it!"

A charge that has already been levelled against me is that I am a "mere antiquarian." If this means that my main research interests center on the pre-industrial era, then I can only reply with yet another twist, "If this be antiquarianism, then make the most of it!" Is it a crime to be concerned with the past rather than the present? Are historians mere antiquarians? It seems to be a crime most *Material Culture* subscribers are guilty of and I am proud to count myself one of them.

Before proceeding, let me give one justification for what I have finished saying. The view that I have presented concerning the exclusion of four kinds of material culture from our subject is not an idiosyncratic one. Read through the past issues of this journal; read through the past issues of other journals such as *Folklife* and *Pennsylvania Folklife.* What does one find? The majority of articles conforms to the guidelines I have just laid out. Our journal, as far as I know, has never explicitly stated that the material culture of the rich and the aristocratic, of exotic peoples, or of American popular culture are excluded, but in actual practice this has been the case—with only a few readily understood exceptions.

Now that I have made these important but preliminary distinctions, let me speak further on some of my points. When I say that the *Material Culture* people should concentrate on the artifacts produced by and used by the great mass of people in the pre-industrial era, my reasons are many. First, it is these people who are the primary source of today's society. It is not the elite society of the past that is primarily responsible for today's society no matter what the historian and the social historian may tell you. It is true that the elite society has influenced today's society in many ways but it is still the old traditional way of life that is today's society's main source. Let me cite a single example: child rearing in the elite society and the folk society of the past and in the United States today. There is much evidence to show that in the elite society of the past in England and the United States, the parents had little to do with their children once they were born. A newborn infant was put out with a "wet nurse," the aristocratic mother fearing that suckling her infant might "ruin her figure." The weaned infant was turned over to a "nanny" and then to a governess. At an early age, usually eight, boys were sent off to boarding schools. By the Victorian era this pattern began to change slightly as motherhood became more fashionable. It is important to remember that this pattern was followed by only a tiny percentage—less than five—of the total population for obvious reasons—you had to have plenty of money if you were going to follow it. On the other hand, children were raised at home and sent to nearby one-room schools by the vast majority of people. What of today's society? I believe I am correct in saying that, to most people today, the ideal is that children should be close to their parents. I realize that there are many circumstances when this closeness is impossible, but it still seems to me that family closeness is the ideal. Contemporary American society, then, in this important area follows the traditional society of the past and rejects elite society. It is true that most writers misunderstand or ignore traditional society and turn to elite society when they want to generalize on "how people used to live," ignoring the fact that they are talking about far less than five percent of the total population when they deal with the elite.

Second, I present as a working hypothesis that the main features of traditional society are very old. How old I cannot tell but, for example, when I examine the folk architecture of my region, I find that I can trace its main features back to the east coast, then back to Great Britain, and back to the Middle Ages at least. In other words, in concentrating on the traditional society of the pre-industrial era we are not looking at a brief, transitional stage in society that had a temporary and passing effect on the lives of people. We are looking at a way of life that was the norm for generation after generation. I realize that it is a common practice for the illuminati to leap on a person who has made such a statement and proclaim, "This poor deluded one thinks there was never any change!" I know there was change, but I still insist that the main features of this way of life persisted for a long, long time. Next the cognoscenti say, "But how do you *know* that the main features remained unchanged? This is an assumption that can't be proved." My reply is that I know it is an assumption but that one has to start somewhere. I feel that it is a major goal of future research to test this and many other hypotheses.

Third, it is this traditional society of the past that was so profoundly influenced by the local environment. The elite tried to escape from the local, the vernacular, in their architecture, their furniture, their clothing. The general tendency is for *Material Culture* people to emphasize local patterns in all phases of their study. They try to make some sense out of distribution patterns, stressing migrations, for instance. They have usually ignored the elite material culture, subject as it was to rapidly changing fashions and distributed by printed pattern books and the like.

So *Material Culture* should emphasize the traditional material culture of the past. Notice that I say "emphasize," not "restrict itself to." It is clear, for example, that there was interplay between the traditional society and the elite society in the past. Folk costume was influenced by high-fashion costume, but at various times and in various places high-fashion costume was influenced by folk costume. The plans for the houses of the wealthy came from books on classical or Gothic architecture, but the houses were built by traditional craftsmen. And so it goes. The interplay is there and should not be ignored. However, the traditional material culture is so poorly known at the present, I feel that most of us ought to be discovering what it is and how it worked before we begin seeing how it interfaced with elite material culture.

It is also clear that pre-industrial traditional material culture persists in a variety of ways into the present and interacts with industrial material culture. Indeed, it is the traditional material culture of the past which persists into the present that has been the primary focus of *Material Culture.* How could it be otherwise? It is the buildings and other artifacts on and in the landscape that we examine. Other sources of documentation are woefully inadequate. We have a long way to go, though, before we can really see the relationships with modern material culture. I hope we will continue to emphasize the study of the traditional material culture of the past so we can better understand it. Then there will be time to compare it with modern material culture.

Finally, what of the study of traditional material culture and the study of people? It works both ways. I side with Henry Glassie and others who stress that the study of traditional material culture is vital if we are to understand the people of the past, not the upper two percent who are accessible through written sources, but the vast majority. At the same time, however, we cannot hope to understand artifacts unless we can understand their cultural context. An artifact separated from its cultural context and stuck in a glass case is like a fish out of water. We can measure and weigh the fish and count its scales, but we can never understand what fish are really like unless we can see them swimming in their element. So it is with artifacts. We must do our best to understand how they were made and how they were used, to understand, in short, the people and the society in which they flourished. This is a tough assignment, I realize, but it should be the goal of students of traditional material culture.

Having just said this, I must draw the obvious conclusion that folklife research and the study of traditional material culture belong together. It is only folklife research that is concerned primarily with the traditional society of the past, its persistence into the present, and its influence on the present. People who study traditional material culture in any meaningful way are studying, like it or not, folklife, and anyone studying folklife must concentrate heavily on traditional material culture. The study of traditional material culture should, therefore, never become an independent discipline divorced from the study of people and their society. If one is going to study buildings, he or she is going to have to study the people who built them and the people who lived in them. I firmly believe that there is no other way.

2

The Folklife Research Approach to Textiles

This lecture was presented at a conference on the ways of preserving historic textiles and costumes. The lecture was intended only to give the other participants in the conference who were mainly museum curators some insights into folklife research, its goals and methods, and what assistance folklife research could offer to museums.

*   *   *

Although folklife research is a familiar term in northern Europe, it is not in the United States. Only a handful of universities in this country offer courses in the subject, for instance, and there are no folklife research departments in American universities. Hence, I feel that I should begin with a brief introductory definition.

Folklife research studies the old traditional rural way of life of northern Europe and the United States of the pre-industrial era in all its manifestations. Folklife researchers are concerned also with the persistence of that way of life into modern society and its affects on modern society.

Why the pre-industrial era? Because the Industrial Revolution was a great upheaval that drastically altered the way of life of vast numbers of people, a way of life that had persisted for centuries. Why the rural way of life? Because the pre-industrial way of life was predominantly rural. In the year 1800 in the United States, for example, at least 95 percent of the population lived on farms while only 5 percent lived in towns and cities. Today, of course, less than 5 percent of the population lives on productive farms.

Folklife researchers and historians have, of course, a great deal in common, but there are significant differences. Folklife research makes rural,

---

This article is a revision of a paper originally delivered at the conference, "The Preservation of Historic Textiles and Costumes," held at Indiana University, May 15–17, 1978; and later printed and distributed to participants in the conference in the *Selected Papers.*

pre-industrial life its main concern, for instance. Because rural people in earlier times left few written records, the folklife researcher concentrates on fieldwork. He or she feels convinced that the best way to study folk crafts is to go out and find working traditional craftsmen and interview them. What written records there are can and should be used, but they can give us only a very incomplete picture. They need to be supplemented by other kinds of information and I will cite an example of this sort of situation later.

I should also mention that folklife research has tended to concentrate on material culture—folk architecture and folk crafts—perhaps as a reaction to the tendency of folklore to be preoccupied with oral literature—folktales and folksongs.

Let me turn now to the question of the folklife research approach to textiles. The folklife researcher must be interested in textiles because such a tremendous amount of people's time was spent on textiles in earlier days. I suppose that if we could know how people—especially women—spent their time in the small, self-sufficient communities, we would find that day-in day-out, year-round most time was devoted to raising, preserving, and preparing food. Certainly, the planting, tending, and harvesting of crops, the drying, canning, and pickling of foods, and the preparation of meals was tremendously time-consuming.

Second in importance, however, would probably be the time spent on textiles. The planting, tending, and harvesting of flax and the rearing and shearing of sheep took much time; but there still followed the retting, scutching, and hatcheling of the flax, the gathering and preparing of natural dyes, the spinning of thread, and the weaving of cloth. Small wonder that unmarried women were called spinsters. Probably their lot in life was to work with textiles while their married sisters tended children and prepared meals. If we could count the hours of skilled labor needed to produce an item such as a blanket from the back of the sheep to the finished product we would be amazed.

And if we bear in mind the amount of time needed to produce the linen for a dress, we would know why old houses have so few closets. It was, of course, because people had so few clothes that they didn't need closets. One of the problems facing the person trying to restore an old house and preserve its integrity while making it suitable for modern living is where to put closets, for the Industrial Revolution has made textiles relatively cheap and relatively plentiful.

After saying that the folklife researcher must be concerned with textiles, I must hasten to say that I, myself, have not devoted much attention to the subject. It is not that I lack interest in it, it is a purely practical problem. I have said that fieldwork is the folklife researcher's primary source of information. Certainly, I have done a fair amount of fieldwork in the past and continue to do so as the opportunity arises. It should come as no surprise to you that, in the Indiana countryside, strong notions about sex roles still exist. Certain things are thought to be men's work and certain things are thought to be women's work, and men have only a superficial knowledge about and very little interest in women's work and vice versa. Hence if I tried to interview ladies about textiles, they would feel uncomfortable and so would I as a result. It would take a long time to explain my interest in textiles, and a quilter, for instance, would still feel that she couldn't properly explain something to me that I couldn't do myself—and she would probably be right.

I can talk by the hour to a blacksmith about the tools he uses and why he can do certain things with wrought iron and other things with steel. I have no need to try to explain to him what folklife research is. All I have to do is tell him I'm interested in blacksmithing and that is enough.

Hence when I am out in the field with some of our female students, I can hang around in the corner of the room while a woman explains to them how to make quilts, trying to overhear what is being said without appearing too curious. It is far more common for the man of the house to expect me to sit out on the porch with him, talking about crops and the weather while the women-folk in the parlor discuss the matters that concern them.

For this reason I can give only a few samples of the kinds of information that I have run across in my fieldwork and other research. These must serve as examples of the kinds of information that the folklife researcher finds when trying to study all aspects of a way of life that persists in the present in a largely fragmentary way.

First, let me report that a place name can give information in a roundabout way about textiles. Several years ago I was over in eastern Greene County about 25 miles from Bloomington looking for the site of an old watermill that had long since disappeared. Most of the people in the area knew the location. They said, "Yes, it's down by the Sheep Washing Hole." The name "Sheep Washing Hole," of course, intrigued me so I asked what it meant. Everyone we talked to knew its location, but no one could explain how this specific spot in the river got its name.

I knew from reading books on English folklife that it was customary in earlier days to wash sheep in some convenient pool shortly before shearing. This was a communal effort for no one family alone could normally muster enough men to do the job. Hence, several families in a neighborhood would pool their resources (no pun intended). On the appointed day the families would bring their sheep to the water hole. One man would stand out in the water while others herded the sheep and pushed them in from one bank. The man in the water would souse them up and down and send them on to men on the opposite side who would drag them out. Let us hope that a warm spring day was chosen for this task and that the man deep in the water was relieved at frequent intervals.

The fact that people I talked to knew the name but not what the name meant told me that sheep raising and the communal washing had once flourished in the area but had died out before the memory of most living men. Later I was interviewed by a local newspaper reporter and mentioned, for some reason, the Sheep Washing Hole. After the name was published in the paper an elderly lady wrote me that she had been born and raised near the hole and that she remembered as a very young child hearing the men laughing and shouting as they washed sheep at the hole. This dated things pretty well. The custom had lasted until about 1900.

I know from other sources that the home production of cloth was common well into the second half of the nineteenth century. In an old house built in 1870, for instance, bundles of flax were found in the attic and I have a locally made hatchel with the date 1864 stamped in it. It seems likely, then, that woolen textiles were still being produced in this rural area of Greene County as late as 1900.

As a sample of the way in which data on textiles can throw light on other aspects of folklife, let me read a brief quotation from a book written by the first professor at Indiana University, Baynard Rush Hall, about his experiences in Bloomington and vicinity in the second and third decades of the last century.

In speaking of a family named Ashbaugh, Hall says: "They all were, too, thrifty and ingenious. Unable in the early times of their settlement to obtain hemp or flax, they gathered a peculiar species of nettle (called there nettleweed) which they succeeded in dressing like flax and in weaving it into cloth." Textiles were made from nettles in Europe. I have heard that Germans during World War II experimented with raising nettles for cloth when their supplies of cotton were cut off. This is the first report I have encountered of this use of nettles in the United States.

At first thought, the expedient to which the Ashbaugh family was reduced would seem to reinforce the notion that pioneer life in Indiana was harsh and crude. However, another way of looking at things is that this family was able to make cloth nearly as soon as they arrived in the new area. If they could make cloth, they certainly had a loom, probably a spinning wheel, and other pieces of equipment. Where did they get them? They probably brought them with them. If they didn't bring them with them but made them as soon as they arrived, someone must have been well supplied with tools, for one doesn't hew a spinning wheel out of a log with a broadaxe. Hence, information about textiles can tell us that the picture of a pioneer setting out into the woods with an axe over his shoulder and a few small possessions on his back probably is not a very true portrait.

It might come as a surprise to someone not familiar with the Indiana countryside to learn that weaving as a traditional craft still flourishes. By a traditional craft, I mean one handed down from generation to generation, often within one family, rather than one learned in school or from books. The traditional weavers still working in Indiana make rag rugs that are woven on the loom like any other textile. It is possible for this craft to flourish today because the weaver can earn a modest income from it. Because the raw materials—rags—cost nothing, it is possible for a weaver to produce durable and attractive throw rugs and sell them at a price that is competitive with manufactured rugs.

There is, however, another reason why these rugs are popular today in southern Indiana; they have been woven here from the earliest days and native Hoosiers are accustomed to them and like them. In the folk architecture of this region it was a common practice to place a house—it might be a log house or a house of wooden frame construction—well up off the ground with stone pillars at each corner. People knew from past experience that unless the houses were built in that way, the bottom timbers would rot and be attacked by termites. It may have been comfortable in the summers to have the wind blow freely under the house, but it certainly wasn't in winter. It was customary in the fall to put on the floor a heavy layer of straw and to cover that with a wall-to-wall carpet. This carpet was made of long, narrow strips of rag rugs sewn together. In the spring the carpet was taken up, the straw discarded, and the floor was left bare throughout the summer. As is often the case, folk architecture and folk crafts reinforce one another. Because it was possible to weave rag rugs, a house could be protected from decay and yet kept reasonably warm in the winter. Because people are accustomed to rag rugs, they are still being made.

Let me cite one other reason why the study of textiles is important to folklife research. Using information of various kinds drawn mostly from fieldwork, I had some reasonably solid but still tentative conclusions concerning the general status of folk crafts. A new book on Indiana coverlets written by Pauline Montgomery has recently appeared. I will try to show briefly how information on Indiana coverlet weavers reinforced my earlier conclusion.

First, I had concluded that most craftsmen in the past lived in the countryside and were farmers first and craftsmen second. That is, they worked at their craft in the winter months and at other times of the year when they were not busy in the fields. As a result, the usual written records do not tell us anything about these people as craftsmen. Many of the Indiana coverlets have the name of the weaver woven into the fabric at two corners. Yet in many cases, the written records—census reports and the like—show that these weavers considered themselves farmers. Even though proud enough of their craft to include their names in the coverlets they wove, they nonetheless told the census-takers that they were farmers, not weavers. It is clear, then, that historical records are not reliable sources of information about traditional craftsmen.

Second, I had concluded that Indiana was insulated from the effects of the Industrial Revolution for several decades because of the cost of transportation. An item could be made in an eastern factory for far less money than an Indiana craftsman could make it, but when the cost of transportation was added, the factory-made object got pretty expensive by the time it reached Indiana. This generalization is directly supported by the biographies of coverlet weavers. Many of them left Scotland, for example, in the early decades of the nineteenth century because factories in Scotland had begun producing textiles so cheaply that the hand weavers could not compete. Some of them moved to Indiana because they could work at their craft here and earn a decent wage by doing so. And, they were able to work in Indiana for many decades.

Finally, when did the Industrial Revolution begin to affect Indiana by forcing craftsmen to leave their crafts? On the basis of architectural and other evidence that I will not detail, I had previously decided upon the date of approximately 1875. I am happy to be able to report that data on coverlets nicely corroborates that date. There are many dated coverlets from the 1840s and 1850s, a few from the 1860s, and a tiny handful from the 1870s. By 1875 improved transportation had made Indiana much less isolated, and factory-made textiles finally forced the hand weavers to leave their looms.

Let me close with a few general remarks about this conference. I am happy to see regional conferences of this sort held. National conferences which keep people in touch with what is going on are, of course, very valuable, but regional conferences have their place, too. Because there are special regional problems, they are needed.

Let me mention briefly some experiences I have had in the area of architectural preservation and restoration. It is, unfortunately, true that many people are deeply in awe of the written word, so much so that they often prefer to trust a book rather than their own powers of observation. There are numerous books on restoring and preserving old houses. They emphasize areas such as New England and stress the eighteenth century. A person in the midwest may not always appreciate the old buildings in his own area because they do not resemble the houses he sees in books or in visits to old house museums. Furthermore, when he tries to restore an old house and turns to books for guidance, he may get misinformation because the books deal with a different area and a different time period.

In one example that I noted, some people in Indiana were trying to restore a building that was probably built around 1870. The floorboards in the building seemed to me to be part of the original construction and they were fairly narrow as one would expect for that time period. However, the people had decided on the basis of their reading that all old buildings should have wide floorboards, which may well be true for eighteenth century New England buildings. So they tore up the original narrow boards and replaced them with wide boards salvaged from an old barn. Had there been adequate information available to them on midwestern architecture of the nineteenth century, they probably would not have made that mistake.

I realize that one doesn't find wide boards and narrow boards in textiles. Nonetheless, I hope that a regional conference of this sort will lead to an appreciation of regional resources and will help disseminate appropriate information about them.

3

Fieldwork: Recording Material Culture

While there had been many articles and a few books on collecting oral forms of folklore, little had been written in the United States concerning recording material culture. This essay was written to partly fill that void. It was one of a collection of short essays designed to serve as introductions to various topics in folklore and folklife, essays which a beginning student or interested layman would find useful.

*　　*　　*

The importance of fieldwork and recording in the area of traditional material culture cannot be too highly stressed. Several generations of folklorists have warned that folkloristic items are disappearing without leaving a trace behind. This warning is, if anything, more applicable today than ever before, especially in connection with material culture. More and more traditional artifacts and techniques are outmoded by accelerating technological changes. Those displaced are soon cast away and forgotten. In the United States, the spread of cities and highways continually engulfs farms and farm buildings, and the bulldozer buries valuable material and data. Elsewhere, when large reservoirs and artificial dams are constructed, responsible governmental agencies work with archeologists to uncover and register aboriginal material; and yet the traditional material culture of contemporary inhabitants is usually destroyed without a backward glance. In recent years there has been an increased interest in architectural preservation. Many individuals and organizations have rescued fine old buildings and even large groups of buildings from the wrecker's ball, and these buildings have often been restored and preserved for the future. Nearly always, however, the preservationists have saved examples of academic architecture, the mansions of the wealthy, while few have spoken out in favor of preserving examples of the traditional architecture of the

This article originally appeared in *Folklore and Folklife: An Introduction,* edited by R. M. Dorson (Chicago: The University of Chicago Press, 1971), pp. 431–44. Reprinted by permission of the publisher.

common people. Surely there is a desperate need for competent fieldworkers to collect and record traditional material culture. The Industrial Revolution spelled the doom of most folk crafts and the traditional ways of life associated with them. Modern urban life threatens to obliterate much of what has persisted into the present.

The importance of fieldwork and recording in the area of traditional material culture needs stressing also because so little work of this sort has been done in Great Britain and the United States. This fact has been underlined in other sections of this work and need not be treated here. We need, however, recordings of many different kinds. Ideally, all aspects of the traditional ways of life of a given area should be recorded. Only in this way can one comprehend the true function and significance of the various interrelated parts. As an example, the tools used in harvesting, the customs of cooperative labor involved in harvesting, the beliefs associated with harvesting, the harvest festivals, the songs sung while harvesting and at the festivals, and the place of harvest time in the entire seasonal round of life all need to be studied together along with many other associated items in order to see their true significance. One could hardly isolate harvest songs, for instance, and study them outside their context without missing a great deal of their meaning. At the same time, it must be admitted that a study of all aspects of the traditional ways of life of even a small geographical area is immensely time-consuming and would involve the cooperative efforts of a number of specialists, for it is the rare fieldworker who is equally competent in, let us say, recording the techniques of a folk craft and the music of a fiddle tune. In actual practice, therefore, fieldworkers tend to concentrate on one subject or a group of closely related ones without ignoring the remainder, and fieldwork of this sort can be extremely fruitful. Even when one concentrates on one specific subject, however, the recording must be done in detail and in depth, as will be pointed out below.

Before one begins actual fieldwork, a considerable amount of preparation must be done. The exact preparation will, of course, vary from one collecting subject to another and from one geographical locality to another, but some generalized suggestions can be made. First of all, the prospective recorder must gather as much information as he can about the area in which he is going to work and about the subject he is going to record. As for the area in which he is going to record, one can talk with other collectors who have worked in the area or with someone who lives in or has lived in the area and read what written sources are available. In addition to any earlier collections or other folkloristic sources, local histories, guidebooks, and the like may prove useful, though one must be careful not to go out with preconceived notions that might influence his approach or lead him to ignore some data. Formulating a thesis and going out in the field to test it is a useful device for some types of collecting. By and large, there has been so little accurate fieldwork done with traditional material culture that it is necessary to do the basic recording before formulating theses.

The prospective recorder must also find out as much as he can about the subject he plans to record before he ventures out into the field. If he intends to concentrate upon a specific folk craft, for example, he must have some general information about that craft so that he will know, in a broad way, what to look for, so that he can ask meaningful questions, and so that he can attempt to gather all pertinent information. In interviewing a craftsman, for instance, one can hardly expect him to volunteer all pertinent information about his craft. One must question him about such topics as where he gets his raw materials, what the sources of his designs are, and where he has learned his craft. At the same time, a craftsman will usually talk much more freely to a person who has some knowledge of the craft than he will to a person who professes or shows complete ignorance of the craft. In this connection it often proves helpful to prepare a collecting guide in advance to insure that the recorder will not overlook some important type of information while in the field. One may become so engrossed in taking notes, making sketches, measuring, and photographing that only later does he realize that he has forgotten to investigate some aspects of his subject. A preliminary collecting guide should always be subject to revision as work in the field progresses and as the recorder gains more knowledge of his subject, and the guide should never be referred to so frequently that the informant gets the impression that he is being asked a number of cut-and-dried questions to be entered on a form. Still, a well-prepared and intelligently used guide can be a definite assistance to the recorder.

Before actually setting out to record, one should, if at all possible, obtain both contacts and leads. A contact is, normally, a person who lives in the area where recording is to be done and who is familiar with the area. He may or may not have information on the subject the recorder is looking for, but he can often suggest other people who do have useful information. When the recorder approaches an informant, he can say, "So-and-so told me that you might be able to help me," and the informant is then much more likely to be cooperative than otherwise. A lead is a person who actually has information or who possesses an item of interest. Other collectors and government, agricultural, and forestry agencies are possible sources of contacts and leads.

The recorder of material culture also needs a certain amount of equipment, varying with the work he intends to do, besides a reliable form of transportation. Under normal circumstances the fieldworker does not collect actual artifacts in the course of trips, although the occasion may arise when he can purchase some items either for himself or for some sponsoring institution. Instead, he accumulates photographs, measurements, and other data. He must, therefore, have a reliable camera and be familiar with it. It is at best discouraging to return from a long field trip to find that one has either poor quality photographs or none at all due to a malfunctioning camera or some human error. The exact type of camera equipment one uses will be dictated by the work he intends to do. A motion picture camera would prove useful if craftsmen at work are to be studied, but a still camera is adequate for most collecting. A camera equipped with extra lenses is certainly desirable. A wide-angle lens can be used to advantage in photographing the interior of a house or a craftsman's workshop, while a telephoto lens, for example, may be needed to take a picture of the details of the roof construction of a barn. If one expects to take some photographs in dark interiors, and some craftsmen's workshops are poorly lighted, flash equipment or very fast film is needed. The decision as to whether to use color film or black and white again depends on the subjects sought. If one is likely to photograph gaily painted barn decorations, for instance, color film is a necessity, but unless colors are important, black and white film is to be preferred, for it is more versatile and does not fade over the years as color films tend to do, especially when not properly stored. Some fieldworkers are able to carry two cameras with them when collecting, one loaded with color film and one with black and white film, using either as the circumstances dictate. Whatever photographic equipment is decided on, the prospective fieldworker will do well to take a roll of photographs and have them developed before setting out on his trip to be sure that his equipment is functioning properly and that he knows how to use it. When actually in the field, it is well to use the camera liberally, for film is a negligible investment compared to the time and expense of most field trips.

Since measurements are important data, measuring devices appropriate to the task must be taken into the field. For architectural work a fifty-foot steel tape and a six-foot folding wood rule are most useful. For investigating a craft, a six-foot rule may be adequate. With it one can measure a workshop or a tool equally well. It is also useful to have a clearly marked rule, preferably with alternating black and white solid rectangles marking the inches, that can be placed beside a small item to be photographed so that the marking on the rule will appear in the print. In this way the size of the item is clearly indicated without recourse to separate notes.

For some types of fieldwork a tape recorder is also a valuable tool. In recording data on processes, to be discussed below, a great deal of oral information must be gleaned. When one is talking with a craftsman about his work, for example, and how, when, and where he learned it, a tape recorder is obviously far more useful than a notebook. At the same time, of course, the fieldworker must bear in mind that some informants will hesitate to talk freely when faced with a tape recorder. Many informants can record a set or memorized performance such as a folksong with comparative ease. It is another matter, however, to have them talk clearly and easily into a microphone when they are searching their memories for details about their craft. The fieldworker must use his own judgment in this matter with each informant, balancing the ease of recording and the desirability of having the informant's own words on tape as against the possibility that the informant may be embarrassed and hesitant about speaking into a microphone.

Maps are needed both to help one find his way and to record the exact location of an item such as a house in case it is necessary to revisit it or so that someone else can find it. In the United States, U.S. Geological survey maps are invaluable for they are of such a scale and in such detail that they give the actual location of each house and barn in the countryside, identifying them by small squares. They need to be supplemented only in one way: they do not always give the local names of rural roads, and one will nearly always be given directions in this manner. Hence a local map giving these names is very valuable. A compass may be necessary, not that one is apt to get lost without it, but so that one can indicate the direction a building faces or so that the relationships between the various buildings on a farm can be given. Binoculars can save time in helping one decide whether to walk a long distance across a field to a remote barn, for instance. Finally, I personally carry a snake-bite kit with me in warm weather, for snakes love old houses and barns. I have never had to use it, but I usually feel better for having it when I tramp through the high weeds surrounding an abandoned barn.

There are two general kinds of recording that the fieldworker in material culture may collect. One involves recording data on artifacts, be they as large as a barn or as small as a thimble, while the other involves recording descriptions of processes such as the way a blacksmith makes a hinge or a farmer plows a field. The range of artifacts that may be recorded is so great that it is probably better to discuss one subject in detail rather than to attempt to generalize. Recording data on a house can be taken as an example with the hope that it will also give some insight into the problems of recording data on other artifacts. Recordings for a house can be of three kinds: measured plans, photographs, and sketches. Each has its own uses, and they can supplement one another.

Ideally, the data to be recorded on a building should be so complete that the building could be reproduced down to the last detail in case it were destroyed. Recording this much data on even an average house, however, would require many days of work. From a practical standpoint, the type of research that is being undertaken can dictate the amount of detail to be recorded. One must always bear in mind, however, that other workers may make use of one's recordings and that each generation of folklorists has tended to be critical of the preceding generation because it has not included enough detail in its recordings. It is certainly wiser to err on the side of being too detailed than to err in recording too little detail.

Measured plans cannot, of course, be completed in the field, but the measurements can be made and recorded on a rough plan, later to be transferred to a scaled plan. A floor plan for each floor should be made, giving the location and dimensions of such features as room partitions, doors, windows, fireplaces, stairways, and the like. A scaled elevation for each of the four sides of the house should also be made, showing the location and dimensions of doors, windows, exterior chimneys, and so on. A practical problem arises with heights such as the height of the ridgepole above the ground or the height of the chimney above the roof. Ladders to allow one to actually measure heights are usually not available, and owners are understandably reluctant to have strangers clambering around on their roofs. The recorder can always measure up six feet and then hold his rule above his head thus gaining a measured height of twelve feet. The remaining height can usually be estimated reasonably accurately. If the building is made of brick or if it has horizontal siding regularly applied, it is possible to determine the size of each course and count the number of courses, thus assuring reasonable accuracy.

Photographs and sketches can usually supplement one another. In most instances a photograph is preferable because it is not only more accurate but also takes far less time to obtain. Photographs should be taken of all four sides of the exterior as well as of interior details such as the foundation, doors, windows, and trim. Inside the house, one should try to photograph typical details such as doors, moldings, fireplaces, staircases, and the like. It is often necessary to sketch features that cannot be photographed either because one cannot get into a position to take a picture or because there is insufficient light. In many ways, J. F. Kelly's *Early Domestic Architecture of Connecticut* (New Haven, 1924) can serve as a guide to the fieldworker who is recording data on houses. First of all, Kelly gives excellent photographs and measured drawings that can serve as models. The thoroughness with which Kelly treats the various aspects of architecture is noteworthy. One can also profit by following Kelly's outline that includes such subjects as the house frame, roof framing, masonry, the outside covering, windows, front entrances, interior woodwork, paneling, mantels, cupboards, the stairs, moldings, and hardware.

In addition to measurements, photographs, and sketches, one should record other data of various kinds. The placement of the house in relationship to other buildings, roads, and features of terrain such as streams and springs can be shown by a rough sketch. Any information that the owner or people living nearby can give about the history of the building such as date of construction, name of builder, and names of past owners should be noted down. Moreover, any evidence from the building itself that might aid in determining its age should be recorded. Unfortunately, evidence of this sort is not always immediately apparent and takes considerable experience to evaluate properly, but some indications of the type of evidence that can be useful in this connection can be given.

First of all, one must always be aware of the fact that material in a house may not be contemporaneous with the building of the house. Materials may have been salvaged from earlier buildings and used in the construction, and many changes may have been made in the house after it was built so that material much newer than the house may be found in it. Kelly reports on the basis of his experience in Connecticut, "Rooms were panelled, ceilings plastered, fireplaces reduced in size, stairs rebuilt, mantels introduced, and entrances changed or added during the years after the original house-building." Often the evidence that can be gleaned from the house itself, however, is the only source of dating that one can use.

One source of evidence involves the way in which timbers and boards have been cut. The telltale marks of the broadax indicate that a timber has been hewn, while the straight saw marks left by the up-and-down blade of a water-driven sawmill differ noticeably from the curved saw marks of the modern circular saw. One needs, of course, to examine timbers exposed in the basement or attic or to examine the bottom sides of floorboards seen in the basement and the like, for the marks of broadax or saw have been removed by planing in most finished parts of a house. On places where many coats of paint or long wear has not obscured them, one can often find the somewhat irregular marks of the hand plane or the faintly rippled surface left by a power-driven modern planing mill. Unpainted closet shelves and the backs of closet doors are good places to examine for plane marks. Masonry can also be examined for evidence of age. The use of concrete, for example, indicates modern work. Uncut fieldstone can be used in any period, but if cut stone has been used, one can distinguish between stone that has been shaped or "picked" by hand and that sawed with modern machinery. If brick has been used, one can distinguish old, hand-made bricks from factory-made bricks because the hand-made bricks are more uneven and irregular and show greater variation in color. In older masonry work, too, clay was often used in place of mortar, especially where it would not be exposed to rain such as in a chimney built in the center of a house. If plaster has broken loose any place, or if it is possible to examine the back side of plastering either in a closet or a basement stairway, some indications as to age may be obtained. If animal hair is used in the plaster itself it is an evidence of age. Older lath will either be rived, usually from oak, or sawed in broad sheets and then spread out accordion fashion by being split partially through. Sawed lath that is regular in size and shape indicates modern construction.

Windows and doors should also be examined. Old window glass was thinner than modern glass and filled with streaks and bubbles. Very old glass often shows a metallic iridescence. In general, too, the smaller the panes are, the older the window is. Modern window frames are more complicated than older ones, for in older work the upper sash was fixed and only the lower sash could be raised. While it is usually difficult to examine the actual construction of the window sash, it is possible to see how doors were constructed. Older doors were often of the "board and batten" type in which vertical boards are held together by means of two or three horizontal boards nailed across the back. A more complicated form of door construction in which panels are set into a frame was often used also in earlier houses. The same type of door is still manufactured today, though hand-made doors can usually be recognized because the tenons of the rails pass completely through the stiles. Pegs were usually driven through the entire joint. Nails and hardware should also be examined. There are three general types of nails. The earliest is the hand-wrought nail that can be recognized by its irregularity. The head of the most common type is large and usually shows the marks of the blacksmith's hammer while the shank of the nail is square in cross-section and tapers unevenly to a point. But nails in use throughout most of the nineteenth century are much more regular in appearance. The head of the most common type is rectangular, and the shank is rectangular and tapers towards a blunt point on two sides only. Wire nails have been used mainly in the twentieth century. They have round heads and round shanks that taper very abruptly to a point. (Anyone attempting to establish dates of construction on the basis of the type of nail used should consult Lee H. Nelson's "Nail Chronology as an Aid to Dating Old Buildings," American Association for State and Local History Technical Leaflet 15.) It is usually possible to recognize hand-wrought door hinges and latches that are the earliest type. Cast-iron hinges and latches replaced hand-wrought ones, replaced in their turn by modern steel ones. Sometimes hardware of solid brass was used in earlier houses, especially in such an important place as the front door, while much modern hardware is brass-plated steel. If it is possible to remove a wood screw, one can usually tell whether it is a modern, machine-made screw by its general smoothness and its point. Old screws that were hand-made are very irregular and early machine-made screws are blunt.

Another type of recording involves processes such as those involved in various crafts. Here, again, statements that could apply to all processes are so generalized that it is better to indicate some of the steps in recording data about a single craft such as cabinetmaking. Here there are various types of information to be recorded about such topics as materials used, tools and their use, designs and their sources, and the craftsman and his customers. After the fieldworker has had the opportunity to visit the cabinetmaker and become acquainted with him, he can begin recording information. A natural preliminary step is to ask for biographical information, stressing especially the ways in which the cabinetmaker learned his craft. Whenever possible, the fieldworker should try to find out as much as he can about changes that have occurred in the course of time that the informant remembers or that he has heard about from older craftsmen.

The materials the cabinetmaker uses are, of course, mainly wood. The fieldworker should try to find out where the cabinetmaker gets his wood of different kinds, how he seasons it, and why he uses different kinds of wood for different purposes. Information should also be recorded about the other kinds of materials the cabinetmaker may use such as hardware, glue, and finishing materials like varnish and lacquer.

Detailed information on the tools of the cabinetmaker and their use may require a number of visits. Unless the craftsman has a great deal of free time at his disposal and can demonstrate how each tool is used, the fieldworker will simply have to try to be present when the tools are being used in the normal course of the craftsman's work. A wise preliminary step would be to make a measured floor plan of the workshop showing the location of work benches, stationary tools, storage areas, and the like. If possible, an inventory of the tools should be made giving the craftsman's name for each tool and any information he may be able to give as to its age, where he got it, and how often he uses it. When time permits, each tool should be measured and photographed. As the occasion arises when the craftsman is actually using his tools, as many photographs as possible should be taken. If a motion picture camera is available, it should be used to show the tools in use. Any explanations that the craftsman can give as to why he uses certain tools in certain ways should likewise be recorded. Henry C. Mercer's *Ancient Carpenters' Tools* (Doylestown, Pa., 1929) is an excellent source to use for general information in this regard.

Gathering detailed information on the designs or plans the cabinetmaker follows in building his furniture is a time-consuming but vital task. One should undoubtedly begin by locating, photographing, and measuring as many of the craftsman's products as can be found. This will entail visiting his customers and getting their permission to examine the furniture the craftsman has made for them. The owners of the furniture and the cabinetmaker himself may be able to supply information about the dates when the furniture was made.

A second step would involve an investigation of the sources of the craftsman's designs or plans. As time permits, the fieldworker should talk with the cabinetmaker and record any information he can give as to which designs he has drawn up himself and which he has acquired in a traditional way either from those from whom he learned his craft or from other craftsmen. One must bear in mind that information from the craftsman himself must be treated with some caution, though it must be recorded in detail. A craftsman who has been making a certain type of chair for many decades may firmly believe that he designed the chair himself in the first place, whereas in actual fact it may be a reasonably exact replica of chairs made by earlier craftsmen. The cabinetmaker may also be able to give information concerning changes he has made in designs over a period of time and the reasons why he has made these changes. Many cabinetmakers also have in their shops detailed plans, sketches, and full-sized patterns made of heavy paper, cardboard, or thin wood for parts or entire pieces of furniture. These can be photographed or copied in other ways, and the craftsman may be able to tell where he obtained them. The fieldworker should not overlook the possibility that some of the cabinetmakers' designs may have come from books and magazines or that some of his designs may have been influenced by printed sources.

If it is at all possible, the fieldworker should attempt to document the influences on the cabinetmaker's designs by investigating the tradition in which he is working. For the sake of simplicity, let us assume that the cabinetmaker has learned his trade from his father. Any pieces of furniture made by his father that can be located should be photographed and measured so that comparisons can be made. Moreover, the furniture made by other cabinetmakers in the area whose work the informant may be familiar with should also be investigated.

Finally, the fieldworker should try to discover whether or not the cabinetmaker knows and uses a general or traditional principle of design or knows an inherited rule of thumb that he follows in making new designs. As an example, let us assume that the cabinetmaker has been asked to make a chest of drawers unlike those he has made in the past. How does he determine the general proportions, i.e., width, height, and depth, assuming that these have not been specified by the purchaser? How high are the legs or the base? Since all the drawers are usually not the same size in a chest, how does he decide what the height of each drawer is? How thick is the top and what size should be the moldings under the top and elsewhere on the piece? It may well be, of course, that the cabinetmaker will answer queries of this sort by saying, "I've always done it that way," or "That wouldn't look right," and be unable to give any further information. He may, however, know the rule of thumb that, in a chest of drawers, the height of each drawer should be less than the one below it by an amount equal to the size of the piece of wood separating them. (As a simple illustration, take a chest with four drawers: if the strip of wood between drawers is one inch in height and the bottom drawer is seven inches in height, the next drawer should be six inches in height, the next five inches, and the top drawer four inches.)

Information about the craftsman and his customers should also be obtained, for it is a subject that has been almost totally neglected in the past. Some of this information can be gleaned from the cabinetmaker himself, but his customers should also be interviewed if it is at all possible. Some points to be investigated in this connection include: to what extent have the customers determined the designs and specifications of furniture the cabinetmaker has made; how do his customers regard his furniture in comparison with that of other craftsmen or that made in factories; how has furniture made by the craftsman in years gone by held up in actual use; does the craftsman regard his customers as friends and acquaintances whom he is happy to oblige or are they thought of in more impersonal terms; and is the craftsman admired for his skill and considered an important person in the community? It may be well to stress once again the importance of detailed recording of this kind. Traditional crafts that are of great antiquity are on the point of disappearing. They represent an important part of a traditional way of life that is also being submerged by a new and different way. The few craftsmen who still carry on their crafts should be studied as thoroughly as possible while there is still time.

In addition to the work that he carries out in the field, the student of material culture must consider how best to store and file his accumulated records. Much will depend, of course, upon how extensive his fieldwork is, how many different types of material he is recording, and other factors, but in general some sort of file or archive will be necessary. Two general principles should guide the person who is trying to decide how to organize his recorded data: the material should be easily accessible, and related materials should be kept together. It is beyond the purpose of this paper to describe how a large archive for an entire state, for example, should be set up, although many of the ideas that apply to a small collection can apply also to a large archive.

First of all, the data—photographs, drawings, measurements, transcriptions of tape recordings, or other notes regarding one item or one craftsman—should be placed in a large envelope or folder. The way in which these envelopes or folders is arranged in sequence will vary according to the subject. At least three methods can be cited. If the fieldworker is recording many different kinds of material, the arrangement should probably be based upon the kinds of material. For example, his file might contain a section on architecture, another on agriculture, a third on crafts, and so on. If the fieldworker is concentrating on one subject, architecture, let us say, it is probable that a geographical arrangement will prove most satisfactory. With this system, all the buildings recorded in one township, for example, can be filed together. If, on the other hand, craftsmen are being visited and interviewed, it is quite likely that an alphabetical arrangement based upon the informants' names will be most useful. Whatever basic scheme is used, a system of cross-referencing should also be considered. If the system is based upon the kinds of material investigated, some type of geographical cross-reference should be developed, as well as an alphabetical list of names of informants or of the owners of the material investigated. For a geographical cross-reference it may be possible to use a map or some arrangement of file cards may be worked out, while for personal names a file card system is obviously best. If, on the other hand, the basic filing system is a geographical one, a cross-reference index for subject matter and another for personal names should be used. As an example, let us assume that architecture is being recorded and that the folders containing data on the individual buildings are filed according to their geographical location. A separate file of cards covering the different kinds of buildings—dwelling house, barn, smokehouse, and so on—keyed to the main file should be developed together with another file of cards listing alphabetically the owners' names. Finally, if the basic system depends upon the owners' or informants' names, separate cross-reference indexes should be drawn up for the geographical location and the type of material. In any case, it is wise to keep a map on hand giving the location where fieldwork has been done as an aid in planning one's work and laying out future field trips.

Bibliography and Selected Readings

Evans, G. Ewart, *Ask the Fellows Who Cut the Hay.* London: Faber, 1956. An excellent book concerned with the recording of oral tradition in East Anglia. Ewart Evans's other books, *The Horse in the Furrow,* London: Faber, 1960, and *The Pattern Under the Plough,* London: Faber, 1966 are also very valuable.

Fenton, Alexander. "An Approach to Folk Life Studies." *Keystone Folklore Quarterly* 12 (1967): 5–21. Contains practical suggestions for fieldwork in material culture based upon the author's experiences in Scotland.

Higgs, J. W. Y. *Folk Life Collection and Classification.* London: The Museum's Association, 1963. Reproduces in condensed form the classification scheme used at the Museum of English Rural Life and gives sample questionnaires.

Jenkins, J. G. "Field-Work and Documentation in Folk-Life Studies." *The Journal of the Royal Anthropological Institute* 90 (1960): 250–71. Valuable information based upon the author's own fieldwork in England and Wales.

————, ed. *Studies in Folk Life.* London: Routledge and Kegan Paul, Ltd., 1969. Contains a series of twenty essays presented to Dr. I. C. Peate. The essays are by European scholars and cover material, linguistic, and social aspects of folk life.

————, ed. *Traditional Tools and Equipment.* Transactions of the Museum Assistants' Group, No. 5. London, 1965. Contains brief articles by several different scholars with emphasis on collection and classification.

Owens, T. M. "The Recording of Past Social Conditions." *Folk Life* 4 (1966): 85–89. Deals with the use of the tape recorder to collect oral data on a wide range of social topics.

Peate, Iorwerth C. *Folk Museums.* Cardiff: University of Wales Press, 1948. A description of folk museums in Europe and of the Welsh Folk Museum at St. Fagans.

————, ed. *Gwerin.* Vols. 1–3 (1956–61). Contains numerous articles relating to folk collections. The successor to *Gwerin* is *Folk Life* (edited by J. Geraint Jenkins), published annually by the Society for Folk Life Studies.

Scottish Studies. School of Scottish Studies, University of Edinburgh, 1957–. A bi-annual journal devoted to Scottish folklore and folklife.

Ulster Folklife. Ulster Folk Museum; Dublin. A quarterly journal dealing with folklife studies of northern Ireland.

The handbooks of folk museums such as the Welsh Folk Museum, The Museum of English Rural Life, the Luton Museum, the City of Gloucester Museum, and the Castle Museum, York, are useful for information on the collections of those museums.

4

Hoosier and Family Names

The question as to how the term "Hoosier" used for inhabitants of the state of Indiana originated is constantly being raised. Almost never is a truly satisfactory answer forthcoming. In order to provide what I, at least, consider a more satisfactory answer than that usually given, I composed the following essay which also incorporates some reasons why folklife researchers and folklorists should be interested in family names. The original essay was written as part of a special issue tribute to my old friend, William Koch, at the time of his retirement from a lifelong career of teaching and studying folklore of the plains. It has been revised and updated at appropriate places to reflect current observations and thoughts on the subject.

*   *   *

Folklorists, it seems, have completely ignored surnames in the past. Placenames and the legends connected with them have interested a number of folklorists in the United States over a period of years.[1] Some attention has also been given to nicknames and the like,[2] but I have been unable to find any folklorist who has treated family names as folklore or who has suggested that family names might belong in the canon of folklore.

The reasons for this neglect of family names by folklorists are not hard to find. Families in Great Britain assumed or were given their names so long ago that these names are simply taken for granted. It is a rare person in the United States who tells legends about the origins of his family name. The British placenames from which so many family names are derived are remote and generally meaningless to Americans, and the fact that a family name may indicate that one's ancestor came to England with the Norman conquerors doesn't seem to interest many Americans even though it may interest the English. (The fact that one's ancestors came over on the Mayflower interests Americans, but the situation regarding the family names

---

The original version of this article appeared in *Kansas Quarterly* 13, no. 2 (1981): 78–82; © *Kansas Quarterly,* 1981.

of the Pilgrim Fathers is rather different. Their names are generally English, but so are thousands of other American names.)

This neglect of family names by folklorists seems to me to be unfortunate. I would propose that any scholar working in folklore or folklife research should be at least aware of some aspects of family names and I would like to advance some justifications for this proposal.

Before proceeding further, I must make some disclaimers and give some restrictions. First of all, my academic training was in folklore and I have trained myself in folklife research. I am not a specialist in family names by any stretch of the imagination. I consider myself to be a folklife researcher who is at least aware of family names and who wants to make other folklorists and folklife researchers aware of them. Moreover, a detailed knowledge of the history of the languages spoken now or at one time in Great Britain is absolutely essential to anyone doing serious research with British family names. Otherwise, the changes over the centuries in spelling, pronunciation, and meaning of names can be understood only with great difficulty. My knowledge of the history of the English language is very minimal and my knowledge of the other languages of the British Isles is nonexistent. If, for example, a French miller with a name something like Moulineux ended up in Ireland, and the name became Mullinix eventually, I am unable to explain why the "x" is retained in the name. If, therefore, some of my remarks seem naive and uninformed to those who have the training and knowledge I lack, I can only beg them to remember my disclaimer and my purpose.

I shall deal here mainly with the names of Americans of European descent in southern Indiana. The reason for restricting myself to names of this sort is simple: it is among those people I have done most of my fieldwork.

To return now to my reasons why folklorists and folklife researchers should be aware of family names, my first one is a suggestion that much could be learned from an analysis of surnames about the folklife and material culture of the period (roughly 1250–1450) when family names were being taken or given. This is a period that is difficult to find information about. The usual sources that help us with the folklife and material culture of later periods (fieldwork, written records, and the like) are out of the reach of most Americans, but family names are as near at hand as the telephone directory.

For example, family names can tell us what crafts, trades, and professions flourished in that earlier period and can even give us some indication of the relative frequency of craftsmen and others in that period. When we find names such as Fletcher (arrow maker), Weaver (or Webster), Dyer, Turner, Carpenter and a host of others, we know that many crafts still flourishing in the nineteenth and twentieth centuries were flourishing centuries earlier (Carpenter, for example) while some such as that of Fletcher have pretty well died out. When we reflect how common a name Smith is, we must conclude that there were great numbers of smiths (mostly blacksmiths) in that earlier period, but when we see how comparatively rare the name Painter is, we must conclude that paint and the specialists who applied it were either rare or non-prolific. This matter of relative frequency must be applied with some caution, however.

Why have I never found a person named Cabinetmaker? Does the absence of this name, at least in my experience, mean no one made furniture in that early period? Certainly not. It is probably because a man who devoted much of his time to making furniture would have been called a joiner. But because even Joyner is a fairly uncommon name we should probably conclude that carpenters and wheelwrights made a great deal of the furniture in that period. And what about the absence of (in my own experience, at least) Basketmaker as a family name? Didn't people have baskets in that early period? I'm sure they did. I believe that basketmaking was practiced by great numbers of people as a sideline, people who were farmers primarily, probably, and that basketmaking was not commonly regarded as a specialized craft. Even today in my fieldwork I find that the few traditional basketmakers who still work consider basketmaking a sideline, something to do when other work is slow.

The list of kinds of information that could be culled from family names as to folklife and material culture in that earlier era is practically endless. Take the name Boltinghouse, common in the Bloomington area, as an example. It tells us that in some area in England, at least, flour must have been bolted in a building separate from the mill in which it was ground. But limitations of space force me to leave such a list to the interested reader.

Another reason for folklorists and folklife researchers to be aware of family names is that placenames and family names in the United States are intimately connected. One can hardly study placenames, and folklorists, as I have previously mentioned, do study them, without some awareness of family names. Take the southern Indiana town Cumback, for instance. One might think that some booster named the town as an invitation to the tourist to return for another visit—unless he knew that Cumback is a family name. Or Beanblossom, Indiana. Was it named because the early settlers found beans in blossom (the Indians had planted them, presumably) as is generally believed, or because of an early settler named Beanblossom? I incline to the family name as the explanation. I cannot cite any family named Beanblossom or Bean Blossom currently living in the area, but there are a number of families with that name living in and around Corydon, Indiana, about 100 miles south. Moreover, the 1850 census lists seven people named Beanblossom living in Harrison County, whose county seat is Corydon, as well as three in Noble County in northeast Indiana.

And what about Solsberry, some 20 miles west of Bloomington? It is pretty well accepted in this area that the place was once named Sol's Berry Patch but that, over the years, the "Patch" was dropped off. A placename scholar should know, however, that "Solsberry" is a phonetic spelling of the common pronunciation of "Salisbury."[3] (My desk dictionary gives the pronunciation of Salisbury as "SÔLZ'BERI.")[4] The town might have been named for Salisbury, Maryland, by someone who spelled as he pronounced, a common practice until relatively recently. Or it could also be named for a person whose surname was Salisbury or Solsberry because his ancestors lived at Salisbury in England. Basil Cottle lists Salisbury as a British surname with Salisberry as a variant spelling.[5]

One final example of family names as placenames will have to suffice. In western Monroe County a county road runs straight up hill and down and true north and south for at least three and a half miles. It is named Hartstraight Road, Hart Straight Road, or Hart's Trace Road depending on whom you ask, what map you consult, or what road sign you look at. At one time different road signs at different intersections gave all three possibilities. People who favor one form of the name over the others usually have a legend to support their choice. These legends involve a pioneer logger named Hart who built a straight road to haul his logs, an Indian named Johnny Hart, or a trace (as in Natchez Trace) beaten down by harts (i.e., male deer).

A few years ago I was asked by a man who lived along that road to appear at a meeting of the county commissioners to set them straight on the proper form of the name. He, of course, assumed that I would support his spelling and etymology based upon the logger named Hart. I declined. I feared that my explanation would please no one, but would probably unite the warring factions in an attack on me. The name of the road, I suspect, is derived from the family name Hartstrait. I say this because, although there is now no family with that name living on or near the road, there are families with that name not too far away. A recent candidate for mayor in Bedford, 20 miles south of Bloomington, was named Hartstrait, for instance. Moreover, many of the county roads in Monroe County are named for families or individuals that live or once lived on them.[6]

A third reason why folklife researchers and students of material culture in general should be aware of family names is that they are closely, and often confusingly, bound up with craft objects, craft tools, processes, in short, the whole world of material culture. If a fieldworker asked a woodworker what the tool he was using was called, and was told that it was a "badger plane," said fieldworker might wonder for a long time how the plane resembled the animal. He would probably never guess that it was named for its inventor, one Charles Badger, a "member of the firm of Badger & Galpin, of No. 1 Stargate, Lambeth, in 1863."[7]

There are other examples. Much has been written about the sailor's folk art called scrimshaw which involves carving and engraving ivory and whalebone. Several writers have tried to explain how this art got its name and what the name means.[8] None, as far as I know, has pointed out that Scrimshaw is a family name. It's not a common one, of course, but it is one. I do not intend to claim a simple, direct connection between the folk art and the family name; that is, I am not saying that a sailor named Scrimshaw invented it. I do, however, suggest that anyone writing on the origins of the term "scrimshaw" ought to be aware of the family name. Again, numerous other examples could be cited, but these two must suffice.

I want to turn now to another topic, namely, the concept of initial occupancy and family names. Folklife researchers and cultural geographers are rightly much concerned with the concept of initial occupancy. It holds that the first settlers in a region in the United States will establish a number of patterns in such elements of culture as architecture, agriculture, and speech. These patterns will be like those in the areas the first settlers came from. Later immigrants to the area will tend to conform to the patterns established by the first settlers even though the later comers may have been from an area with rather different patterns. This concept is of great importance in dealing with many aspects of folklife and folklore.

Some examples from one geographical area will have to suffice. My mother was born in England and came to the United States when she was twenty years old. My father was born and grew up in North Carolina. The newlywed couple moved to a small town in Maine where I was born and grew up. Not surprisingly, I grew up speaking not with an English or North Carolina accept, but a Maine accent. (After I moved to another part of the country, my friends used to ask me to say, "Park your car in Harvard Yard" and then double up with laughter at my pronunciation.) My mother must have adapted to the local patterns in folk cookery rather quickly. As long as we lived in Maine we had baked beans every Saturday night just like all our Yankee neighbors. Baked beans, I hasten to say, are virtually unknown in the traditional cooking of North Carolina (the canned variety has been introduced in recent years, of course) and of the part of England my mother came from.

That one family moving into a new area should have adopted many of the traditional patterns of that new area is to be expected. But what makes the concept of initial occupancy more significant is the fact that great numbers of French Canadians had moved into the area in the early 1900s to work in the mills. While the older French Canadians spoke French among themselves, when they spoke English they spoke it with a Maine accent, as did their children, and they all ate baked beans on Saturday night. Moreover, even later in the 1900s substantial numbers of Finns moved into the area. The terrain, rocky, hilly, with many small lakes and birch trees, perhaps reminded them of their homeland. At any rate, when they spoke English they spoke it with a Maine accept (they, too, would have said, "Pahk yuh cah in Hahvud Yahd") and they ate baked beans on Saturday night.

The concept of initial occupancy needs much more study and research, but it obviously is of importance to folklife research and folklore as well as to other academic disciplines. How does one determine who were the initial occupants (after the Native Americans, of course) and where they came from? History books and census records will help, of course, but so will local telephone directories. Once one discovers what the common family names are in an area, he is well on his way to determining who the initial occupants were in the area and where they came from as well as being able to identify later immigrants. (A small town with a large university in it like Bloomington presents some special problems of course, but the college faculty and foreign graduate students in the telephone directory can be sorted out if one is willing to take the time.)

It is generally accepted that the largest number of the early settlers in southern Indiana were of Scotch-Irish ancestry.[9] There are many family names probably indicating Scotch-Irish ancestry in Monroe County whose county seat is Bloomington. Many of these names do not appear in the usual reference books on family names, so that it is impossible to be certain. However, a large number of very common names in the county appear to be of Pennsylvania German origin. Such are: Bohall, Deckard, Holtsclaw, Kinser, Swango, Wampler, and Zikes. These names are not only common in the telephone directories but also are names found in old, rural cemeteries. They show that the initial occupants who established important patterns in the county were clearly not a homogeneous group for large numbers were Scotch-Irish while large numbers were Pennsylvania German. It is likely that the family names cited are the best sources of information on this topic.

In general, I would suggest that there is a real need for studies of American surnames. Such studies would be a great help to researchers in many fields including folklife and folklore.[10]

Let me now make some very tentative suggestions about a family name that has caught my interest—Hoosier. It is not a very common name, but I have found it in the telephone directories of several large American cities, including St. Louis and Cincinnati. The Indianapolis directory is a case in point. Tucked in among a long listing of commercial firms with names such as Hoosier Electric Company are six listings for individuals named Hoosier and seven named Hooser, probably a variant spelling. Hoosher also is found and may be another variant spelling.

The term "Hoosier" has long been applied to residents of Indiana and has been widely accepted in the twentieth century by most residents of the state, many of whom are proud of it. For instance, when the 1976 Indiana automobile license plate appeared bearing the legend "Indiana, the Heritage State," a somewhat vague reference to the exploits of George Rogers Clark and his stalwarts who captured a British garrison at Vincennes, a Bloomington resident wrote an indignant letter to the local paper about the phrase "Heritage State." The resident complained that Indiana was well known as the Hoosier State and ought to be proud of it, and asked sarcastically whether the Indiana University football team was going to be called "The Fighting Heritages" from now on.

Indiana University has, in the last few decades, adopted the term "Hoosier" with enthusiasm. Not only are various athletic teams called the Fighting Hoosiers, the Hurrying Hoosiers, and the like, but a large chorus is called the Singing Hoosiers. Because the word Hoosier is so well known in athletic circles, I am a bit surprised to learn that the term "Big Red" seems to have been used more and more in the last couple of years. Not only do local sports writers refer with increasing frequency to the Big Red teams but the slogan "Go Big Red" has gained prominence. Names, of course, reflect all sorts of things, and a large liquor store that opened in Bloomington a few years ago is called Big Red Liquors. Perhaps five years ago it would have been named Fighting Hoosier Liquors or something similar. In the most recent Bloomington telephone directory there are five businesses using Big Red in their name, including Big Red Disposal Service Inc. I hasten to add that there are twenty-seven businesses listed in the directory with Hoosier in their name.

I suspect that the drift away from Hoosier as a nickname for athletic teams is partly a matter of fashion. A nickname may lose its appeal after a few decades and seem slightly old-fashioned and a bit dowdy. There also, however, has been a real problem in visualizing a Hoosier, and an athletic team really needs a visual symbol such as a mascot to be paraded around the field. A couple of decades ago there were decals on automobile windows embodying the word Hoosier and showing an obviously benign but not especially intelligent-looking schoolmaster wearing glasses with octagonal lenses and carrying an upraised ruler in one hand. This was a reference, lost on many, I suspect, to Edward Eggleston's novel, *The Hoosier Schoolmaster* (1872), which was very popular in its day and helped make Hoosier a well-known term.

More recently an uncouth figure called "Mr. Hoosier Pride" has cavorted around the field during halftime at Indiana University football games. This is a male figure with a large head and a rather nondescript face topped by a broad-brimmed, shapeless hat. About all one can say about the face is that it represents a "Caucasian" male with a prominent chin and a blank expression. This attempt to visually represent a Hoosier has met with little enthusiasm from local football fans.

In 1987 two events combined to arouse new interest in the word "Hoosier": the Hoosiers won the NCAA basketball championship and a movie entitled *Hoosiers* received wide acclaim. This new interest called forth a number of explanations to join the many already in existence as to why inhabitants of Indiana are called "Hoosiers." Some of the explanations are seemingly tongue-in-cheek, some serious.

The origin and original meaning of the word "Hoosier" have been much debated in the past and there were already several interesting humorous etymologies current. A lack of space precludes a full survey of these. The explanation for the term most accepted in scholarly circles and the one that makes most sense to me was presented by H. L. Mencken a number of years ago.[11] He pointed out that, before the state was founded, "hoosier" was used "in Tennessee, and the Carolinas and even in parts of Virginia to indicate a mountaineer or any other uncouth rustic" and that it is still used in that sense there. During the first half of the nineteenth century more or less opprobrious nicknames were applied to residents of several midwestern states. As a case in point, Baynard Rush Hall, himself a Presbyterian minister, wrote of a church meeting he attended in 1824 in Vincennes, Indiana:

> The Protestant assembly was a gathering of delegates principally from the land of Hoosiers and Suckers [Illinois]; but a smart sprinkling of Corn-crackers [Kentuckians], and a small chance of Pukes [Missourians] from beyond the father of floods, and even one or two from the Buckeye country [Ohio].[12]

As time went on, some of these nicknames stuck, but the more obviously opprobrious ones (Pukes and Suckers) have pretty well died out. The original meaning of Hoosier—rustic, uncouth person—was largely forgotten in Indiana. As a result, the term was retained by residents of the state who now, as I have said, are mostly proud of it.

One of the problems with the accepted explanation of the term is that if "hoosier" was a word in wide use in the mid-South before Indiana was settled, before 1800 that is, why is the word not known in Great Britain? No British dictionary or dialect dictionary has ever listed the word. The dialect word "houster," also spelled "hooster," meaning "a badly-dressed, untidy person,"[13] is about the closest one can come to it.

No one who has written on the term "hoosier" has, as far as I know, mentioned the family name Hoosier and its possible significance in showing how old the term may be. There are three generalizations that are of importance here. 1) Most family names in England were established by 1450, though the process continued for at least another century in Ireland, Scotland, and Wales. 2) Some family names are opprobrious terms applied by neighbors, we hope in a good-natured way. Witness such obvious examples as Lawless, which means exactly what it seems to mean, and Toplady, which, Cottle says, is an obscene name for a libertine, "sadly inappropriate to the author of *Rock of Ages*" (Rev. Augustus M. Toplady [1740–1778]).[14] 3) There is absolutely no reason to assume that the present bearer of such a family name has any of the qualities that caused his extremely remote ancestor to be given such a handle.

At first glance, then, the family name Hoosier would seem to indicate that the word "hoosier," meaning a wild, uncouth person, has been used in Great Britain for a long time. It was brought to this country and flourished in the mid-South where it retained its meaning. It was eventually applied to residents of Indiana and has been retained until today because its original meaning has been forgotten.

In support of this thesis, P. H. Reaney reminds us that family names, especially ones that are derived from a nickname, can "carry back the history of a word for 300 to 400 years; from time to time they provide us with forms of importance for etymology of the word."[15] To put it another way, a word may not appear in any printed source until fairly recently. Hence the compiler of a dictionary may assume that the word is of modern origin. The use of that same word as a family name, however, means that the word was in use at least at the end of the Middle Ages and simply was not used in any text that the compilers of dictionaries consulted. As a case in point, Reaney cites the word "piffle." The compilers of the famous *Oxford English Dictionary,* who had as one of their goals to show when each word first appeared in English, were able to find the word appearing in print for the first time as recently as 1847.[16] Yet Reaney finds Piffle appearing as a family name as early as 1344. He assumes the bearer of that name was given it because he "piffled around" a great deal.[17]

If such is the case with "piffle" and a number of other words Reaney cites, why could it not also be the case with "hoosier"? Perhaps the word was used in some regions of Great Britain for a long time. It gave rise to the family name and it was brought to America by people from those regions in Great Britain where it was used. They settled mostly in the mid-South where the word has been used until the present day. But the word has never been written down in Great Britain, so it does not appear in British dictionaries.[18]

There are other cases where a development closely parallel to that I have suggested for "Hoosier" can be traced. For example, the word "tyke" or "tike" originally meant "a mongrel dog." It became an English family name. Probably it was a more-or-less good-natured nickname (cf. Stinky) which finally became permanent as a surname. As early as 1700 it was applied in a probably derisive way to the inhabitants of Yorkshire. Today, however, the term "Yorkshire Tyke" is proudly accepted by the people of Yorkshire.[19]

The main problem with this explanation for the name "Hoosier" is that it is far too complex to be widely dispersed and accepted. Consequently, it is likely that the many simpler explanations will remain current as will also, of course, the humorous ones. The family name Hoosier as proof of the age of the word and the parallels with other state nicknames will probably never gain wide acceptance.

Notes

1. See the useful bibliography in Jan H. Brunvand, *The Study of American Folklore: An Introduction.* 2nd ed. (New York: W. W. Norton, 1978), p. 50.

2. Ibid., pp. 50–51.

3. The authors of the standard book on Indiana placenames either did not know this or did not care, for they do not mention it in their entry on Solsberry: Marvin D. Carmony and Ronald L. Baker, *Indiana Place Names* (Bloomington: Indiana University Press, 1975).

4. *Webster's New World Dictionary of the English Language* (Cleveland, Ohio: The World Publishing Co., 1964).

5. *The Penguin Dictionary of Surnames* (Baltimore, Md.: Penguin Books, 1967), p. 247.

6. Hence Rock East Road, named, of course, for Mr. Rockford East. The road is in the western part of the county and runs generally north and south. The namers of the road must have concluded that calling it just "East Road" would have been confusing.

7. R. A. Salaman, *Dictionary of Tools* (New York: Charles Scribner's Sons, 1975), p. 304.

8. See for example, Edouard A. Stackpole, *Scrimshaw at Mystic Seaport* (Mystic, Conn.: The Marine Historical Association, 1958). Stackpole writes, "The term scrimshaw is in itself of uncertain origin. It is thought to be a derivative of early terms—'skrimshander,' 'scrimshonter,' and 'scrimshorn.' ... So far as may be ascertained, this word appears to come from the Dutch *Skrimshander,* meaning one who indulges too much in laying [*sic*] around or a 'lazy fellow'" (p. 7).

9. See E. Estyn Evans, "The Scotch-Irish: Their Cultural Adaptation and Heritage in the American Old West" in E.R.R. Green, ed., *Essays in Scotch-Irish History* (London: Routledge & Kegan Paul: 1969), p. 74 and fig. 1.

10. Elsdon C. Smith, *American Surnames* (Philadelphia: Chilton, 1969) is a useful beginning.

11. *The American Language,* Supplement II (New York: Alfred A. Knopf, 1948), pp. 620–21.

12. Robert Carlton [pseud.], *The New Purchase,* ed. by James A. Woodburn (Princeton: Princeton University Press, 1916), p. 294.

13. William Grant and David D. Murison, *The Scottish National Dictionary,* V (Edinburgh: 1960), p. 202.

14. Basil Cottle, *The Penguin Dictionary of Surnames* (Baltimore, Maryland: Penguin Books, 1967), p. 286.

15. P. H. Reaney, *The Origin of English Surnames,* p. 224.

16. *The Oxford English Dictionary* (Oxford: Oxford University Press, 1933).

17. Reaney, *The Origin of English Surnames,* p. 224.

18. I should admit that there is at least one other possible derivation for the family name Hoosier. It may be a variant spelling of the name Hosier, "a maker or seller of hose." I cannot, of course, find Hoosier in any reference work dealing with the origin of names, as was the case with other family names cited above. Nor can I find any indication in any works I have consulted that "hosier" was ever pronounced as "hoosier." Hence, I believe that my thesis as outlined has a good chance of being a valid one.

19. Reaney, *The Origin of English Surnames,* p. 262.

Folk Arts and Crafts from a Folklife Perspective

5

Folk Crafts

There are very few general surveys of folk crafts in the United States. When one considers how much interest craft displays elicit at folk festivals and the like, it is surprising that so little of a general nature has been written. This very brief survey was prepared as an introduction for beginning students and interested people in general.

*   *   *

In dealing in limited space with a topic as broad as folk crafts, one can only generalize and enumerate the various crafts. The first consideration must be: what are folk crafts? Here the element of tradition is of primary importance, and one can say generally that folk crafts are traditional crafts. It is, indeed, in the crafts that one can observe with special clarity the operation of tradition. Until relatively recent times, craft techniques and designs were passed down within one family for many generations or were transmitted by the apprentice system wherein a boy learning the craft served for as long as seven years under a master craftsman. Only fairly recently has the older, traditional system of transmitting the skills and knowledge of a craft been partially supplanted by formalized training in schools and by printed manuals and books.

The strong traditional element in the crafts is also apparent in the great antiquity of many crafts. The making of pottery, for example, is immensely old and has changed little over the centuries, while the flint knappers of England who in mid-twentieth century were still producing shaped flints were using a craft technique of unknown antiquity. Tradition usually has a geographical as well as an historical spread; that is, while an element of folklore is passed from one generation to the next within any given area, it also usually spreads from one part of the world to another. So it is with the crafts, some of which are of worldwide diffusion. The expansion of

This article originally appeared in *Folklore and Folklife: An Introduction*, edited by R. M. Dorson (Chicago: The University of Chicago Press, 1971), pp. 233–52. Reprinted by permission of the publisher.

European culture has made it difficult to ascertain distribution patterns. Thus pottery was made in most parts of the world prior to the spread of European culture, and the production of flint knives and arrowheads was also practiced all around the world in prehistoric times. While it is certainly impossible to prove in every case, folklorists are convinced that most folklore elements that are widely distributed were not invented or created at one time and in one place and hence spread by the migrations of people or were passed from one group to the next over a long period of time.

Certain general requirements will determine when a craft is a folk craft. The element of tradition is more important than the element of age. Every craft item that is old is not necessarily a product of a folk craft. It would be incorrect to consider such famous eighteenth-century cabinetmakers as Chippendale to be folk craftsmen. At the same time, many traditional crafts still flourish today. While there is, obviously, a strong correlation between antiquity and folk crafts, one cannot assume that everything old is folk while everything new is non-folk. In order to be considered a folk craft, too, a craft must have been in fairly general use and not restricted only to the upper layers of society where learned, academic, or sophisticated modes of transmission exist. The craft of the goldsmith, therefore, probably lies outside the realm of folk crafts. Although there are strong traditional elements in goldsmithing, the goldsmith catered to the very wealthy and drew his designs often from printed rather than traditional sources. Finally, crafts in which primarily one man creates and designs the finished product have a better claim to consideration as folk crafts than those processes involving mass production, with one man repeating a single operation over and over making only one small part, or with machines doing most of the work.

Another, broader question involves the distinction, if any, between a craft, an art, and an occupation. Although there is much confusion in terms (for example, the term "manual arts"), in general practice the so-called fine arts are distinguished from the crafts. Hence painting and sculpture when traditional are considered as folk art rather than folk craft. Moreover, occupations such as mining and logging are usually not deemed crafts, for the miner, for example, simply produces the metals with which the blacksmith and the tinsmith work while the craftsman produces the finished product. Moreover, the craft demands, on the whole, a greater degree of training and skill than does the occupation.

Although much has been written on folk crafts in certain European countries, especially in Scandinavia, relatively little has been written of a scholarly nature in Great Britain and the United States. A number of popular works, especially "how-to-do-it" books for hobbyists, have been published over the years. In Great Britain earlier works dealt with the history either of crafts in general or of a particular craft, while only a few, such as Norman

Wymer's *English Country Crafts* (1946), attempted to describe on the basis of fieldwork the traditional crafts still practiced. In the last decade there have appeared a number of important works, most of them by members of the Society for Folk Life Studies, organized in 1962. Two books by J. Geraint Jenkins illustrate two primary research methods in folklife research. *The English Farm Wagon* (1961) is an exemplary survey of a single topic based in large part upon questionnaires and fieldwork. *Traditional Country Craftsmen* (1965) covers a number of crafts and is based almost exclusively on fieldwork. In the United States even less has been done. Excluding the "how-to-do-it" books, scholarly American works on folk crafts have mostly emphasized the history of crafts, especially in the seventeenth and eighteenth century, as does Carl Bridenbaugh's *The Colonial Craftsman* (1950), Henry C. Mercer's *Ancient Carpenters' Tools* (1929), and a number of brief articles by various authors in the journal *Pennsylvania Folklife.*

In times past, prior to the Industrial Revolution, folk crafts played an immensely important role in traditional society, for practically everything the individual could not produce for himself was produced by craftsmen living in his own locality.. It would be fair to say that the folk society of Europe was characterized by the extended family unit, the self-sufficient farm, and traditional crafts. Stores or shops as we know them today hardly existed in the countryside in earlier times, and if a farmer needed an item that could not be produced on the farm, he went directly to the craftsman to obtain the item or the craftsman came to the farm to produce it. Traveling peddlers did bring craft products to farms, but poor roads made it difficult for them to carry around large or heavy items in any quantity. Occasionally farmers traveled to nearby towns to sell or barter their excess produce and to purchase ready-made items, and in many areas fairs at which craftsmen set up their booths and sold their wares were a regular event eagerly looked forward to.

In the majority of cases, there was close personal contact between the craftsman and his customer. The visit of the farmer to the craftsman to order or pick up an item was a social event as well as a business matter. In many areas, too, craft shops such as the smithy served as social centers where men tended to gather to discuss news and local events and to tell stories. In those instances where craftsmen traveled from farm to farm, they also lived with the family during their stay and were a valuable source of news, stories, and the like. In many areas, for instance, a weaver went to a farm when the wife had accumulated a sufficient quantity of thread that she had spun herself. There, on his own portable loom or on the loom already at the farmhouse, the weaver wove cloth for all the family's needs or wove certain specialized fabrics requiring more skill than the average farmwife possessed. In the same way, the shoemaker often journeyed from farm to farm making shoes for the entire family from the store of leather that had been accumulating since his last visit. Under such circumstances the craftsman and his customer usually developed a special relationship. The craftsman knew his customer and the family needs, while the customer bartered produce of various kinds to suit the needs of the craftsman and his family. The customer received craft items made specifically to suit his special needs and could be sure of receiving serviceable and reliable items, for often his family had known the craftsman's family for several generations, while the craftsman, on the other hand, was eager to produce satisfactory items, for he knew his customers and was anxious to serve them again. A scythe handle, for example, had to be made to match the height and arm length of its user. Small wonder, then, that craftsmen often played important and influential roles in the rural societies of earlier times.

Before we enumerate the various folk crafts, some general statements should be made. The first involves the Industrial Revolution, its effects upon the crafts in general, and the plight of the craftsman at the present day. As manufactured goods began to flood the countryside in the eighteenth and nineteenth century, the craftsman was, of course, immediately affected. When it became possible to buy factory-made goods at a price lower than the craftsman could make and sell his products, most people, of course, began buying the cheaper goods. Unable to sell his products at a decent price, the craftsman, by and large, ceased being a maker and became a repairer of manufactured objects. The watchmaker, for example, no longer actually made watches but repaired factory-made watches, while the shoemaker rarely made shoes but repaired worn factory-made shoes. The date at which factory-made goods supplanted those made by the craftsman differs from place to place and from craft to craft. In most areas in the United States, it was not the progress of manufacturing but the progress of transportation that determined whether a craftsman could still receive a decent return for his work. As long as transportation costs were high, the purchaser who lived some distance from a factory could often buy an item made locally by a craftsman more cheaply than the manufactured item. During the second half of the nineteenth century, cheap and efficient transportation spelled doom for the age-old system of craft production wherein the craftsman produced items as needed for his own neighbors. At this time, too, factory-made items often had a certain glamor or prestige that hand-made items lacked, so that the purchaser was happy to pay extra for the factory-made item. Now, however, in many instances the hand-made item commands a higher price.

In proof that ancient traditions and ways of life are tenacious and cannot be destroyed overnight by changing economic situations, the folk crafts still survive in contemporary society in the United States. In some areas, remote from contemporary urban society, some crafts survive with something approaching their original vigor. Two examples will indicate their diversity. In the southern mountain regions, chairmakers are still producing and selling their distinctive chairs of traditional design because the customer can barter produce for a chair rather than paying cash, and because the raw materials used for the chairs are plentiful and cheap. No better-paying jobs being available, the craftsman continues with his craft and lives on an income pitifully small by standards of other parts of America. Among the Amish, who are surrounded by and yet apart from contemporary society because they have chosen to cling to the old ways of life for religious reasons, many crafts such as blacksmithing survive. The Amish cannot purchase factory-made items in the old-fashioned designs they demand, and they refuse to make use of motor-driven tools and other mechanical equipment. The well-known Amish buggy is a case in point. Because there is no large demand for it, local carriage-makers, wheelwrights, blacksmiths, and harness-makers find employment producing a limited number of vehicles that a factory would find unprofitable to make.

Second, some craftsmen still flourish in areas where they repair factory-made items, although not all crafts survive in this way. Weavers, for example, do not mend torn or worn-out cloth (the specialists who re-weave cigarette burns in garments use entirely different equipment and techniques) but survive in other ways, and basketmakers do not customarily mend worn-out or broken baskets. To survive by doing repairs, many crafts have had to change their operations. The cabinetmaker in most areas usually does more refinishing of furniture and reupholstering than anything else, while the blacksmith generally spends much of his time welding with modern equipment and tools.

Craftsmen also manage to survive for various special economic and technological reasons. It is economically feasible for some weavers in southern Indiana to weave rag rugs at their looms because the raw materials—rags—cost little or nothing and hence they can sell their rugs at a price comparing favorably with even the cheapest factory-made rugs. From the technological standpoint, some crafts manage to survive because machines have never been developed that can do the work of the hand craftsman. No machine presently makes baskets, so basketmakers still flourish in some parts of the United States even though factory-made containers of paper or plastic have largely replaced baskets and even though foreign baskets can be imported and sold more cheaply than the local basketmaker's product.

A fourth reason the crafts survive today in many areas is that a hand-made item has, for many purchasers, a prestige or glamor that factory-produced items cannot match, quite apart from the question of better workmanship. As a result, craft shops flourish in districts where there are many tourists and where craftsmen can find a market for their products. Craft production of this type does not always represent any noteworthy tradition, for in some cases the craftsmen have learned their craft in schools or in some other formalized way and the items they produce sometimes do not follow traditional designs. A number of organizations and foundations have stimulated craft production of this sort, finding or training craftsmen, supplying designs, and arranging for marketing. At Berea College in Kentucky, for instance, the teaching of crafts is emphasized. While many traditional designs from the surrounding areas are used, some copies of eighteenth-century New England furniture are produced. Henry Glassie cites the case of southern mountain craftsmen making Dutch colonial chairs and Tyrolean baskets following designs introduced to them from urban sources. See his *Pattern in the Material Folk Culture of the Eastern United States* (Philadelphia, 1969), p. 1.

Certain crafts exist today in yet a fifth way, for pottery-making, weaving, silversmithing, and several other crafts have been elevated to the status of fine arts and are taught in art schools. Here again, while the techniques are undoubtedly mainly traditional, emphasis is upon creativity in design rather than upon the observance of tradition.

Finally, in the United States today many crafts are practiced as hobbies because many individuals find great personal satisfaction in making useful or decorative items for their own use or for their friends. Numerous books on weaving, furniture-making, tinsmithing, and the like explain the rudiments of these crafts and supply designs for the hobbyist to follow. While crafts pursued as hobbies testify to the vitality of the crafts and to the important social role they once played in providing an outlet for individual talent and creativity, the element of tradition is largely lacking when designs and techniques are learned mainly from books, so that we would not be justified in considering hobbies as folk crafts.

Another point on the crafts in general concerns the individual—the farmer—as his own craftsman. For practically every craft to be enumerated below there were specialized craftsmen, such as blacksmiths, coopers, wheelwrights, and so on, but many farmers had the ability and the tools to carry on to some extent these specialized crafts themselves (fig. 5.1). The situation varied a great deal from individual to individual, but many farmers could make simple items from metal, wood, and leather, or repair broken or worn items without requiring the services of a specialized craftsman, and it is likely that a farmer with the tools and a special ability in a craft such as blacksmithing would assist his neighbors even though it remained a sideline with him and he never became a specialist. At the same time, craftsmen were also usually part-time farmers who had some land on which they grew crops and raised animals, devoting time to their own farm when they could.

Hence it is difficult to draw a hard and fast line between the farmer and the specialized craftsman. The specialized craftsman, however, devoted much more time to his craft and derived a significant amount of his income from it in comparison to the average farmer.

The list of different crafts to be given below is not exhaustive but suggestive. It might prove impossible to list every specialized craft that ever flourished in Great Britain and the United States, to say nothing of other countries, but we mention most of the crafts widely practiced over a long period of time, with their common names based upon American usage. (Variant names for different crafts, especially as they relate to family names, is an interesting topic, but beyond our present scope.) The crafts are arranged loosely according to the main material with which the craftsman worked, such as wood or metal. If he used more than one material—for instance, a clockmaker can make clocks with both wood and metal parts—a decision was made on the basis of what seemed the more important. The crafts covered are those that flourished during the eighteenth century and continued on at least into the nineteenth century in the United States.

Throughout history, wood has proved to be an immensely important raw material for mankind. Light in weight, durable, easily worked, elastic, smooth to touch, capable of absorbing shock, and possessing many other useful qualities, wood has served man in an astonishingly wide variety of ways. Since woods possess different qualities, craftsmen have needed to know what wood is best for which use and how best to work with different woods. Hence we begin our listing of crafts with those primarily utilizing wood. The cabinetmaker or joiner comes immediately to mind. While some cabinetmakers who catered to the wealthy drew some of their designs from printed sources such as the famous design book of Chippendale, most cabinetmakers relied heavily upon traditional designs. Designs and a sense of proper proportion were part of the lore transmitted from one generation of craftsmen to the next, and one can discover many furniture designs or types made by a number of cabinetmakers over a period of at least one century over a wide geographical area. While a country cabinetmaker usually fashioned all sorts of furniture and made complete pieces, other craftsmen who also worked on furniture are sometimes separately identified. Chairmaking in many areas was a distinct craft, for in making chairs somewhat different techniques are used than in making case pieces such as a chest of drawers. Turning is important in making the round legs and other parts of chairs, and whereas the builder of a chest of drawers works almost exclusively with right angles, the chairmaker seldom uses right angles, for in order to be comfortable the back of a chair, for example, cannot be at a right angle to the seat. Country chairmakers usually employed a few designs, the most common being the Windsor chair and the

Figure 5.1. A Farm Blacksmith Shop, Fulton County, Georgia

This shop is located on the farm of Homer Martin, north of Alpharetta. When it was extensively photographed in November 1966, this small shop (it measures only 8½ by 17 feet) was no longer in use; it was, however, in perfect condition, with its forge at one end, a workbench at the other, and an anvil in the doorway. Mr. Martin, who is pictured at the anvil, was genially available for interview. Mr. Martin used the shop primarily to repair his own farm equipment, although he did some blacksmithing—sharpening plowshares mostly—for his neighbors.

(Fieldwork and artwork by Henry Glassie)

slat-back chair. Turning was often a separate craft, for turners made on their lathes many other items such as turned wooden bowls and wooden buttons in addition to chair parts. The woodcarver was sometimes called upon to use his talents in the decoration of furniture: in seaports he was likely to carve ships' figureheads, and in cities to make carved shop signs, including cigar-store Indians.

The carpenter, either house carpenter or ship's carpenter, represents a craft working with wood still very much alive although considerably changed by the developments growing out of the Industrial Revolution. Prior to the nineteenth century, the carpenter and the cabinetmaker used very much the same techniques, for both joined pieces of wood, whether delicate table parts or huge barn timbers, with the mortise and tenon joint, in which a protruding member on one piece of wood (the tenon) fits into a matching cavity (the mortise) in the other. The development of cheap nails largely put an end to this technique in carpentry, in the United States at any rate. Modern, power-driven saws have likewise supplanted the age-old technique of shaping wood in the direction of the grain by splitting and hewing, while other technological developments have radically changed the craft of the carpenter in other ways.

Before the nineteenth century, when containers were still made by hand, the cooper together with the basketmaker were important craftsmen. Great quantities of barrels in many sizes were needed for the storage and transportation of solids and liquids. In some areas a distinction was made between the tight cooper who made barrels to contain liquid and the slack cooper who made barrels for solids. From staves held together by hoops the cooper made many other containers, both large and small, bearing names now largely forgotten—piggin, noggin, and firkin. Emerson's line, "The meal's in the firkin, the milk's in the pan," preserves one of these terms.

It is probably simplest to place under the heading of wainwright all crafts devoted to making such wheeled vehicles as carriages and wagons. One of the best books available in English on any craft, *The English Farm Wagon* by J. Geraint Jenkins, shows the wide variety of vehicles of traditional design that were developed in response to special needs and the differing requirements of varying terrain in many localities. Often farm wagons as well as carriages were painted in traditional colors and with traditional designs. Closely allied with the wainwright was the wheelwright, who also worked closely with the blacksmith, for an important step in making one type of wheel involved heating an iron tire of the correct size until it expanded. Then it was slipped over the wooden wheel and immediately doused with water so that it contracted and forced the wooden parts of the wheel almost inseparably together. The interdependence of many crafts is shown also in the fact that the blacksmith supplied the wainwright with many iron fittings, hinges, and similar parts needed for the vehicles.

Until the twentieth century many utensils and containers used in the kitchen, dairy, and dining room were made of wood rather than pottery or metal. These wooden bowls, churns, spoons, trenchers, and mugs are generally classified together as treenware. Some of these were made of staves and hoops by the cooper, and some were turned on a lathe by the turner, but many were carved or chiseled from different kinds of wood by the treenware-maker or by the farmer himself during the long winter evenings. Nearly unbreakable and easily cleaned, such treenware had many practical advantages.

The agricultural implement-maker of the past produced such items as rakes, grain cradles, and grain scoops. Many implements made largely of iron at the present, such as rakes and spades, were once made either entirely of wood as in the case of rakes or mainly of wood and shod with iron as in the case of spades. Makers of ax handles, scythe snaths, and the like can also be placed in this category, although often the individual farmer kept a pattern for the utensil handle that best suited his personal requirements and made his own handles from ash, hickory, or other suitable woods.

Other craftsmen who worked mainly with wood include the millwright, who constructed the gears, wheels, and shafts for water and windmills; the fiddle-maker, who shaped other musical instruments besides fiddles; and the clock-maker who, in the early era of factory production, used many wooden parts in the works of his clocks.

A number of other crafts used metals of various kinds. Certainly the most common of the metal-working crafts was blacksmithing, and the smithy was a familiar feature in small communities and towns, whether or not it stood "under the spreading chestnut tree." The knowledge of how to work with iron, transmitted from one generation to another, was, of course, of crucial importance to the progress of civilization, for with tools and implements of iron farmers could raise more foodstuffs and build a greater variety of structures. Items of iron made by the blacksmith were important to many other crafts, for not only did the blacksmith make many of the tools that the carpenter, for instance, used in his work, but also the blacksmith provided the iron nails and hinges that the carpenter needed in building a house. In the twentieth century blacksmiths were largely occupied in shoeing horses, but in earlier times horseshoeing was done by another craftsman, the farrier, who depended upon the blacksmith to supply the necessary shoes and hence worked in close connection with him. When factories began to supply more and more ready-made iron items, many blacksmiths gradually assumed the role of farrier.

Another metalworker especially important during the pioneer periods in various parts of the United States was the gunsmith. The famous Kentucky rifles, actually made mostly in Pennsylvania, played a key role in the period of expansion when the pioneer was forced to contend with Indians and to secure a large part of his food supply from wild game. Guns have generally been regarded as decorative as well as purely utilitarian objects, and the gunsmith chose beautifully grained wood for gun stocks and also used metal inlays and engraving for decoration.

The pewterer, the tinsmith, and the coppersmith all made items that were used in the farm dairy and kitchen and at the dining table. Many families owned a certain number of pewter plates and bowls, and even spoons were often made of pewter. The metal is relatively soft, of course, but if a pewter item were damaged it could be returned to the pewterer who would melt it and recast it. Pewter buttons were also frequently used in an earlier age. The tinsmith made a wide variety of pots, pans, and other containers as well as funnels, strainers, lanterns, and the like. In the eighteenth century, painted tinware, called tôle, in the form of trays and coffee pots became popular. The coppersmith supplied the large copper kettles essential to such diverse household tasks as cheese and apple-butter making. In many places traveling tinkers repaired worn or damaged household wares.

Other craftsmen working in metal include the locksmith, the cutler, the sawsmith, and the bell maker. Certain metal crafts that catered to the wealthy and flourished in the large urban centers should probably be considered outside the realm of folk crafts. These are goldsmithing and silversmithing.

A number of crafts that used mainly various vegetable fibers can be considered together. Basketmakers wove containers of many sizes and shapes for a wide variety of uses. They also employed raw materials of many kinds depending, of course, on what raw materials were available. Varieties of willow especially suitable for basketry were cultivated in some areas, while in other areas certain kinds of wood, especially ash, were used that separate into long thin strips when pounded along the grain. Tree bark of various kinds and straw and grasses were sometimes used to weave baskets, and a special technique of braiding straw and grass and building up a container from such coils was also practiced. Weaving chair seats of fiber would seem to be closely connected with basket-weaving. Certainly the same materials and techniques are used in each craft. Chair seats woven from wild rushes were common where rushes were available in sufficient quantities, though basketmakers did not make much use of rushes.

Ropemakers also used many kinds of fibers, though hemp was the mainstay of those craftsmen in seaports who supplied the great quantities of rope needed aboard sailing vessels. In the countryside, however, ropes were often made from straw, flax fibers too coarse for textiles, bark, animal sinews, leather, and other substances.

Although they used other substances as well, both broom-makers (fig. 5.2) and thatchers made extensive use of straw. Special varieties were cultivated to supply the straw used in these crafts, but brooms were also made from twigs and reed was often used for thatched roofs. Thatching seems to have been used very little in the United States, for the abundance of suitable kinds of wood for splitting shingles made shingle roofs common as early as the seventeenth century, and their popularity has continued in most parts of the country into modern times.

Wherever suitable clays could be found, potters supplied local needs; the countryside used to be dotted with small potteries operated often by a single family. Brick and tile makers also worked where suitable clay was available, though often brick for a house was made right on the site where a house was built, using the clay excavated when the cellar was dug. Clay pipes were also made by specialists.

Wherever suitable stone could be found, masons also were in demand. Masonry can be of many types. A structure, be it a building, a chimney. a foundation for a building, or a fence, can be made of stones that are gathered and used in their natural shape (fieldstone, for example) or artificially shaped pieces of stone quarried from the ground or brick. The masonry can either be fitted together without mortar (dry laid), or mortar of various kinds can be used. In many areas these various kinds of masonry are found side by side. Stone fences or walls of fieldstone laid without mortar, for example, may surround fields, while foundations of houses may be made of field stone laid in mortar and chimneys may be made of shaped stones or bricks laid in mortar. Of these various techniques, the naturally occurring stone laid without mortar must be the most ancient, but it is still being used at the present time.

Another use of stone in building was made where naturally occurring slate made slate roofs possible. Stone was useful in other ways, for grindstones, whetstones, millstones, and gravestones, while containers were often made from soft, easily worked soapstone.

Leather was another raw material for several crafts. The tanner had to work with the animal hides before they could be used in many ways, though rawhide was often used in small quantities for light ropes and cords. Tanned leather was essential for the shoemaker who, as mentioned previously, sometimes traveled from farm to farm making shoes for the entire family from the store of tanned leather that had accumulated since his last visit. The harnessmaker and the saddler also required tanned leather. Frequently

Figure 5.2. Mr. L. A. DeWitt Making Brooms in His Workshop near
            Birdseye, Indiana, August 1979
            In the foreground is a pile of broomstraw ready for
            use. Mr. DeWitt grows broom corn but mostly makes
            brooms for his neighbors, who bring him their old
            broom handles and the broomstraw they have grown.
            On the brooms Mr. DeWitt makes from the broom-
            straw he grows he affixes a label bearing the trade
            name, "Hoosier Pride."
            (Fieldwork and photograph by the author)

leather garments were worn, and some craftsmen, such as blacksmiths, required leather aprons, and these, as well as leather gloves, were supplied by the glover.

A few other crafts associated with other raw materials may be mentioned briefly. Glassblowers were very uncommon outside large urban areas because their products were both fragile and expensive and because glassblowers worked in groups rather than singly. A large furnace was needed to produce the molten glass, and it was not feasible for a single craftsman to maintain such a furnace for his own use. A group of men working together needed to be near a city to find a large enough market for their products. Animal horn was another substance used by occasional craftsmen to produce horn combs and spoons, while powder horns were, of course, also made from animal horns.

Other crafts practiced not by specialized craftsmen but by practically every farmer and his wife need separate treatment. Although not often recognized as crafts, the daily tasks of the farmer may be called subsistence crafts and the daily work of the farmer's wife may be considered household crafts. Both may be treated briefly here because of their importance and because they do not fall under other categories.

The subsistence crafts of the farmer cover a wide range of activities and each activity required considerable skill and a sound knowledge of the traditional lore associated with it. In addition to raising crops, most farms carried on dairying, animal husbandry, and poultry raising. Fruit was grown, the different kinds depending to some extent on the locality, though the apple was probably most important. Berries also were cultivated. Practically every farm had a number of beehives. In most of the eastern United States this source of sweetening was supplemented by maple sugar and by sorghum syrup. Other subsistence crafts were practiced on the average farm, but those mentioned will give some notion of the wide variety of basic crafts.

Where the natural environment made it possible, fishing, hunting, and trapping were also practiced. Under fishing would come such matters as the making of nets and their use, eel-spearing, ice-fishing, and turtling. Trapping involves a great deal of lore concerning different kinds of snares and traps, while under the general topic of hunting and trapping may be listed all sorts of subjects connected with survival in the woods such as the construction of temporary shelters, the kindling of fire, the use of pack-baskets, the making and use of snowshoes, and the training of hunting dogs. It is in this sphere of human activity that much research remains to be done on the relationships between the white man and the American Indian. While the European settler borrowed a great deal from the Indian in the New World, the question of how much he brought from the Old World, how his importations were modified, and what, if any, the Indian borrowed of woodland lore from the white man has never been adequately explored.

If the farmer practiced many crafts in the course of his daily tasks, so also did the farmwife in her daily duties. In preparing foods she drew heavily upon traditional recipes and techniques. In addition, the preservation of foods was mainly her work. In the long history of human life, the discoveries of various ways to preserve foods take on great significance. In a northern climate, foods are abundant at harvest time but scarce at other times of the year, especially in the winter. Great effort was devoted to preserving foods when they were abundant so they would last throughout the year. Methods of preservation include drying of fruits and meats, smoking of meats, conserving of fruits and berries with sugar, pickling of meats and vegetables, spicing as in the making of sausages, and storing root crops in cool root cellars or straw-lined trenches in the ground. Cheese-making may be considered here too, for when milk is plentiful during the summer months cheeses are made to be eaten during the winter. Cider-making and vinegar-making are also ways of preserving apple products past the harvest time.

Another group of crafts practiced in practically every farmhouse are those devoted to producing textiles. In an earlier era, practically all textiles used in the home were produced in the home, and it was a rare occasion when a piece of cloth was purchased. The textiles in common use were linen and wool. Practically every farmer kept enough sheep to provide the wool for his family, while flax also was grown practically everywhere in the eastern United States. The first step in producing cloth was preparing the fiber, shearing the sheep, washing the wool and carding and combing it, or retting, swingling, and combing the flax. Next came spinning the fiber into thread, a time-consuming process. A spinning wheel or two, a smaller one for flax and a larger one for wool, stood in practically every farmhouse, and the women members of the family spent so much time in spinning that the distaff became the symbol for women. Weaving also required much time, and in larger houses a special room was allocated to the loom so that it could be used over a period of time. In most households, however, the loom was set up for shorter periods and then dismantled and stored. In some areas, as previously noted, professional weavers traveled from farm to farm weaving patterns too complicated for the average farmwife or bringing with him to be set up a large loom capable of producing wider webs of cloth than the family looms could produce. Dyeing was another important step in producing cloth. The cloth could be dyed after it was woven, or the thread could be dyed before weaving began so that a colored pattern was produced in the weaving. Most dyestuffs were grown on the farm or gathered in field and forest, and there were many traditional recipes for preparing batches of dye. Various nuts, for instance, produced different shades of brown, while the indigo plant was often cultivated for the sake of the blue dye it produced. Many garments were knitted rather than woven from wool, and fulling was a step in the production of woolen cloth in which moisture, heat, and pressure were used to shrink and thicken the cloth.

A certain number of textile crafts are practiced largely for decorative purposes. These include embroidery, crewel work, needle-point, and crocheting. Girls also made samplers that involved intricate decorative needlework. While it is true that these decorative techniques were frequently used by the young ladies of well-to-do families and were taught in schools, they were also traditional and practiced in leisure hours by most women.

A final group of textile crafts may be termed "salvage" crafts. These include quilting, hooking rugs, braiding rugs, and weaving rag rugs. Sound portions of garments outgrown or worn beyond patching and scraps of leftover material were used in all these crafts. There are several different kinds of quilting, but a common one, the patchwork quilt, involved a pattern of usually different colored pieces of cloth of different sizes sewn together. Not only is the technique of quilting traditional, but designs of great variety, often with colorful names, were also passed from one quilter to the next. In hooking, braiding, and weaving rugs, pieces of cloth useless for other purposes are cut into long, narrow strips. For hooked rugs these strips are worked through a coarsely woven piece of cloth leaving loops protruding. For hooked rugs also traditional patterns are widely known and used. In braided rugs, the strips are braided into coils that are sewn together while for a woven rag rug the strips are woven on a loom very much as any cloth is woven.

Other household crafts include such tasks as brewing, soapmaking, and candlemaking. Prior to the religious revivals of the late eighteenth and nineteenth century ale was brewed in many households and drunk at home as well as at inns and taverns. Wines and cordials such as elderberry wine and dandelion wine were often homemade. Whiskey was also distilled, and eighteenth and early-nineteenth-century American records and travelers' accounts testify to the large quantities that were consumed. Soap was made at home from animal fats treated with lye obtained from wood ash. Candles were also made from animal fats as well as from waxes including that obtained from the bayberry. Candles were made either by dipping lengths of string into molten fat or wax or by using candle molds. All in all, the household of an earlier era was a busy place. The farmer and his wife must have gained considerable personal satisfaction from supplying the needs of their families by their own hands, guided by their inherited knowledge of necessary techniques and patterns.

Bibliography and Selected Readings

United States

Bridenbaugh, Carl. *The Colonial Craftsman.* New York: New York University Press, 1950; Chicago: The University of Chicago Press, 1961. Included as the best example of a number of works by historians on early crafts and industries. The craftsman, his social position, and the role of specific craftsmen in historical events are the themes of this book rather than the traditional aspects of craft techniques and products or the crafts in traditional culture.

Eaton, Allen H. *Handicrafts of the Southern Highlands.* New York: Russell Sage Foundation, 1937. Although designed primarily to encourage the revival of handicrafts as "leisure-time occupation" and "therapy for grown-ups," this work does give the best available survey of surviving traditional crafts in that area in the United States that is probably the richest in such survivals.

————. *Handicrafts of New England.* New York: Harper, 1949. The companion volume to the above work for another rich area.

Glassie, Henry. *Pattern in the Material Folk Culture of the Eastern United States.* Philadelphia: University of Pennsylvania Press, 1969. While emphasizing architecture, much material on folk crafts is included in an attempt to block out tradition areas. The method used is that of the cultural geographer rather than the folk atlas technique. The book incorporates the best available bibliography on folk crafts in the eastern United States but is difficult to use since the bibliographical section of the book is arranged alphabetically by author.

Kettel, Russell H. *The Pine Furniture of Early New England.* Garden City, New York, 1929. The best available work on furniture of traditional design made both by traditionally trained craftsmen and by nonspecialists for their own use. Lavishly illustrated.

Kovel, Ralph and Terry. *American Country Furniture, 1780–1875.* New York: Crown, 1965. The Kovels use the term "country furniture" in the antique dealer's sense, i.e., in contrast to the high-style furniture made for the wealthy in the cities. Although the book contains a number of examples of relatively late, factory-made pieces, nonetheless it does contain a fair number of examples of traditional designs.

Lord, Priscilla S., and Daniel J. Foley. *The Folk Arts and Crafts of New England.* Philadelphia: Chilton Books, 1965. Although poorly written and superficial, this work does bring together photographs covering a number of traditional crafts and is a useful supplement to Eaton, above.

Mercer, Henry C. *Ancient Carpenters' Tools.* Doylestown, Pa.: The Bucks County Historical Society, 1929, 1960. The best American book in the field of folk crafts. Mercer, a self-trained scholar, used all the techniques of the comparative folklorist: distribution and historical studies, functional concepts, extensive fieldwork.

Needham, Walter, and Barrows Mussey. *A Book of Country Things.* Brattleboro, Vt.: Stephen Green Press, 1965. Of special interest to the folklorist in that Mussey tape-recorded Needham's reminiscences about his grandfather and what he taught him. The recordings appear to be reproduced with substantial authenticity. Good coverage of the crafts practiced on the farm in the nineteenth century.

van Wagenen, Jared. *The Golden Age of Homespun.* Ithaca, N. Y.: Cornell University Press, 1953. Covering upstate New York, this book is the best general American survey of the nineteenth-century crafts of the countryside including professional craftsmen, crafts carried on in the home, and subsistence crafts.

Great Britain

Evans, E. Estyn. *Irish Folk Ways.* London: Routledge and Kegan Paul, 1957. Describes and illustrates many aspects of material culture and traditional crafts, in such chapters as "Furniture and Fittings," "Hearth and Home," and "Home-Made Things."
Grant, Isabel F. *Highland Folk Ways.* London: Routledge and Kegan Paul, 1961. Contains discussions of Highland weavers, spinners, tinkers, woodworkers, and other craftsmen, with many text figures.
Jenkins, J. Geraint. *The English Farm Wagon.* Lingfield, Surrey: Oakwood Press, 1961. A model work, sponsored by the Museum of English Rural Life. Applies the methods developed by Scandinavian scholars to English material.
————. *Traditional Country Craftsmen.* London: Routledge and Kegan Paul, 1965. The best survey in English on crafts that still flourish today.

6

Turpin Chairs and the Turpin Family: Chairmaking in Southern Indiana

In this essay I tried to deal at length with a number of the aspects of a particular folk craft rather than focusing on the products of the craft alone. I tried to give as much information as I could find on at least two generations of one family in which chairmaking was passed from father to son, information gathered from the only written source I could find, the censuses, and information gathered from living family members and neighbors who had known the family. I also tried to locate as many chairs as possible that were made by the two generations to describe those design features each family member used as his "signature," and to show how the chairs were made on the basis of interviews with the sons of one of the chairmakers, men who had helped their father in their youth. I tried likewise to give some history about the types of chairs the family made. Finally, I talked about the cultural context of the chairmaking and the changes in the milieu that affected the chair designs and the craftsmen. When I offered the paper to the *Indiana Magazine of History* their experts in Indiana history objected to the general approach I had used and said that I should simply show a few pictures of chairs and explain why anyone should pay any attention to them. This episode shows that historians and folklife researchers have different perspectives on material culture.

* * *

The term "Turpin chair" is familiar to a number of people living in northeastern Greene County, northwestern Monroe County, and southeastern Owen County in southern Indiana.[1] Not only is the term familiar, but also many people in these areas own Turpin chairs. These so-called slat-back chairs are all hand made[2] and share a number of design and construction features, which will be described later. More important to the people who own them, however, is the fact that they are strong, durable, comfortable, and light in weight. Many of the owners cherish them as family heirlooms.

The original version of this article appeared in *Midwestern Journal of Language and Folklore* 7, no. 2 (1981): 57–106.

I became interested in Turpin chairs originally for several reasons. First of all, I knew that much furniture that had been made by hand in Indiana was treasured by Indiana families, but I also knew that very little had been written about the makers of this furniture. For example, when Betty Lawson Walters published her book, *Furniture Makers of Indiana, 1793 to 1850* in 1972,[3] she was able to cite only one other work on Indiana furniture makers, Arthur Whallon's article, "Indiana Cabinetmakers and Allied Craftsmen, 1815–1860," published in 1970.[4] Both of these works consist of names of craftsmen culled from census reports, newspaper advertisements, county histories, and similar sources. While this research is of great value, it is only rarely that it is possible to associate the name of any specific craftsman with a piece of furniture he made. For example, Walters was able to find the names of 2,176 furniture makers who worked in the period she studied, but only about 25 of these can be identified as the makers of specific surviving examples of furniture. In the years since Walters' and Whallon's works were published, little further has been written on Indiana furniture. It seems to me, therefore, that it would be useful to identify specific furniture makers and to connect them with surviving examples of their work.

Soon after I became interested in Turpin chairs I was told that Jim Turpin, the last of the family to make chairs, had died as recently as 1955 and was making chairs almost to the time of his death. It seemed to me that the Turpin family presented a fine opportunity to investigate a whole complex of related problems such as the effects of the Industrial Revolution on the southern Indiana countryside and the people who lived in it, the persistence of older patterns into the modern era, the role of the craftsman in society, and the like. Studies have been made of cabinetmakers of the eighteenth and early nineteenth centuries[5] it is true, but such studies have had to rely on sparse written records as a source of information about the craftsmen. I knew that in this case I would be able to talk with many people who had actually known Jim Turpin.

The Turpins: A Family of Chairmakers

Several people gave me information about Jim Turpin, his father, Joe, and his brother, Bill, all chairmakers. By using census records it has been possible to compile something of a family history. There are some minor inconsistencies in the census records concerning the ages of people listed, but by and large the records are clear.[6]

John Turpin was living in Garrad County, Kentucky, about thirty miles south of Lexington by at least 1798, for one of his sons who was born in that year is said to have been born in Kentucky. He was married, and his wife, whose name is not given, was about his age. They were the parents eventually of four sons and a daughter. James was the oldest son, and Henry the next to youngest. This James was born in 1798 and Henry in 1817. John and his family moved to Franklin Township, Owen County, Indiana, shortly after 1830. James, who was already married, moved with him. The date of the move to Indiana can be established by the fact that the family is not listed in the 1830 Indiana census and by the fact that James' oldest child, Sarah, was born in Kentucky, while his next child, Andrew W., was born in Indiana in 1832.

John Turpin died between 1840 and 1850, and James and his family moved from Owen County to Beech Creek Township in Greene County, a move of only a few miles. They settled in a valley since called Turpin Hollow. James' wife, Elizabeth, was born in 1800 in Virginia. There were five children, including two sons, Andrew W., born in 1832, and Josephus, born in 1840. Andrew W. lived very near his father in Turpin Hollow. Born in 1832, he married Louisa Ison on August 14, 1851. She died shortly afterwards, and on January 24, 1855, he married Isabel Brown, who in turn died in a few years so that he married Mary E. Barton on September 5, 1859. Some time between 1860 and 1880 he moved away from Turpin Hollow, seemingly to some other state. Josephus, born in 1840, lived with his father until his father died. He continued to live on the family farm in Turpin Hollow after his father's death. He married Susan J. Martindale November 10, 1864, and married again later in life in 1886. His second wife was named Martha. His first wife bore him two sons, William W., born in 1866, and James R., born in 1868. Josephus (also called Joseph or Joe) was still living in 1900, but his date of death could not be ascertained. Census records do not reveal very much about William W. except for his birth date. However, there is good evidence that he was working in the town of Mt. Tabor in northwest Monroe County around 1895. This evidence will be presented later. James R. lived on the family farm in Turpin Hollow after his parents died. He never married and died March 2, 1955.

In 1900 Joseph M. Turpin, born in October 1864, was also living in Beech Creek Township, Greene County, with his wife, Mary, and four children. He was probably a cousin to James R. and had moved to the township after 1880, for he is not listed as living in the township in the census of that year.

Since many of the censuses list the occupation of adult males (adult females are usually noted to be "keeping house"), it is possible to see from the records that many of the Turpins in several generations were chairmakers. It is necessary, however, to supplement the information on occupation that the censuses provide. The census takers were probably instructed in most cases to list the primary occupation of adults; hence, James R. Turpin is listed in the 1900 census at age 31 as a farm laborer. According to the testimony of many people living today, however, he made chairs all his life, beginning by helping his father when he was only seven years old.

Around 1900, then, there were four Turpins who were making chairs within a few miles of one another. Joseph, who was 61 years old in 1900, is listed in the census as a chairmaker. His son, James R., was well known as a chairmaker. Another son, William, is also known to have been a chairmaker. Joseph's nephew, Joseph M., is also listed as a chairmaker in the 1900 census.

Joseph's older brother, Andrew W., born in 1832, is also listed in the 1860 census as a chairmaker. He moved away from the county with his wife and children sometime before 1880. The father of Joseph and Andrew, James, born in Kentucky in 1798, is listed in both the 1850 and 1860 censuses simply as a farmer. It is safe to conclude, however, that he was a chairmaker, for his two sons were. It is also possible that the craft was followed by Turpins of earlier generations, but there is no way to determine whether this is true or not.

At least three generations of Turpins, then, were chairmakers. It is not uncommon, of course, for a craft to be handed down within one family for several generations. Indeed, it would seem natural that a boy growing up would help his father and that a father would be interested in teaching his craft to his son.

Jim Turpin, the Last of the Chairmakers

Thanks to the kindness of a number of people, it is possible to give some information about James R., the last of the Turpins to make chairs in Turpin Hollow. Jim, as he was usually called and as I shall call him from now on, was born on the family farm in September 1868. He went to school for several years, for the 1880 census shows that, at the age of twelve, he was attending school. He also, of course, must have helped his father with a number of tasks around the farm. One of these tasks involved making chairs. One of Jim's neighbors who remembers Jim very well showed me a chair that had belonged to her father. She said that Jim had said that he had helped his father make that chair when he was seven years old. In the process of helping his father, of course, Jim steadily absorbed the skills that were to stand him in such good stead throughout his life.

The farm on which Jim grew up was a reasonably prosperous one. Some rough approximation of the relative prosperity of the family can be gained from the 1860 census. The census taker must have ridden or walked along the country roads, visiting each farmhouse in turn. Hence the families listed in the census just before and just after the entry for the Turpin farm must have been their neighbors. If we take the ten nearest neighbors who owned the farms on which they lived, we find that the real estate valuation of four of them is greater than that of the Turpin family, while that of six is less. The real estate valuation of the Turpin property is $1100, while the average for their ten nearest neighbors is $1050.

Jim's father lived until at least 1900, when Jim was 31 years old. Jim continued to live with his parents until they died, farming and making chairs. After the death of his parents he inherited the farm and continued to live on it, following his previous pursuits. He died on March 2, 1955, aged 87, and is buried in a small cemetery, called the Minks Cemetery on county maps, located on the north edge of Turpin Hollow.

Jim was described by everyone who knew him as a kind, friendly man. He was tall and strong, "raw-boned," able to carry out of the woods over his shoulder a log big enough to make a railroad tie. He often walked long distances into Newark, about three miles up some pretty steep hills, carrying a set of six chairs on his back. He always had a big moustache and was a fine singer with a strong bass voice. He would often sing in a quartet of mixed voices at funerals. Everyone who remembers him speaks of him with respect and affection.

As time went on, the countryside around Jim and the people who lived there changed. Progress reached even the hilly, heavily wooded terrain of northeastern Greene County. In the twentieth century many of the smaller, hilly farms which had supported families for a century were abandoned. The farmers who remained mostly enlarged their farms and turned to modern agriculture. The older pattern, wherein a farmer raised enough foods of a variety of kinds mainly to feed his own family and had very little surplus to sell or barter, gradually was abandoned by most people. This pattern gave way to "cash crop" farming, wherein a farmer raised one or two crops, selling most of what he raised and using the money thus gained to supply many of his and his family's needs. Farmers patronized the country stores in such nearby towns as Newark and McVille and probably visited Spencer, about ten miles away, for special purchases. Automobiles and trucks replaced horse-drawn vehicles, and tractors replaced horses. Fashions in clothing changed and, more important for chairmakers, fashions in home furnishings did also; but, as we shall see, people in the area still bought some chairs from Jim Turpin.

In general, the standard of living in the area increased. As people became more prosperous they acquired more possessions. The children and young people attended schools longer, and the education thus received changed their outlook on life. Many felt life in a city to be more attractive than life on a farm and moved away. Those who remained on the farms often became part-time farmers. As roads were improved and cars became more reliable and more common, it was possible for a man to live on a farm but hold a job in town. While it is true that many of the people living in the area retained some of the traits of their forefathers, in many ways they became like people everywhere else in the United States. They wore the same clothes, drove the same cars, listened to the same radio programs, read the same magazines, and watched the same movies.

In such changing times Jim Turpin did not change as his neighbors did. He continued to raise enough foods of various kinds to supply his needs, and, of course, he continued to make chairs entirely by hand. It is not so much that his standard of living decreased, for he probably had at least as many material possessions as his father had. The standard of living of most of his neighbors, however, increased so that Jim seemed the poorer by comparison. Jim undoubtedly seemed to some of his neighbors to be backward, unprogressive, perhaps a bit strange. There is no doubt but that everyone like him and trusted him completely, but in his later years, especially, he must have been regarded as a figure out of the past, somewhat different from those among whom he lived.

Jim made chairs for people in his neighborhood, of course, but also people who lived some distance away would come to him for chairs. A lady who lives about eight miles north of Turpin Hollow told me that when she was married in 1927, her husband went to see Jim and got a set of chairs from him. Jim also made arrangements with the store in Newark whereby people who wanted chairs would leave word at the store. Jim would make the chairs and deliver them to the store where they could be picked up. People who needed a chair bottomed (i.e., a new seat) could leave word at the store. Jim would take a roll of hickory bark, go to the person's home, and weave the new seat. Jim also made some other pieces of furniture, such as tables and cradles, but only for his own family and friends.

The prices that Jim charged for his chairs varied somewhat over the years but were never very high. Prices people mentioned to me ranged from $1.50 to $3.00 for rocking chairs and from 75¢ to $2.00 for straight chairs. I was told that around 1950 he was charging $2.00 for a straight chair. Comparisons are hard to make, but in 1950 a rocking chair somewhat comparable to one of Jim's could be bought in a store for about $7.50, while in 1930 one could be bought for about $3.00. Generally speaking, then, Jim's chairs cost about half what comparable chairs would cost in a store.[7]

Bill Turpin, the Mt. Tabor Chairmaker

I first heard about Turpin chairs from a friend who lives in the little community of Mt. Tabor in northwestern Monroe County. Mt. Tabor was a thriving community in the last century. The 1850 census, for instance, lists eighteen households and a total population of 85 for the town. Today, however, there are only three or four families living in the community. My friend told me that at one time there had been in Mt. Tabor the Turpin chair shop. She was able to point out to me the site of the Turpin shop, and her relatives and friends were able to describe the shop to me since it had been standing as late as 1920. The shop was long and narrow and stood on land owned by Mr. and Mrs. Benjamin Davis. After the chairmaker left, the building was used for storage purposes, but it was torn down in the 1920s.

When I tried to find some written record of the Turpin chair shop in Mt. Tabor, I was completely unsuccessful. No census for Monroe County listed a Turpin living in or near Mt. Tabor, nor were any other records for Mt. Tabor useful. I visited a number of cemeteries in the vicinity of Mt. Tabor, hoping to find a gravestone of a Turpin, but to no avail. Since Mt. Tabor is not far from Owen County, I searched the Owen County censuses, but, again, to no avail.

Fortunately, through the kind offices of a friend, I was finally put into contact with Mrs. Hattie Spicer of Gosport. Mrs. Spicer, at the time I visited her in July 1979, was 88 years old and in excellent health. She owns a small child's chair with arms but without rockers (fig. 6.1) that she said had been made for her when she was a child by Bill Turpin at his shop in Mt. Tabor. She is the first-born of 10 children. When she was three or four years old, her mother decided that Hattie should have a rocking chair of appropriate size. Her father went to the Turpin shop to order a chair, but he ordered the chair made without rockers since he feared she might tip over in a rocking chair and hurt herself. A year or so later, about 1895, when Hattie was riding in a buggy with her parents, her mother pointed to a man on the street and said, "That's Bill Turpin, the man who made your chair."

Bill Turpin, Mrs. Spicer recalls, was a tall and thin man. At his shop he kept on hand straight and rocking chairs, but a special chair such as a child's chair had to be ordered and picked up after it was made. Mrs. Spicer's father had a rocking chair and her mother a set of straight chairs made by Bill Turpin. I have been able to locate a number of other rocking chairs and straight chairs and another child's chair made by Bill Turpin and owned by people living in or who once lived in Mt. Tabor, Gosport, and Stinesville or nearby countryside. Gosport is about three miles from Mt. Tabor, while Stinesville is only about a mile away. Bill (William W.) Turpin was born in Turpin Hollow in 1866, the son of Joseph and the older brother of Jim. He was living at home in 1880 at the age of 14 according to the census of that year. He must have moved to Mt. Tabor, a distance of only eight miles, sometime between 1885 and 1890. Since nearby Stinesville was a growing town at that time, thanks to the thriving limestone quarries and mills there, it must have seemed to him a good location for a chair shop. It is almost certain that he was living in Mt. Tabor in 1890, but the detailed listing of citizens by name for the 1890 census has been destroyed and no copy was made. He must have left Mt. Tabor by 1900, for he is not listed in the census for that year. I have been unable to find any record that would show where he went after he left Mt. Tabor.

Figure 6.1.   Child's Arm Chair Made by Bill Turpin in Mt. Tabor, 1894
Made for and owned by Mrs. Hattie Spicer of Gosport.
The chair has been refinished and the seat replaced.
The front posts have been worn down from the chair
having been dragged along by children using it as a
support while learning how to walk.
*(All chairs, unless otherwise noted, are in the author's
collection, and all photographs are by the author)*

Characteristics of Jim Turpin's Chairs

I have been able to locate and photograph 28 chairs made by members of the Turpin family. Although all these chairs resemble one another in a number of ways, there are some minor differences between the chairs made by different members of the family. Because more information is available about Jim and how he made his chairs, I will begin by describing his chairs and then show what differences there are in chairs made by Bill and Joe.

All Turpin chairs are what is usually called slat-back chairs. They consist of two long back posts, which serve both as legs for the chair and for back supports; two front posts or legs; a number of rounds or rungs, which join all of the posts together and four of which serve as a frame for the woven seat; slats, thin but wide pieces of wood, which join the two back posts together above the seat level and form the back; and the seat, woven from thin strips of hickory bark.

Compared to other southern Indiana chairs, Jim's back posts, front posts, rounds, and slats are of medium size (fig. 6.2). I have seen other chairs both with heavier and lighter members (fig. 6.3). Jim's front and back posts in his straight chairs are $1\frac{1}{2}$ inches in diameter below the seat, while other Indiana chairs I own range from $1\frac{3}{8}$ inches to $1\frac{5}{8}$ inches. In his straight chairs the rounds (those not covered by the woven seats) average $\frac{7}{8}$ inch in diameter at the center, while rounds in other Indiana chairs range from $\frac{5}{8}$ inch to 1 inch. Of course, in larger rocking chairs the pieces are larger. The three straight chairs I own that Jim made are $34\frac{1}{2}$ inches high, measured from the floor to the top of the back post. Chairs by other Indiana makers I own range from $32\frac{1}{4}$ inches to $35\frac{1}{2}$ inches high. It should be mentioned in regard to the height of a chair, however, that a chairmaker may have made a chair for a particularly tall or short person and hence used a height different from his customary one, or the chair may have been cut off or worn down. I have tried to measure chairs that appear to be the same height as when they were made.

All Jim's back posts are bent above the seat both backwards and outwards. On a typical straight chair the backward bend amounts to about $\frac{3}{4}$ inch. The outward bend is about the same. The front of the upper part of the back posts is flattened beginning at a point about an inch above the seat. None of his back posts have finials at the top, partly because the flattening of the front of the posts makes such finials impractical, partly because the backward and outward bend of the posts would make the finials appear to sit at a strange angle. The back posts also taper slightly overall from the greatest diameter near the bottom of $1\frac{9}{16}$ inch to the smallest diameter of $1\frac{3}{16}$ inch at the top. All four posts on straight chairs terminate at the floor in "feet" formed by a more distinct taper. On Jim's chairs the taper begins $3\frac{1}{2}$ inches above the floor, and the diameter of the post is reduced from $1\frac{9}{16}$ inch to $\frac{15}{16}$ inch. The

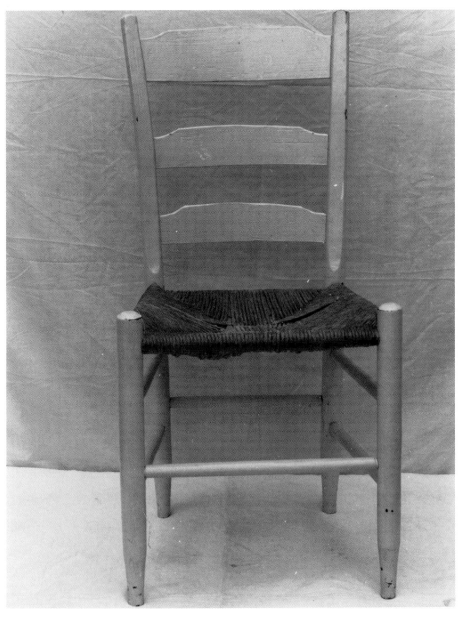

Figure 6.2. Straight Chair Made by Jim Turpin
Purchased at an auction sale in 1952, it had been made
some years prior to that time because the seat had
been worn out.

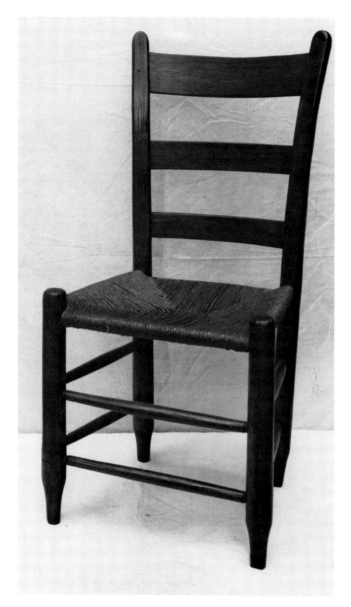

Figure 6.3.   Straight Chair Probably Made in Indiana, Chairmaker
Unknown
Purchased at an auction sale in 1968 east of Bedford.
Probably made before 1900, for the seat was
completely worn out and the chair had been stored in
an outbuilding for some decades. Chair was refinished
and the seat replaced.

tops of the front and back posts are not "domed" as in most chairs made by others. Instead, the very top is flat, and there is a very sharp, straight chamfer surrounding the flat surface (fig. 6.4).

The back posts on Jim's large rocking chairs are similar to those on his straight chairs except they are longer and of somewhat greater diameter. Also the flattened portion begins just above the arms rather than just above the seat. Moreover, the "feet" are different (fig. 6.5). The bottom of the posts does not taper but retains the same diameter as the rest of the post. At the very bottom there is a slight chamfer. If the bottoms of rocking chair posts tapered, the posts would be weak at the point where the rockers are fastened to them. It is often possible to tell whether a chair made as a straight chair has been converted to a rocking chair later. If the bottoms of the posts in such a chair taper to form "feet," the chair was undoubtedly built originally as a straight chair, especially if the rockers are of the type wherein a piece is cut from the side of the post and the rocker is fastened against it with a screw or a bolt.

The slats on Jim's chairs are relatively thin, averaging $\frac{1}{4}$ inch. They bow backwards, the top slat on a straight chair bowing about 1 inch. In his straight chairs Jim used three slats and in his rocking chairs, four. The top slat is wider than the others. In his straight chairs the top slat is about $3\frac{1}{2}$ inches wide, while the other two slats are about $2\frac{5}{8}$ inches. All the slats are "notched"; that is, a piece of wood is cut out of both upper corners.

The front posts are the same diameter as the back, $1\frac{1}{2}$ inch. They do not taper except at the feet on his straight chairs. On his large rocking chairs, however, the front posts are larger at the bottom than at the top, gradually tapering from a diameter of 2 inches at the bottom to $1\frac{1}{2}$ inches at the top. This feature provides for greater strength where the rockers are fastened.

The front posts on Jim's large rocking chairs extend about $8\frac{1}{2}$ inches above the line of the seat. Between the top of the seat and the point at which the arm enters the front post, a long shallow cove is cut (see fig. 6.5). This is about 5 inches long, and the diameter of the post is reduced from about $1\frac{7}{8}$ inches to about $1\frac{7}{16}$ inches at the center of this cove. The center of the arms is about $7\frac{1}{2}$ inches above the seat. The arms are tenoned into the front posts about $1\frac{1}{2}$ inches below the top of the posts. They do not sit atop the front posts as they often do in arm chairs and rocking chairs by other Indiana makers. The arms themselves are turned so that they are larger in the center (about $1\frac{3}{4}$ inches), tapering gradually to about $\frac{7}{8}$ inch at each end. The taper is such that they can be said to be cigar shaped.

Jim used a total of ten rounds for each of his chairs, including the four rounds upon which the seat is woven. There is only one round below the seat, therefore, at the front of the chair. The rounds on his straight chairs are $\frac{7}{8}$ inch in diameter throughout most of their length, tapering slightly at each end. The seats of the chairs were originally woven of thin strips of hickory

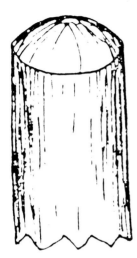 

Figure 6.4.   Tops of Front Posts of Chairs by Bill and Jim Turpin

bark averaging ¾ inch in width. Although the hickory bark is remarkably durable, many of the chairs I have seen now have seats of different materials. The rockers on Jim's large rocking chairs are about ⅞ inch thick and 1¾ inches wide. On some much-used chairs, of course, the rockers have been worn away somewhat. Jim always cut away the outside lower portions of the posts and fastened his rockers in this notch with bolts which pass through both the rocker and the post. The bolt and the nut protrude from the inside surface of the post.

Two men who had helped Jim make chairs when they were boys told me that Jim customarily made his posts and his slats from red oak. The rounds were made of hickory. On request, he would make chairs of sugar maple, but he charged more for these. He never used any varnish or other finish on his chairs, although, of course, many were subsequently varnished, stained, or painted. While he was turning his posts in his lathe, he pressed a pointed instrument against the posts which made a small ring around the posts to mark where the rounds and the slats were to be inserted. These marks are very shallow. If a chair has been refinished, the marks may have been scraped or sanded away.

Figure 6.5. Rocking Chair by Jim Turpin
Original finish and seat.
(From the collection of Mr. Gary Stanton)

I have seen and photographed seven straight chairs and five large rocking chairs Jim made. He also made other types of chairs, such as a small rocking chair, I have been told, but I have not seen any of these other types.

How Bill's Chairs Differ from Jim's

I have seen and photographed thirteen chairs made by Bill Turpin in Mt. Tabor in the 1890s. Eight are straight chairs, three are large rocking chairs, one is a child's arm chair, and one a child's rocking chair. On the basis of these examples it is possible to see that Bill's chairs are very like Jim's in most respects but with some noticeable differences. I will describe only the differences so that if one desires a complete description of Bill's chairs, he or she should read the description of Jim's chairs and substitute the differences noted for Bill's chairs.

The tops of the front and back posts in Bill's chairs are domed, that is, gently rounded (see fig. 6.4). The slats in his chairs are not notched at the corners but are straight across the top. His slats are of different widths, the widest at the top and the narrowest at the bottom. On a rocking chair of his that I own, the top slat is $4\frac{1}{8}$ inches wide, the next $3\frac{5}{8}$ inches, the next $3\frac{1}{4}$ inches, and the bottom one $2\frac{5}{8}$ inches (fig. 6.6). On this same rocking chair the cove motif of the front post is repeated on both the front and the back posts between the rounds so that the front post has a total of three coves (fig. 6.7). Other rockers that Bill made, however, do not have this cove motif between the rounds but only on the upper part of the front posts. The front posts of Bill's rocking chairs do not get thicker towards the bottom as Jim's do.

Bill's arms are set in between the front and the back posts in his arm chairs and rocking chairs just as are Jim's, but Bill's arms are somewhat different. On the rocking chair I own, the arms have what has been called a bamboo turning. That is, they are larger at four different points and gently diminish in size on each side of these points so that they look somewhat like a stalk of bamboo. The arms on his other rocking chairs that I have seen do not use this bamboo motif but are simpler round turnings, larger in front than at the back.

Bill used a total of eleven rounds in his straight chairs so that there are two rounds beneath the seat between the front posts. On his rocking chairs, however, there is only one round beneath the seat between the front posts. On the rocking chair I own, but only on this chair, the front round is larger in the middle than at the ends and has a simple decorative turning in the center consisting of a ball-shaped motif with incised rings on either side. On my rocking chair the rockers are held to the posts with large screws, but on the other two rocking chairs Bill made, the rockers are held on with bolts, as in

Figure 6.6.   Rocking Chair Made by Bill Turpin in Mt. Tabor, ca. 1895
Chair refinished and seat replaced.

Figure 6.7.   Detail of Rocking Chair

Jim's chairs. Bill used far more sugar maple in his chairs than did Jim, for every one of Bill's chairs I have seen has maple posts, while a few also have maple slats.

How Joe's Chairs Differ from Jim's

I have been able to identify with certainty only two chairs made by Joe Turpin, the father of Jim and Bill. One is a large rocking chair. It is very similar to the two simpler large rocking chairs that Bill made except for the slats. They are neither notched at the corners like Jim's nor straight across the top like Bill's, but slightly arched across the top. I own a child's high chair made by Joe that is different in one important respect from every other Turpin chair (fig. 6.8). Indeed, as I will mention later, it is different in this respect from most slat-back chairs made in southern Indiana. The back posts are not bent above the seat. They are not flattened on the fronts, and they have finials at the top. Whether Joe made other chairs with this distinctive feature I cannot say.

How Jim Made Chairs

Thanks to the kindness of two men who helped Jim make chairs when they were boys, it is possible for me to give a reasonably detailed description of how Jim made chairs. The methods he used were essentially unchanged throughout his life, and it is almost certain that his father and grandfather made chairs in exactly the same way. The main reason for this consistency is that they all used hand tools exclusively, and hand tools for woodworkers have changed very little in the last 200 years or so. An example would be a drawknife, a tool which Jim and his forefathers used a great deal (fig. 6.9). In early days a blacksmith would have made the blade, and the woodworker himself would have made the wooden handles fitted to each end of the blade. A modern drawknife is mass-produced in a factory; however, it still has a steel blade and wooden handles, it is the same size and shape as the earlier drawknife, and, of course, it is still used in exactly the same way. Most modern woodworkers make chairs in quite different ways than did Jim and his forefathers, but that is because the modern woodworker has a shop full of machines powered by electric motors. Even if Jim had wanted to buy modern woodworking machines, there was no electricity in Turpin Hollow up until after his death in 1955. I might add that a modern woodworking shop where one or two men can make furniture has at least $8,000 worth of machinery, whereas even today one could buy all the tools that Jim used for less than $150.

Figure 6.8.   Child's High Chair Made by Joe Turpin, ca. 1900
Chair refinished and seat replaced. The front posts
have been worn down to the point that the end of one
arm is visible at the front of the post. The chair was
dragged along by children using it as a support while
learning how to walk.

Figure 6.9. Tools of the Type Used by the Turpins
From left to right: skew lathe chisel, gouge for the
lathe, barking knife, back or mortise chisel, and drawknife.
(All tools shown are from the author's collection)

Jim's first step in making a chair was to go out into the woods to cut down a tree. Jim preferred to cut down trees during those months when the leaves were off the tree because "the sap was down" at that time and insects would not be attracted to the wood by the sugars left after the moisture of the sap dried out. When he made chairs from seasoned wood, as would occur when, for instance, he made a chair in the summer from wood that had been cut in the previous winter, he had to boil the wood. He did this by boiling the rough blanks in a tank so that the wood would cut easily and so that the back posts could be bent.

Jim used red oak and hickory almost exclusively, and he chose smaller trees so that he could carry the logs he wanted back to his workshop on his shoulder. Most important, the tree trunks he chose had to have straight grain and be free of branches, for where there is a branch there will be a knot in the wood. A tree that grows in the open will develop branches close to the ground and hence will be useless to a chairmaker. Trees that grow in the forest, however, usually have branches near their tops and none lower down. Hence they have a long, straight trunk free of knots. Such were the trees that Jim chose.

Once he had located a tree, Jim chopped it down with an axe, cut the trunk to the lengths needed, and carried the logs back to his workshop. There the logs were split into pieces, first with an axe and wedges and then with a froe driven by a club (fig. 6.10). In splitting out the pieces to make chair parts, it was necessary to make a piece that was slightly oversize, but not too much oversize. If the piece were much too large in cross section, much time and effort would be wasted later in removing the excess wood. Since in the splitting process the wood separates along the grain, it is of vital importance to have straight-grained wood for all the parts of the chair.

Once a piece of wood of appropriate size had been split out, it was mounted in the lathe between two metal points so that it was firmly fixed but could be rotated. A piece of wood to make a back post for a straight chair would be 36 inches long and roughly square in cross section with a diameter of about 1 3/4 inches. Once such a piece was mounted, it was worked down with a drawknife until it was nearly octagonal or round in cross section. Then it was ready to be turned in the lathe.

The lathe that Jim used was of very simple construction (fig. 6.11). The body consisted of two heavy planks mounted on posts so that the planks were parallel to the ground and about two inches apart. In the slot formed by the planks were mounted two upright posts that could be moved along the slot to accommodate different lengths of pieces to be worked upon. The posts could be fixed in place by wedges. From the inner surfaces of these two posts there protruded metal pins sharpened at the ends. Each pin could be screwed in and out by a handle. The piece of wood to be turned had a mark made in the

Figure 6.10.   Froe Club and Froe of the Type Used by the Turpins

center of each end and was mounted in the lathe so that a metal pin engaged each mark. A leather strap was wound around the piece of wood. The upper end of the strap was fastened to a springy pole well above the lathe. The bottom end of the strap was fastened to a treadle underneath the lathe. When Jim pressed down with his foot, the piece of wood rotated in one direction. When he released his foot, the springy pole drew the leather strap back up and the piece of wood rotated in the opposite direction. Fastened to the bed of the lathe was a support to hold up a chisel or a gouge. By pressing a sharp gouge against the side of the rotating piece of wood as he pressed down on the treadle, Jim could remove big shavings and could turn the piece of wood into a long cylinder. When the pole sprang back up and the wood rotated in the opposite direction, the gouge or chisel had to be pulled away from the wood.

The type of lathe that Jim used is sometimes called a "pole lathe" or a "boom and treadle lathe." It is a very ancient instrument, for there is an illustration showing one clearly dating from the thirteenth century.[8] There were other types of lathes also in earlier times. Some used a more compli- cated mechanism and operated by foot power like an old-fashioned sewing

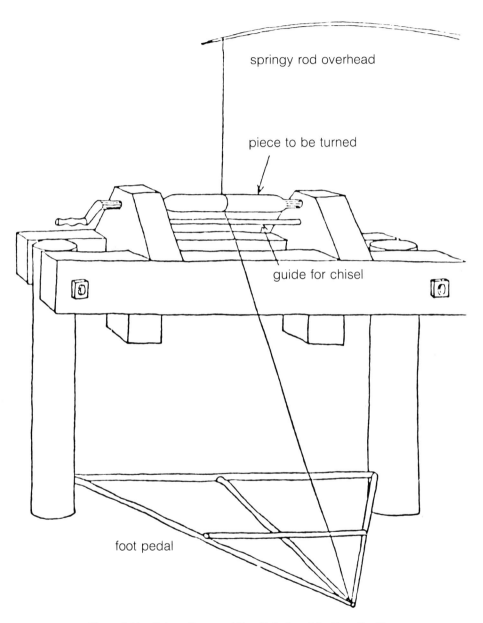

springy rod overhead

piece to be turned

guide for chisel

foot pedal

Figure 6.11.   Pole or Boom and Treadle Lathe of the Type Used by
the Turpins

machine, but these were best for smaller work. Some were driven by a separate wheel cranked by another person. A few lathes were located at water mills and were run by water power. For hundreds of years, however, most woodworkers used pole lathes. They were simple to make, using only wood except for the two iron pins, they could be used anywhere far from a source of water power, and they could be operated by one man. It was not until electric power brought the small, relatively inexpensive electric motor into the workshop that most woodworkers abandoned the pole lathe. The modern, all metal lathe driven by an electric motor that the contemporary woodworker uses turns the piece of wood to be worked upon at speeds around 2,000 revolutions a minute. The pole lathe that Jim used turns at less than 100 revolutions a minute. Yet as one looks at chairs or any other piece of furniture made before about 1875, one should remember that the turned parts were probably made on a pole lathe unless the piece was made in one of the early furniture factories, mostly in New England, where water power was used to run machinery.

Because electricity was not available in many rural areas until quite recently, Jim was not alone in using a pole lathe until well into the present century. Men in England who built small sheds out in the woods so as to be close to the source of supply and turned chair legs there used pole lathes as late as 1960.[9] Allen H. Eaton found many chairmakers in the southern mountains using pole lathes in the 1930s,[10] and a brochure on crafts mentions chairmakers using them in the 1960s in Tennessee.[11] When looked at in this light, it is not too surprising that Jim used a pole lathe. What is surprising, though, is that for at least 50 years while Jim was laboriously and slowly turning chair parts on his lathe, a large chair factory in Bloomfield less than 15 miles away was producing thousands of chairs a year with modern machinery.

As Jim turned the piece of wood in his lathe, he first used a gouge, which is U-shaped in cross section, to remove shavings and finished the work with a skew chisel, which is a flat chisel whose cutting edge is not at right angles to the shaft of the blade but ground at about a 30-degree angle (see fig. 6.9). The piece, if it were a back post for a straight chair, would be $34\frac{1}{2}$ inches long and $1\frac{1}{2}$ inches in diameter. At one end it would taper sharply to form the foot. Starting at the center, it would taper slightly to form the back above the seat. Jim did not finish his turning by sanding the whole piece as it rotated. He relied upon sharp tools and the skill acquired by years of experience to achieve a smooth finish without sandpaper.

The final step in turning the post was to mark it to show where the mortises for rounds and slats were to be cut. For this purpose Jim had a marking stick. It consisted of a stick with a number of nails driven through it so that their points all protruded on one side. When the stick was held with one end even with the bottom of the post and pushed against the post while it was turning, a number of shallow rings were made around the post. By using this marking stick, every post could be marked in exactly the same way. Jim had a number of such sticks, one for the back posts and one for the front for each size of chair he made. Before the post was removed from the lathe, the top half was shaved down with the drawknife to produce the flattened portion found on all his chairs. The post did not rotate during this process, but since it was held firmly in the lathe at each end, it could be worked on conveniently.

After two back posts had been finished in the lathe they could be bent. Jim had a number of forms cut out of heavy planks, each of which could take two posts at once (fig. 6.12). A form was the same length as the chair posts. It was about two inches wide at the bottom. The sides were parallel for about half the length of the form, but from that point the form tapered so that the two sides nearly met at the top. The two posts were placed with one on each side of the form with the flattened portion out. The bottoms of the posts were held with a piece of wood with a notch in it of appropriate size. Then the posts were bent in towards the form until another piece of wood with a notch in it could be forced down over them to hold them in place.

Because the wood was green or was pliable because it had been boiled, it bent readily. Because the post was smaller in diameter in the upper half and because some of the wood had been removed in the process of flattening one side, the post bent at the desired place. If a post were the same diameter throughout and if it were not flattened, it would tend to bend in a symmetrical arc from one end to the other with the maximum bend coming in the center. The flattened portion of the post, therefore, not only contributes to the comfort of the person who uses the finished chair but also makes it possible to put the correct bend in the post.

I own a slat-back chair that, I believe, was not made by hand by a single chairmaker but was mass-produced in a small factory. I estimate that it was made in the 1930s. I bought it in 1951, and it had seen years of use at that time because the seat was completely worn out and had to be replaced. The back posts of this chair are bent, but not flattened, and are the same diameter throughout. They form a perfect arc with the greatest deflection from a straight line coming just below the seat level. I find this chair much less comfortable to sit in than Jim's chairs.

Jim made the rounds for his chairs of hickory wood, and he made them well in advance so that they were thoroughly dried out by the time he assembled a chair. As with the posts, he split out the rough blanks from straight-grained wood, shaved them until they were roughly round, and turned them in the lathe until they were ⅞ inch in diameter. The four rounds over which the seat was woven were not turned to a final smoothness in the

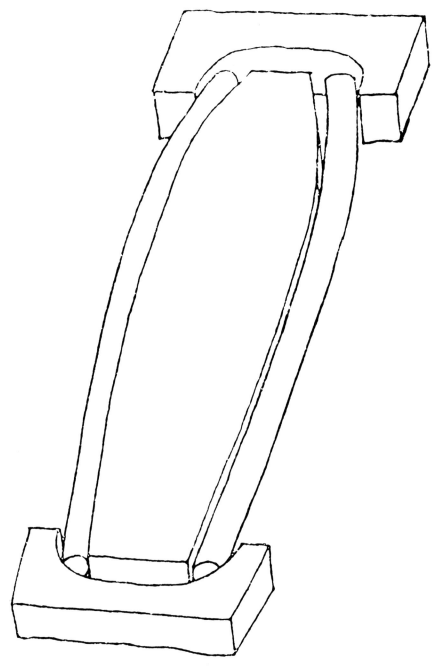

Figure 6.12. Form Used for Bending Back Posts

lathe but were left roughly octagonal, for they were covered when the seat was finished. For each chair there were rounds of three different lengths. For a straight chair there were two rounds for the front of the chair each 15¼ inches long allowing 1⅛ inches at each end to be driven into the posts. There were six rounds for the sides, three for each side, each 12¼ inches long. For the back there were two rounds, each 12½ inches long.

The slats were split out from blanks of straight-grained wood. They were about ¼ inch thick and of varying widths. The wood from which they were made had to be green. For a straight chair one slat 3½ inches wide and two slats 2⅝ inches wide were needed. The slats also are of different lengths, the bottom one being 13½ inches long and the top one 15 inches long, allowing 1 inch at each end to be inserted into the posts. After the slats had been split out they were trimmed and smoothed with a drawknife while clamped in a shaving horse. The notches were cut from two corners with the drawknife. Then they were bent. One end of a slat was put into a crack between two planks, and the top was forced over until the slat was bent with a bow of about 1 inch. After being bent the slats were set aside to dry. No form was needed to hold them while they dried.

Once the parts of a chair were made Jim could proceed to assemble them. The first step was to bore holes in the front and back posts for the rounds. Jim used a ⅝ inch auger to make the holes. Into the edge of the auger he had filed a notch to tell him when he had bored deep enough, a little over 1⅛ inches. The holes were located by means of the shallow rings, described above, which were scribed around the posts while the posts were turning in the lathe. The angles at which the holes were bored were, of course, of great importance, but Jim's skill and long experience allowed him to judge the correct angle without using any measuring device.

The long, narrow mortises to take the slats were begun by boring holes ¼ inch in diameter at each end of the mortise. Then the wood between the two holes was cut out with a special chisel driven by a mallet. The chisel was ¼ inch wide and much thicker than an ordinary chisel (fig. 6.9). Jim called his chisel a "back chisel" because, of course, it was used in making the chair back. This type of chisel is called a "mortise chisel" in reference books on tools.[12]

In order to hold the back posts steady while he worked on them, Jim fitted them into a special device he had made which he called a "press" (fig. 6.13). This press consisted of a heavy piece of plank about five feet long and two feet wide. It had four stout pegs mounted in it so that when the two back posts were placed on the plank parallel to each other and nearly touching there would be two pegs on each side. Then two wedges were driven between the posts, one at the top and one at the bottom. The wedges forced the posts apart and held them tightly between the pegs so that the mortises could be cut in the posts.

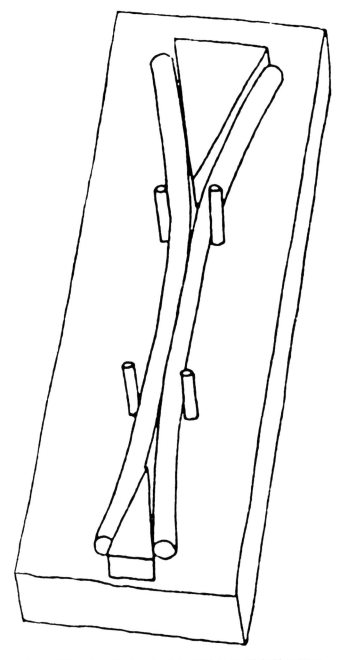

Figure 6.13.   Press Used to Hold the Back Posts While They Were
Being Mortised

The final step in the preparation consisted in shaping round tenons on the ends of the rounds. These tenons were 1 ⅛ inches long and were whittled with a knife. Near their outermost ends they were a full ⅝ inch in diameter. They tapered slightly, however, so that at the innermost end, at the shoulder, they were slightly smaller than ⅝ inch. Jim kept a scrap of wood on hand with a hole bored in it so he could test the size of the tenons to make sure they were just right.

Finally, the rounds and slats were driven into the appropriate holes and mortises and the whole chair assembled. All the parts were driven firmly into place with a wooden mallet. Although the chair was solidly joined together at this point, further seasoning of the chairs would make them even more solid. Since the rounds were thoroughly seasoned before being used, they could shrink no more. Since the posts were either of green wood or had been boiled in water before being made, they would shrink over a period of weeks as they seasoned. Since the tenons on the rounds were slightly smaller at the shoulder than at the ends, the wood of the posts shrank around the rounds at the shoulder. Hence the posts held the rounds in a vice-like grip that cannot be broken. Moreover, the holes for the rounds that hold the seat were bored in such a way that the tenons of the two rounds in each post held one another in place (fig. 6.14). The two holes in each post for the seat rounds were bored so close to one another that the two tenons on the ends of the rounds actually touched one another inside the post. One round was driven home first. As the second round was driven into its hole its tenon slid over the first tenon. This process forced one tenon up slightly and the other down so they were firmly locked in place. Finally, since the seat was woven of flexible strips of bark, when a person sits in a chair, the weight of the body tends to pull all four of the rounds inward. The Turpin chairs, then, were held solidly together without the use of glue, nails, or pegs. Of all the Turpin chairs I have seen, none has ever been loose at the joints. Some have been so abused that rounds and slats have been broken, but the parts have never come loose.

The Hickory Bark Seats

Every Turpin chair I have ever seen originally had a seat of hickory bark even though some now had replacement seats of different materials. There is a period of a few weeks in late spring and early summer when bark will peel easily from hickory trees. Jim would cut down a tree during that period and remove the bark from the trunk and larger limbs. First the rough, scaly outer bark was removed with a drawknife, and then a layer of brown, useless bark was removed with the same tool, exposing the usable inner bark. Jim made a cut, as straight as possible, through this inner bark from one end of the trunk to the other using a pocket knife. Of course, the length of the cut depended

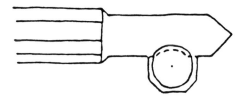

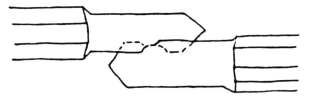

Figure 6.14.   Detail Showing Two Adjacent Seat Rounds in the Front Post
This demonstrates how the two rounds lock one another in place.

on how much of the trunk was free of limbs, but he would start underneath the lowest limb and cut from there to the butt of the trunk. Then he made a second cut parallel to the first and ¾ inch away from it. A long strip of bark could then be peeled off. Once free from the tree, this strip could then be separated into three thinner strips, each ¾ inch wide.

Once the first strip had been removed, Jim could use a special tool called a "bark knife" to cut the other strips from the tree (see fig. 6.9). This tool consisted of a stout bar of wood about 18 inches long and 1½ inches in diameter. In the center of the bar a knife blade was fixed. The point of the blade protruded about an inch from the bar of wood, and the blade was held in place by wooden wedges to that it could be adjusted or removed for sharpening. A piece of metal fixed into the bar ¾ inch from the knife blade served as a guide or fence. Once the first strip of bark had been removed from the tree, the guide of the tool would fit into the groove in the bark thus formed. Then as the bark knife was pulled down the trunk, a second strip ¾ inch wide would be cut, and the strip could be removed. This procedure was repeated around the tree. The green bark strips could be rolled up into balls about the size of a basketball and used later, or the bark could be woven into a seat shortly after it was removed from the tree.

If the seat or bottom was woven within a few days after the bark was removed from the tree, the bark would still be flexible. Bark that had dried could be soaked in water for about a half an hour to make it flexible. I have taken strips of bark from a seat nearly a hundred years old and soaked them in water. After a half an hour the previously stiff bark has become almost as flexible as a piece of leather. Jim was thus able to weave seats throughout the year even though the bark could be stripped from the tree only in the late spring and early summer. As mentioned previously, Jim would take a roll of bark and go to a person's home to weave a new seat on a chair when it was needed.

To weave a seat (Jim would have said "to bottom a chair") Jim first chose a long strip of bark. He tied one end to the rear round at the left post. Then the strip was passed over the front round, up over the back round, and so on until the space between the posts was filled in. If the strip were not long enough, Jim joined a new strip to the end of the old one so the connection was hidden on the underside of the seat. Then strips were woven across the seat. The crosswise strips went over three and then under three of the front-to-back strips both on the top side of the seat and on the bottom side (fig. 6.15).

The resulting product was a strong, flexible, and durable seat that would not stretch or sag in use. The weight of a person sitting on the chair, as I have mentioned, tends to pull the chair together rather than spread it apart. In hot weather air can circulate through the woven seat to cool a person off, unlike a chair with a solid wooden seat. Moreover, a chair with a woven seat is lighter in weight than a chair of comparable size with a solid wooden seat, and there is enough "give" to the woven seat even after the bark is dry to make it comfortable. The light weight of the chair makes it easy to move it from place to place.

The Rockers for Rocking Chairs

Jim made the rockers for his rocking chairs from 1 inch thick oak boards which he obtained from local sawmills. He kept a pattern on hand that he used to mark out the rockers, the same pattern that had been used by his father, Joe. Jim would hew away the excess wood from the board with a hatchet, stopping short of the marked line. Then he would finish the rocker with a drawknife. He did not use any sandpaper, for the sharp drawknife left a smooth surface.

Once the rockers were made, Jim marked the places for notches on the outside surfaces of the bottom of the posts. He cut out the notches with a handsaw and a chisel. The rockers were held in place in the notches while a 1/4 inch hole was bored through both the rocker and the post. Through this a bolt of appropriate length was inserted with the head on the outside of the post and the nut on the inside.

Figure 6.15.   Detail of the Hickory Bark Seat Woven by Jim Turpin
for the Chair Shown in Figure 6.5
A few of the strips of bark have broken off at the
front of the seat.

Woods Used in the Chairs

The Turpins were fortunate to live and work in an area where fine woods for chairs were readily available. The ideal wood for a slat-back chair must have the following qualities:

1. It must be strong and not brittle, for a chair can be subjected to much stress especially when a person tilts back on the two back feet. Too, people sometimes use chairs to stand on when reaching for something on a high shelf or something similar. Although the posts of Jim's chairs are 1½ inches in diameter, when a hole is bored for a round the post is greatly weakened at that point. At the point where the two seat rounds enter the back post, a great deal of wood is removed from the post, and it is at this point that a great deal of stress occurs when a person leans back in the chair. Hence a strong wood that does not become brittle with age is needed.

2. The wood should be hard to resist dents and abrasion. Some of the Turpin child's chairs I have seen have been used as supports by children learning to walk. One lady told me that her children had

dragged their chair along a concrete walk in front of their house time after time as they learned to walk. A considerable amount of wood was worn away from the front posts of this chair, but if it had been made from a softer wood, the chair would no longer be usable.

3. The wood should be smooth. It should be possible to work it smooth with a drawknife and with turning chisels, and it should remain smooth after long use. Some woods become fuzzy and even splintery after use, while others become smoother the longer they are used.

4. The wood must split readily along the grain so that the posts, rounds, and slats can be split out. Were it necessary to saw out these members, it would add a great deal of time and effort to making a chair. Splitting, as I have mentioned, also insures that the grain of each member is straight and unbroken so that it will be strong.

5. The wood must bend readily when it is green or after it has been boiled, and it must retain the bend indefinitely after the wood dries out.

6. The wood should shrink considerably in drying so that the posts can increase their grip on the rounds as they season.

7. The wood should not warp or twist as it seasons because otherwise the back posts might change their shape after the chair was put together as the posts seasoned.

8. The wood should be of the type that can be turned well in a lathe. Some woods do not respond well to turning and are especially hard to cut smoothly with lathe tools.

9. The wood should resist decay. Any wood that is kept dry will not decay. It should be noted that the term "dry rot" is a misleading one because it implies that dry wood will decay. Actually, dry rot occurs when wood is exposed to much moisture even though standing puddles of water cannot be seen on it. Some woods kept in a moist cellar, for example, will decay even though visible water does not get on them. At any rate, chairs made by the Turpins were often used on porches, and rain will often blow onto a porch in southern Indiana. Under such conditions some woods will decay over a period of time.

Of all the woods available in the forests of northeast Greene County, the Turpins used only three: sugar maple *(Acer saccharum),* red oak *(Quercus coccinea),* and shagbark hickory *(Carya ovata).* Jim used mostly oak for his posts and slats, while the other Turpins used maple for posts and hickory for slats. They all used hickory for the rounds. These three woods all have to a high degree the qualities listed above.

Maple excels the others in its smoothness. It turn beautifully in a lathe and becomes smoother and smoother with use. Both oak and hickory are smooth, but they both have a grainy quality that maple does not have. Maple cannot be split quite as easily as the other two woods, and it is not so highly resistant to decay. The Turpins who used it probably chose it because of its many practical qualities listed above, plus the fact that it is an especially attractive wood due to its light color and fine grain.

Hickory is nearly the hardest, strongest, and toughest wood in the United States. It is excelled in these qualities only by trees that never grow to much size and hence do not have long, straight trunks, such as dogwood and ironwood. Since hickory trees had to be cut down for their bark, it was practical to use the wood from the same tree.

Oak is also strong, tough, and hard, slightly less so than hickory, but lighter in weight than hickory. It is probably its comparative lightness that recommended it to Jim for his posts. It is also the most resistant to decay of the three woods. By the time Jim was making chairs, well into the twentieth century, his customers regarded his chairs more as utility chairs than they had earlier. Tastes in household furnishings had changed to the point where many people would not have wanted one of Jim's chairs in their living rooms where upholstered furniture was the norm. His chairs were more likely to be used in kitchens and on porches. Hence the somewhat coarse grain of the red oak was no drawback. Indeed, in the first three decades of this century oak was a popular wood for all sorts of furniture. The ability of oak to resist decay was of some importance, too, for chairs used on a porch.

It is worth noting that the Turpins never used some woods that were popular for other kinds of furniture and in factory-made chairs. Wild cherry and black walnut have always been highly prized woods for most furniture, and Indiana cabinetmakers have made handsome tables, chests of drawers, corner cupboards, and other pieces of these woods. Black walnut was especially admired in the second half of the last century, and factories made large numbers of black walnut chairs. Numbers of large trees of these species were available in northeast Greene County, yet the Turpins never used them for chairs. The reason is not hard to find. These woods were not considered strong enough for chair posts by the Turpins, and the woods are brittle. Cherry and walnut are perfectly strong enough for chests of drawers and for cupboards, and when used in beds or tables the legs are usually of large diameter. Factories might make chairs of black walnut, but the manufacturers could be reasonably certain that the chairs thus made would be used mostly in parlors and dining rooms and not subjected to much hard usage. Factories did not make kitchen chairs or porch furniture of cherry or walnut. The woods were too expensive to be used for cheaper furniture, of course, but when the factories built utility chairs they normally used tough, durable, and inexpensive oak.

Tulip poplar *(Liriodendron tulipifera)* was also used by Indiana cabinetmakers for tables, chests, and cupboards. The tree grew to great size in the Indiana forests so that long, wide boards were readily available, and the wood is light in weight and decay resistant. Although these characteristics may recommend it for some uses, it is far too weak and soft to use in slat-back chairs. Beech and elm are common trees in southern Indiana, and the woods are tough, hard and strong. Both woods, however, warp and twist in seasoning, and elm is notoriously difficult to split. A wood that is excellent for chairs is ash. The large trees can be found easily in Indiana forests, and the wood has all the desirable qualities listed above. Why the Turpins did not use this wood in their chairs I cannot say.

The History of the Slat-Back Chair

The slat-back chairs made by the Turpins represent a striking example of the way in which a traditional design can be passed along from one generation of craftsmen to another over a period of hundreds of years. It is impossible to document the history of this chair type in great detail for three reasons. First, these chairs have probably always been considered to be simple, utilitarian objects. They have not often been passed down within one family as treasured heirlooms in the same way that larger, more impressive pieces of furniture have been, such as tall-case or "grandfather" clocks. Second, these chairs have not been highly esteemed by most collectors of antique furniture. Not only have collectors helped preserve old pieces of furniture that might otherwise have disappeared, but also when some class of artifacts has been extensively collected, research will be done on that artifact and books will be written on it. There are, for example, several books that attempt to deal with the history of the Windsor chair that has been widely collected,[13] but no books deal with the history of the slat-back chair. Finally, I have never heard of a slat-back chair on which the maker has marked his name or the date of construction. It is true that most antique furniture is not so marked, but at least there are places on most furniture where the maker can put his name and the date if he so wishes. For example, the underneath side of the broad wooden seat of Windsor chairs provides a place where names and dates are sometimes placed. On a slat-back chair there simply is no place to carve, brand, or write a name and date.

Despite the paucity of detailed information, it is still possible to give some general indications as to the history of the slat-back chair. Some slat-back chairs are shown in early art, for example. The earliest I know of is a mid-fourteenth-century English manuscript showing a school scene with the schoolmaster seated upon what appears to be a slat-back chair.[14] A Dutch slat-back chair is clearly shown in an illustration of a wood turner's workshop published in 1610.[15] An English author states that "Ladder-back chairs were frequently depicted in seventeenth-century Dutch paintings."[16] This type of chair, then must have been well known in western Europe before the first settlers began coming to America.[17] The English settlers in particular who came to America must have been thoroughly familiar with this type of chair, for from the very earliest days these chairs were made all along the East Coast.[18] There are substantial numbers of seventeenth-century slat-back American chairs that have survived, especially from New England and Pennsylvania.[19]

At some time, probably around 1800, southern chairmakers developed a marked change in the way they made their chairs. As far as I have been able to tell, all slat-back chairs before this time had been made with straight back posts. Because these back posts were turned in a lathe, of course, it was possible for the turner to ornament them. Many have turned rings and grooves between the slats and a turned finial at the top (fig. 6.16). For a skilled turner such ornamentation requires little additional effort. The new development consisted in bending the back posts so that they curve out-wards and backwards above the seat. As I have said, in order to facilitate bending, the chairmakers made the posts smaller in diameter above the seats and flattened the fronts of the posts above the seats. Because of the flat surfaces on the fronts of the posts, these chairs do not ordinarily have ornamental turnings between the slats nor do they have finials. The bent back posts with their flattened surfaces make for a more comfortable chair.[20]

The idea of bending and flattening the back posts may have come to the southern makers of slat-back chairs as a result of the popularity around 1800 of the Sheraton fancy chair, as Henry Glassie has suggested.[21] Certainly, the fancy chair became very popular around 1800, and such chairs do have flattened and bent back posts without finials (fig. 6.17). It is reasonable to assume that this development in slat-back chairs came about in the South, for such chairs have been very popular in the Mid-South and in those parts of the Midwest settled from the Mid-South. On the other hand, they seem to have been less popular in the North.

I should stress that we do not have a simple North-South pattern with straight-back chairs in the North only and bent-back chairs in the South only. Instead, it appears to have been in the nineteenth century a matter of preference. For example, the northern Shaker colonies made and sold great numbers of straight-back chairs, while some small shops in New York state turned out small quantities of bent-back chairs.[22] In the southern mountains and in the Midwest the bent-back chair was made in large numbers, but some straight-back chairs were also made.[23]

Figure 6.16.   Rocking Chair Made in New England in the
Mid-Eighteenth Century

Figure 6.17.   Fancy Chair Made in the Midwest, ca. 1840
Original painted and decorated finish. Note that the
back posts are flattened and bent above the seat line.

When we turn to southern Indiana we find, first, that in the early decades of the last century the fancy chair with its flattened and bent back posts but without the characteristically placed slats of the slat-back chair was very popular. Many of the chairmakers who settled in the towns in that period advertised in the newspapers that they made "fancy chairs" and occasionally used a crude woodcut in their advertisements depicting such a chair.[24] Only two such Indiana chairmakers advertised that they made "slat-back" chairs: William Bullock, working in Lafayette in 1838, and Joseph I. Stretcher, working in Indianapolis in 1841.[25] Among their products, some of these chairmakers listed "split-bottom" chairs, which were probably slat-back chairs,[26] and some listed "common" chairs, which probably also were slat-back chairs.[27]

Nonetheless, the bent-back slat-back chair was very popular in southern Indiana. At farm auction sales, in antique shops, and in private collections it is old slat-back chairs with bent posts that I see in great numbers. Fancy chairs and slat-back chairs with straight posts are very rare. If, as the advertisements show, the chairmakers in towns made few slat-back chairs, it must have been chairmakers living in the countryside who produced many of the chairs of this type that survive today in large numbers. Certainly, the Turpin family alone over a period of 125 years must have made a large number of these chairs, and there must have been many other chairmaking families like the Turpins.

A word remains to be said about one chair made by Joe Turpin, a child's high chair (see fig. 6.8). It is different from all other Turpin chairs I have seen and from most southern Indiana slat-back chairs in one important way. The back posts are straight, not bent, they are not flattened on the front sides, and they have finials atop them. In other words, this chair is of a type much more favored in the North than in the South and the Midwest. It shows that the Turpins, and probably most other traditional chairmakers, knew both designs, even though most often they followed only one.

This particular type of slat-back chair, which I call the "obelisk" pattern, with its wide spread legs for stability, is very old. There are seventeenth-century English and American examples known as well as examples from later centuries. These strongly resemble the Turpin chair.[28] This is another indication that the Turpins followed traditional designs, designs that had proved their practicality because they had been used day in and day out over a period of centuries.

It may be seen, therefore, that the Turpins represent a traditional pattern, the farmer-chairmaker who worked in his fields when the season and the weather demanded it, but who made bent-back, slat-back chairs at other times of the year. The Turpin family is unusual only in that Jim, the last of his family to make chairs, continued to work right into the 1950s. The designs of their chairs are very similar to those used by other chairmakers in southern Indiana, the Midwest, and the Mid-South even though there are small individual touches that I have described above that distinguish their chairs from those of other makers.

Rural and Urban Chairmakers: Some Comparisons

The farmer-craftsman who lived and worked in the countryside differed in some respects from the craftsman who lived and worked in the towns. The town craftsman, unlike the rural craftsman, worked full time in his shop. It is true that most people who lived in towns in the first half of the nineteenth century had gardens in their backyards and fruit trees, kept a few chickens, a cow, and perhaps a horse, and may even have raised a few pigs. The craftsmen who worked in towns probably followed this pattern. Nonetheless, they cannot be said to have been farmers in the same sense as the craftsmen living in the countryside were farmers. The town gardens could be tended in the evenings and on weekends. They did not keep the craftsman from working in his shop on a full-time basis year-round. The only reason why a town craftsman would not be in his shop full time would be if business were slow. If business were slow, the town craftsman turned to whatever gainful pursuits there might be open to him in the town. He could not, however, farm because his location in town precluded that possibility. The farmer-craftsman, as we have seen, followed a different pattern. The nature of the season and the crops dictated that farming would have to be done at specific times. He would work at his craft when he did not need to work in his fields.

Since the town craftsman normally worked in his shop full time, he could and did produce a far wider range of items than could the farmer-craftsman. The information compiled by Walters bears out this generalization. If we exclude the cabinetmakers who also made chairs and look only at those town craftsmen who term themselves chairmakers, we still find that they made a wide range of different styles and types. For example, Joseph I. Stretcher of Indianapolis advertised in 1841:

> He has removed his Chair Establishment to the 2 story building on Washington street, one door west of the Indiana Journal office and nearly opposite the Post Office, where he keeps constantly on hand a large and splendid assortment of Fancy and Windsor chairs, as follows: Black Walnut Chairs; Upholstered do [ditto]; Large Cane back and Cane seat Rocking Chairs; Large Boston style Rocking do; The most approved patterns of Upholstered Rocking do; Maple Stools, cane seats, for Hotels or Canal Boats; Upholstered Lounges; Cane seat do; Large Writing Chairs; Fancy Grecian Cane seat do; Fancy Grecian seat Chairs; Regular Sweep Fancy do; Round post Cane seat do; do do Flag do do; Large Windsor Rocking do; Small do do do; Windsor Scroll Top do; do Slatback do; do Common do; do Table do; do Children's do; do Settees of all patterns. P. S. Cabinet Furniture, carved or plain, kept constantly on hand. *Sofa Springs* also kept constantly on hand.[29]

Obviously, this is a far wider range of styles and designs than the slat-backs of the Turpins. I should note that all chairmakers, whether they worked in the town or the countryside, replaced worn-out seats and repaired broken chairs. They also, on occasion, made or repaired a wide variety of other wooden items for the household, shop, and farm.

Not only did the town chairmaker make a wide range of chairs, but also some of his customers were well-to-do people who were aware of the latest fashion in chairs. The town chairmaker, therefore, had to try to keep abreast of what was fashionable in eastern cities and try to make examples for his fashion-conscious customers. Samuel S. Rooker, another Indianapolis chairmaker, advertised in 1835: "Having just received a supply of materials from the city of New York, he will be able to execute fancy work in a style superior to any before offered in this place."[30] Exactly how an Indiana chairmaker learned the precise details of the latest fashions in chair designs in eastern cities it is hard to say. At any rate, the town chairmaker tried to follow fashion and hence added to and dropped from his repertory designs from time to time. The Turpins and other country chairmakers, on the other hand, were largely impervious to changing fashions.

Another important difference between the town and country chairmakers lies in the fact that country chairmakers were making chairs by hand long after the town chairmakers had ceased doing so. As I will show, in the 1930s there were four chairmakers still at work in one small rural area in northeast Greene County. I have never heard of an urban craftsman making chairs anywhere in southern Indiana in the twentieth century. The town chairmakers, in other words, felt the impact of the Industrial Revolution at an earlier date. Railroads were built from town to town, and it was the railroads that brought factory-made goods to the towns. Furniture dealers were established in many Indiana towns before 1900. Factory-made chairs could be sold in towns more cheaply than the hand-made product. Moreover, it is probably true that, at the end of the last century, the factory-made chair had a glamorous appeal to the town dweller that the chair made by hand by a local craftsman could not match. For reasons I will detail, however, chairmakers living in the countryside continued to make chairs by hand for their neighbors well into the present century.

In contrast to Jim Turpin, his brother Bill tried to move away from the old home place and establish a chair shop in Mt. Tabor where he was within a few miles of the towns of Gosport and Stinesville. We know that he made chairs for Stinesville customers also. He probably moved to Mt. Tabor between 1885 and 1890, for he was working there around 1895. Although there may have been other reasons why he left Mt. Tabor by 1900, it is quite likely that he found that more and more people in Gosport and Stinesville were buying factory-made chairs by 1900 so that there was less and less demand for his chairs. I have been unable to find out where he went after he left Mt. Tabor, but many people at that time were leaving the countryside and the small towns, moving to cities, and becoming factory workers. Perhaps that is what Bill did, too.

Finally, it seems likely that, during most of the nineteenth century, there were more country chairmakers working than there were town chairmakers. While this generalization is important for the study and understanding of folk crafts, it cannot be supported by specific figures. As we have seen, the farmer-craftsmen often told census takers that they were farmers so that there are no written records to which we can turn to discover just how many chairmakers were working in the countryside. To do fieldwork all over southern Indiana in order to find how many chairmakers were working in rural areas would be an impossible task. My fieldwork in northeast Greene County, however, has produced evidence to support the generalization that there were far more rural than urban chairmakers. Around 1900 there were three chairmakers working in Turpin Hollow: Joe Turpin and his two sons, Jim and Bill. A few miles away Joseph M. Turpin was also making chairs.

Early in the present century, Joe and Jim Turpin still were making chairs in Turpin Hollow, while Joseph M. Turpin was also still making chairs. Within a radius of a few miles three other chairmakers were also active. These were Doug Turpin, probably the son of Joseph M., Bill Greenwood, and Henry Boruff. As late as the 1930s, Jim Turpin, Doug Turpin, Bill Greenwood, and Henry Boruff were all making chairs. There is no reason to believe that this small area had a much higher concentration of chairmakers than did the rest of rural southern Indiana. I have heard of many other rural chairmakers elsewhere in southern Indiana, but I have not had the opportunity to carry out extensive investigations in other areas.

For reasons I have already given, census records are not reliable indicators of the numbers of rural craftsmen. It is worth noting, however, that in her search through census records and other written sources, Walters found only six chairmakers for the whole of Greene County. All six were working in rural areas, none in Bloomfield, the county seat, for example, and all were listed only in the 1850 census.[31] When we also realize that in 1850, 95.5 percent of the population of the state of Indiana lived outside urban areas,[32] it is clear that country craftsmen must have been far more numerous than those who worked in urban areas. Granted that some of those people who lived on farms acquired chairs from town chairmakers, still the percentage of the population living in the countryside is so high as to leave no doubt as to the preponderance of rural chairmakers.

Many who have written about crafts in the United States have based their discussions solely on town craftsmen.[33] The reason is not far to seek. It is the town craftsmen who advertised in newspapers and the like, who left written records of other kinds behind, and who told census takers they were craftsmen, not farmers. Yet it is clear that craftsmen who lived in urban areas were not typical of all craftsmen, and any broad generalizations about crafts in the pre-industrial era should take this fact into account.

Why Did Jim Turpin Continue Making Chairs until Such a Late Date?

Why did people buy hand-made chairs from Jim Turpin well into the twentieth century when almost all the other artifacts they bought had been produced in factories? Or, to put it another way, why was Jim able to maintain the old pattern of hand craftsmanship and hold out against the Industrial Revolution when all around him old patterns were crumbling? The reasons why people bought Jim's chairs were many. First of all, Jim's chairs were cheap, costing about half what a comparable factory-made chair would cost. At that low price people got comfortable, sturdy, lightweight, and durable chairs. Moreover, they got chairs of a style they were accustomed to, a style that their parents and grandparents had known and liked. It is true that a subtle change in people's attitudes towards the chairs had developed. The earlier generations had thought Turpin chairs were appropriate for use anywhere in their houses, and Turpin rocking chairs undoubtedly occupied a position of honor beside the fireplace in many a home. In the twentieth century, however, most people thought Turpin chairs were more appropriate for the kitchen and the porch. In the best rooms in their houses they preferred to have more stylish factory-made furniture, especially upholstered chairs.

Jim was able to gain a livelihood even though he charged so little for his chairs. One must remember that a rocking chair he sold for three dollars represented many hours of work. To make that chair he had gone out into the woods, cut down a tree, and carried the logs back to his shop. He had split out the pieces and shaped and joined them as I have described. To make the seat, he had cut down another tree and peeled off long strips of bark before he began weaving the seat. It is impossible to estimate with any exactness how many hours of skilled work went into making a chair, but I would suppose that when he sold a rocking chair for three dollars, Jim was earning about 15 or 20 cents an hour for his labor.

The income Jim derived from his chairs was supplemented by occasional odd jobs of other kinds. For instance, many of his neighbors raised tobacco. Jim would split out sticks on which the tobacco could be hung while it was curing. Most important, of course, was the fact that he raised most of his own food. He always planted a garden. He raised pigs, kept a cow, and raised poultry. Jim was able to maintain a standard of living comparable to that of his father and grandfather. In the eyes of others he may have seemed poor because he had no automobile, no truck, and no tractor, for example. Yet Jim preferred living on the old home place to moving to a city, and he preferred making chairs to finding a job in some town and commuting back and forth.

Many people also bought chairs from Jim because their parents had bought chairs from Jim's father and because their grandparents had bought chairs from Jim's grandfather. They knew Jim, and they knew his chairs were good chairs. Why take a chance on an unfamiliar product by buying chairs in a store when Turpin chairs and their qualities were well known? Some people may also have felt that by buying chairs from Jim they were helping out a neighbor, as indeed they were. No one, as far as I know, ever bought chairs from Jim because they thought his chairs were quaint or picturesque. No one either ever thought of buying a chair because it might some day be considered an antique. Yet today, within 25 years after Jim's death, people who live in the area surrounding Turpin Hollow are beginning to appreciate Jim's chairs as antiques, and Turpin chairs are once again regarded by many with respect and pride.

The Importance of Tradition for the Turpins

In the Turpin family and their chairs we can see an ancient pattern, the farmer-craftsman, a pattern that must have existed in Great Britain before the immigrants came to this country but whose exact age it is impossible to determine because of a lack of records. The general pattern of the person who farmed much of the year when the time and weather were right and who worked at his craft at other times is traditional. Traditional also were the tools and techniques the Turpins used, and so were the designs of the chairs. Many factors help explain why tradition was so important in the case of the Turpins. For example, by working only part time at their craft they could still supply as many chairs as the people needed who lived within a reasonable distance. Even so, Jim often carried a set of chairs on his back several miles to deliver them. Had he produced many more chairs than he did by working full time year-round at chairmaking, where would he have sold his chairs? His brother Bill tried to become a full-time chairmaker by moving to Mt. Tabor where there was a growing population needing chairs. Jim, however, preferred to remain on his farm and make chairs part time. If Jim used the same tools and techniques that his forefathers did, it is because the techniques he used were closely connected to the tools he had and because the tools he had were exactly like those of his forefathers. The basic designs of axes, drawknives, and pole lathes had evolved long before Jim's time, and there was no way they could be improved or changed until electricity became available. Of course, an electric-powered lathe or saw would not have been of any use to Jim when he had no electricity.

Finally, Jim also used the same basic designs for his chairs as his father and grandfather had used. A minor revolution in the design had occurred somewhere around 1800, it is true, but still the basic design was very old. It is possible to see in this case that a design had evolved over a period of time that was difficult to improve upon. As long as the raw materials were the same, the tools and techniques the same, and the uses to which the chairs were put the same, these comfortable, durable, strong, lightweight chairs had reached a point in design where no further improvements could be made. If some people in the area bought factory-made chairs instead of Turpin chairs in the twentieth century, it was not because the factory-made chairs were more comfortable or stronger or lighter in weight. Indeed, they were probably inferior to the Turpin chairs in these and other qualities. People bought factory-made chairs even though they were more expensive because the concept of fashion so important in modern life had begun to affect them. Factory-made chairs were fashionable, and Turpin chairs were not. In the modern world where factories produce thousands of chairs of many different designs and fashions change rapidly, Jim and his chairs were both anachronisms. Yet some people who knew good, simple, solid chairs when they saw them kept on buying chairs from Jim as long as he kept on making them. Fortunately, many of his chairs have survived and once more are being appreciated for their design and construction.

The Turpins and the Environment

It is possible to say that the Turpins were in a state of ecological balance with their natural surroundings. The number of trees they needed to cut down for wood or bark was comparatively small. While they could use only the straight, lower trunk of a tree for chair parts, the remainder of the tree was used often for firewood as, of course, were any waste pieces produced in the splitting and shaping process. Jim never had any problem in finding kindling wood for his fire. Moreover, the tools the Turpins used were very simple. The most complicated piece of equipment, the lathe, was almost entirely wood. Whatever energy used was, as we have seen, all manpower. In other words, the chairs they built did not represent a great drain on the environment.

In sharp contrast to the Turpins and the age-old tradition they represent stand the furniture factories of Bloomington and Bloomfield. It was not until after the Civil War that large factories such as these could flourish, for they were dependent on the network of railroads for their existence. Because these factories were not close to the sea, to a large navigable river, or to a canal, they needed the railroads to carry the vast amounts of furniture they produced to customers spread over a huge area. They needed also, of course, vast supplies of lumber from the forests in Monroe and Greene Counties. In the production of this lumber there was a great deal of waste, and the forests in these counties were incapable of sustaining that yield for very long. By the end of World War II the virgin forests had been cut down. Since the high quality hardwoods such as oak, sugar maple, and hickory grow back very slowly, by 1950 the factories had virtually ceased producing furniture.

When one thinks of the overall history of man and his effects on the environment, it is clear that the furniture factories in Monroe and Greene Counties represent a temporary phase, while the Turpins represent the really old, long-lasting pattern. What is truly unusual is that the Turpins were making their chairs laboriously by hand before the factories opened, for nearly a century they continued working less than twenty miles away from the factories, and after the factories shut down, Jim was still pumping away at his treadle lathe in Turpin Hollow. It took hordes of men, mountains of machinery and equipment, and unbelievable quantities of energy for the factories to produce chairs. Jim did it all by himself with the simplest of equipment, but using at every step the skills inherited from his forefathers and honed by long practice. And I have a feeling that long after the factory-made chairs have worn out or been broken and discarded, people will still be using and cherishing the chairs the Turpins made.

Notes

1. A number of people were kind enough to give me information of various sorts as I tried to learn about the Turpin family and their chairs. Many showed me their chairs and allowed me to photograph them. I want to thank especially the following: Mrs. Dale Britton, Mrs. Alta Brunner, Mr. and Mrs. Orville Childers, Miss Ruth Davis, Mr. and Mrs. Charles Glidden, Mr. and Mrs. David Hovius, Mr. Arthur Michael, Mr. James Michael, Mrs. Olif Pegg, Mrs. Pat Powell, Mrs. Hattie Spicer, Mr. Gary Stanton, Mr. Millard Watkins, and Mr. and Mrs. Russell Wells. I would also like to thank Sarah L. Roberts for her help with the drawings used as illustrations in this paper.

2. The term "slat-back chair" seems to be commonly used by American writers who have treated chairs from a historical standpoint or have written about chairs as antiques (see, for example, John Cummings, "Slat-Back Chairs," *Antiques* 72, no. 1 [July 1957]: 60–63). Comparable British writers generally use the term "ladder-back chair" when writing of the same type of chair (see Ivan G. Sparkes, *The English Country Chair* [Bourne End, Buckinghamshire: Spurbooks, Ltd., 1973], pp. 114, 121). American writers on antique furniture, however, prefer to use the term "ladder-back chair" to apply to another type of chair, a Chippendale design fashionable among the wealthy between about 1750–80 (Albert Sack, *Fine Points of Furniture: Early American* [New York: Crown Publishers, 1950], p. 47). In the Southern Mountains a special variety of the slat-back chair, the type the Turpins made which I will describe in detail below, is called a "mule-ear" or a "settin'" chair (Henry Glassie, *Pattern in the Material Folk Culture of the Eastern United States* [Philadelphia: University of Pennsylvania Press, 1968], pp. 229–32). Chairmakers who advertised in Indiana newspapers in the first half of the nineteenth century called this chair a "common chair" (see below, n. 26).

People whom I have talked with who knew Jim Turpin, the chairmaker, or who own chairs he made use no generic term for this type of chair. They distinguish, of course, between "kitchen" or straight chairs, rocking chairs, etc., but they do not seem to use any term for the slat-back chair as a type as distinct from other chairs such as the Windsor chair.

3. Betty Lawson Walters, *Furniture Makers of Indiana, 1793 to 1850* (Indianapolis: Indiana Historical Society, 1972).

4. *Antiques,* 98, no. 1 (July 1970): 118–25.

5. See, for example, Charles F. Hummel, *With Hammer in Hand* (Charlottsville: The University Press of Virginia, 1968). This is a detailed study of three generations of craftsmen, the last of whom worked in the early decades of the nineteenth century.

6. I used the microfilm copies of the federal census records in the Indiana University Library.

7. I own five large catalogs issued by the Belknap Hardware Company of Louisville, Kentucky. This company supplied hardware and a broad range of other goods to hardware and general stores all over southern Indiana. Some hardware stores in Bloomington, for example, currently carry the Belknap Company's line of "Bluegrass" tools. The catalogs I own were intended for the use of store owners. They include a "porch rocker" similar in size and design to Jim Turpin's large rocking chairs. The Belknap rocking chairs were made in small factories in Tennessee. While these catalogs give the wholesale price, they do suggest what the retail price should be.

8. Reproduced in Henry C. Mercer, *Ancient Carpenters' Tools,* 3rd edition (Doylestown, Pa.: The Bucks County Historical Society, 1960), p. 220.

9. R. A. Salaman, *Dictionary of Tools* (New York: Charles Scribner's Sons, 1975), p. 258.

10. Allen H. Eaton, *Handicrafts of the Southern Highlands,* new edition (New York: Dover Publications, 1973), pp. 157–161.

11. *Tennessee Mountain Crafts,* Division of Information, Nashville. Undated, but ca. 1965, unpaginated.

12. Mercer, *Tools,* p. 168.

13. See Wallace Nutting, *A Windsor Handbook* (Saugus, Mass.: Wallace Nutting, 1917) and Thomas H. Ormsbee, *The Windsor Chair* (New York: Deerfield Books, 1962). Michael Owen Jones, *The Hand Made Object and Its Maker* (Berkeley and Los Angeles: The University of California Press, 1975), deals with Kentucky makers of slat-back chairs but says very little about the history of the type. A recent book, John H. Alexander, Jr., *Make a Chair from a Tree* (Newtown, Conn.: Taunton Press, 1978), describes how to make slat-back chairs but largely ignores their history.

14. John Gloag, *The Chair: Its Origins, Design, and Social History* (South Brunswick and New York: A. S. Barnes, 1967), p. 43.

15. Reproduced in Mercer, *Tools,* p. 218.

16. Jane Toller, *English Country Furniture* (South Brunswick and New York: A. S. Barnes, 1973), p. 45. The term "ladder-back chair" seems to be the commonly used term in England for this type of chair.

17. See Sigurd Erixson, "West European Connections and Cultural Relations," *Folk-Liv* 2 (1938): 157, for information on the areas in which the slat-back chair is found in western Europe.

18. Glassie, *Pattern,* p. 228. Although I have found no detailed information on seventeenth-century English slat-back chairs, Sparkes (pp. 114, 121) shows examples from the eighteenth century and Toller mentions seventeenth-century slat-back chairs (p. 45). She believes the Dutch introduced this type of chair into England in the seventeenth century, but she must have been unaware of the mid-fourteenth-century English example mentioned above, n. 12.

19. See Cummings, "Slat-Back Chairs," pp. 60–63, and Wallace Nutting, *Furniture of the Pilgrim Century (of American Origin) 1620–1720* (New York: Dover, 1965).

20. A number of slat-back chairs made by the northern Shakers after 1800 have bent back posts; but the posts are not flattened on the fronts, and they do have finials. In order to get the posts to bend above the seat line, the Shaker chairmakers made the back posts smaller in diameter above the seats. They do not bend as markedly as chairs with flattened back posts. See Edward D. and Faith Andrews, *Shaker Furniture* (New York: Dover, 1950), pls. 15, 18. A chair made by southern Shakers at the South Union Colony in Kentucky has bent and flattened back posts without finials and resembles very strongly southern slat-back chairs made by non-Shaker chairmakers. Ralph and Terry Kovel, *American Country Furniture* (New York: Crown Publishers, 1965), pp. 92–93.

    Benno M. Forman, "Delaware Valley 'Crookt Foot' and Slat-Back Chairs," *Winterthur Portfolio* 15, no. 1 (Spring 1980): 57, shows and discusses a "raked-back" chair, an eighteenth century slat-back armchair whose back posts bend dramatically and sharply just above the seat line. The bend in these Pennsylvania chair posts was produced by a special and complicated technique while they were being turned in a lathe. Forman says, "Raked-back turned chairs are extremely rare in American colonial furniture." He convincingly shows that the chair is the result of German influences. Because this type of chair post is produced by a different method and because it is very different in appearance, it is unlikely that it could have had any influence on the development of the bent-back, slat-back chair.

21. Glassie, *Pattern,* p. 232.

22. See E. D. and F. Andrews, *Shaker Furniture,* pp. 103–9. Kathleen Cairns, "Stencil Decorating and Caning Chairs," The *Chronicle* of the Early American Industries Association 3, no. 3 (April 1945): 27, describes a two-man shop in Middletown, N. Y., that made bent-back slat-back chairs up until 1880.

23. Glassie, *Pattern,* pp. 230–31.

24. Walters, *Furniture Makers,* pp. 57, 120, 141, 145, and passim.

25. Ibid., pp. 59, 202.

26. Ibid., pp. 145, 157, 165, 206.

27. Ibid., pp. 57, 59, 141, 145, 157.

28. An English example is shown in Toller, *English Country Furniture,* p. 144. Seventeenth-century American examples are shown in Robert Bishop, *Centuries and Styles of the American Chair* (New York: E. P. Dutton, 1972), pl. 35, and in Nutting, *Pilgrim Century,* figs. 391, 396, and also in *Antiques* 59, no. 5 (May 1956): 460. An eighteenth-century American example from Salem, Mass., is shown in *Antiques* 88, no. 4 (October 1965): 488, and an example from North Carolina dating from around 1800 in *Antiques* 91, no. 1 (January 1967): 92.

29. Walters, *Furniture Makers,* p. 202.

30. Ibid., p. 184.

31. Ibid., numbers 151, 152, 153, 203, 874, 878.

32. John D. Barnhart and Donald F. Carmony, *Indiana: From Frontier to Industrial Commonwealth* (New York: Lewis, 1954), I, 422, n. 37.

33. See, for example, Carl Bridenbaugh, *The Colonial Craftsman* (Chicago: University of Chicago Press, 1961). Because he is writing about such an early era, Bridenbaugh is forced to rely on written records of different kinds. Hence he describes mainly urban craftsmen.

     Forman, in his previously cited article (n. 19, above), discusses an active and popular Philadelphia chairmaker of the early eighteenth century. This man's shop produced large numbers of chairs, and he employed many workers. Forman gives the impression that this busy craftsman in one of the largest urban centers of the time is typical of all chairmakers. He says, "Equally devastating to the romantic ideal is the way in which this account book systematically destroys the fondly held image of the individual craftsman toiling away in splendid solitude, producing with his own hands the chairs he sells to earn his livelihood" (p. 45).

7

Social Customs and the Crafts: A Note

To show that, just as it is possible to identify folklore in literature, so also is it possible to identify folklife in literature, the following piece was written. It appeared in a double issue of a journal in order to honor an old friend and one-time colleague, William Hugh Jansen.

*   *   *

Anyone interested in traditional crafts must be deeply impressed by the items produced by craftsmen in the late eighteenth and early nineteenth centuries. From that period a great quantity of furniture, silver, china and the like has survived. Some of it is utilitarian; much of it is highly ornamented, of the finest materials and of exquisite workmanship. The work of English craftsmen in that period is particularly esteemed. The names Chippendale, Hepplewhite, and Sheraton in furniture come immediately to mind, for instance.

Antique collectors for at least a hundred years have been searching out, purchasing at high prices, and cherishing furniture and other household items from this period. Indeed, for many decades in the twentieth century authorities maintained that the term "antique" could only properly be applied to an item made before 1835, though this rule was frequently ignored and now has been largely abandoned. The designs developed by craftsmen in the late eighteenth and early nineteenth centuries have been so esteemed that these designs have been copied and reproduced with greater or less care by nineteenth- and twentieth-century manufacturers. Innumerable books illustrating antiques from the era have been published, as have countless magazine articles and several magazines dealing almost exclusively with these antiques.

It should be mentioned that the household furnishings produced in the era can be placed roughly into two categories; for purposes of simplicity we

This article originally appeared in *Kentucky Folklore Record* 23, nos. 3–4 (July–October 1977): 72–78.

can call one category "vernacular." Items in this category were, for the most part, produced for the lower and middle classes. They were simple and utilitarian in design though usually very well made and of good materials, for they were intended for daily use and were not quickly discarded. Usually they were made by country craftsmen. Even though the Industrial Revolution was well underway in England, great numbers of people still lived in the countryside and transportation was such that they patronized local craftsmen. These craftsmen were strongly influenced by tradition in their designs and in all aspects of their work.

A second category can be called "high style." In this category are the items produced mostly for wealthy patrons by city craftsmen, especially London draftsmen, as London seems to have been a style center for the period. These craftsmen undoubtedly followed tradition to a large extent in their methods of work and their choice of materials, but the designs which they used were constantly changing and hence were less often traditional. The items which they made were often elaborate and highly decorated. They were intended to be used, of course, but they were also intended to impress the beholder.

If one were to survey the antiques which fill museums, antique shops, and the homes of collectors and which fill the pages of books and magazines, he would probably find that the high style antiques are much more numerous than the vernacular. During the actual decades of the era, however, far more items we would call vernacular must have been produced, for the really wealthy who could afford to patronize the high style craftsman must have represented only a tiny fraction of the total population. Actually, a process of selection has been going on for some time. The simple vernacular pieces often were not appreciated by subsequent generations and were discarded, while the elaborate high style pieces were often cherished and even though out of style, retained. Moreover, collectors have sought out the high style pieces and, until recently, overlooked the vernacular ones. Museums and writers have, for the most part, followed the same trend.

Despite this fact, it is clear that an amazing quantity of high style household furnishings were produced in the era. Wealthy people had huge houses which had to be filled. Fashion dictated that the old or not so old had to be replaced even though still in excellent condition. The not so wealthy felt they had to emulate the wealthy. It is clear that wealthy people, then as today, felt they had to furnish their houses so as to impress their invited guests. What is not so often recognized, however, is that they also had to impress large numbers of uninvited visitors.

During the late eighteenth and early nineteenth centuries there must have existed a social custom which seems to be largely dead today. People of a certain social status traveling through the English countryside felt it perfectly in order to stop at mansions on or near their route to look over the grounds and be shown through the houses even though they had not the slightest acquaintance with the owners. Likewise, it seems to have been a fairly common practice to arrange an excursion to look over the grounds and be shown through the house of utter strangers. No wonder that wealthy people felt constrained to furnish their houses in the finest manner possible and to patronize the finest craftsmen possible. No wonder that high style craftsmen were encouraged to procure the finest materials and follow the latest styles.

If we are to understand why crafts flourished in this era and why there are so many magnificent antiques which have survived from this era, it behooves us to examine this social custom more closely. As is so often the case, novels of the period provide us with excellent information.

In Jane Austen's *Pride and Prejudice,* published in 1813, though written in 1796 and 1797, and in Charles Dickens' *Bleak House,* published in 1853, there are accounts of people visiting the country houses of utter strangers. Jane Austen's account occurs in volume III, chapter 1, while Dickens' account is found in chapter 7. In addition, there are brief references to the custom in Jane Austen's *Mansfield Park* (1814), chapter 9, and *Sense and Sensibility* (1811), chapter 12. In *Pride and Prejudice* the visit occurs while the heroine, Elizabeth Bennett, and her uncle and aunt, Mr. and Mrs. Gardiner, are taking a summer vacation tour through Derbyshire. Their route passes within a few miles of Pemberley, the estate of Mr. Darcy. On the spur of the moment they decide to visit Pemberley:

> Elizabeth, as they drove along, watched for the first appearance of Pemberley Woods. . . .
> They gradually ascended for half a mile, and there found themselves at the top of a considerable eminence, where the wood ceased, and the eye was instantly caught by Pemberly House, situated on the opposite side of a valley, into which the road with some abruptness wound. . . .
> They descended the hill, crossed the bridge, and drove to the door. . . . On applying to see the place, they were admitted into the hall. . . .
> The housekeeper came; a respectable-looking, elderly woman, much less fine, and more civil, than she (Elizabeth) had any notion of finding her. They followed her into the dining-parlour. It was a large, well-proportioned room, handsomely fitted up. Elizabeth, after slightly surveying it, went to a window to enjoy its prospect. . . . As they passed into other rooms. . . . from every window there were beauties to be seen. The rooms were lofty and handsome, and their furniture suitable to the fortune of their proprietor; but Elizabeth saw, with admiration of his taste, that it was neither gaudy nor uselessly fine, with less of splendor, and more real elegance, than the furniture of Rosings. . . .
> She longed to enquire of the housekeeper, whether her master were really absent. . . . At length, however, the question was asked by her uncle. . . . Mrs. Reynolds (the housekeeper) replied, that he was, adding, "But we expect him tomorrow, with a large party of friends."

Her aunt now called her to look at a picture. She approached, and saw the likeness of Mr. Wickham suspended, among several other miniatures, over the mantlepiece.... The housekeeper came forward, and told them it was the picture of a young gentleman, the son of her late master's steward who had been brought up by him at his own expense. "He is now gone into the army," she added, "But I am afraid he has turned out very wild."
. . .

"And that," said Mrs. Reynolds, pointing to another of the miniatures, "is my master—and very like him. It was drawn at the same time as the other—about eight years ago." . . .

Mrs. Reynolds then directed their attention to one of Miss Darcy, drawn when she was only eight years old.... Mrs. Reynolds, either from pride or attachment, had evidently great pleasure in talking of her master and his sister.

"Is your master much at Pemberley in the course of the year?" (asked Mr. Gardiner).

"Not so much as I could wish, Sir; but I dare say he may spend half his time here; and Miss Darcy is always down for the summer months." . . .

"If your master would marry you might see more of him."

"Yes, Sir; but I do not know when *that* will be. I do not know who is good enough for him."

Mr. and Mrs. Gardiner smiled. Elizabeth could not help saying, "It is very much to his credit, I am sure, that you should think so."

"I say no more than the truth, and what everybody will say that knows him," replied the other. Elizabeth thought this was going pretty far; and she listened with increasing astonishment as the housekeeper added, "I have never had a cross word from him in my life, and I have known him ever since he was four years old." . . .

She (Mrs. Reynolds) related the subject of the pictures, the dimensions of the rooms, and the price of the furniture, ... Mr. Gardiner, highly amused by the kind of family prejudice, to which he attributed her excessive commendation of her master, soon led again to the subject; and she dwelt with energy on his many merits, as they proceeded together up the great staircase....

On reaching the spacious lobby above, they were shewn into a very pretty sitting-room, lately filled up with greater elegance and lightness than the apartments below; and were informed that it was but just done, to give pleasure to Miss Darcy, who had taken a liking to the room, when last at Pemberley....

The picture gallery, and two or three of the principal bed-rooms, were all that remained to be shewn.... In the gallery there were many family portraits, but they could have little to fix the attention of a stranger....

When all of the house that was open to general inspection had been seen, they returned down stairs, and taking leave of the housekeeper, were consigned over to the gardener, who met them at the hall door.

ᴗ

In *Bleak House* Chesney Wold is the country seat of Sir Leicester Dedlock, "the most powerful baronet in the land." Mrs. Rouncewell is the housekeeper and Rosa is an especially favored young maid whom Mrs. Rouncewell, because of her advancing years, has trained to conduct visitors through the mansion. Watt is Mrs. Rouncewell's grandson.

"What company is this, Rosa?" says Mrs. Rouncewell.

"It's two young men in a gig, ma'am, who want to see the house—and if you please, I told them no!" in reply to a gesture of dissent from the housekeeper. "I told them it was the wrong day, and the wrong hour; but the young man who was driving took off his hat, and begged me to bring this card to you."

"Read it, my dear Watt," says the housekeeper.

"Mr. Guppy" is all the information the card yields.

"Guppy!" repeats Mrs. Rouncewell. "Mr. Guppy! Nonsense, I never heard of him."

"If you please, he told *me* that!" says Rosa. "But he said that he and the other young gentleman came from London only last night by the mail, on business at the magistrates' meeting, ten miles off, this morning; and that as their business was soon over, and they had heard a great deal said of Chesney Wold, they had come through the wet to see it. They are lawyers. He says he is not in Mr. Tulkinghorn's office, but he is sure he may make use of Mr. Tulkinghorn's name, if necessary."

Now Mr. Tulkinghorn is, in a manner, part and parcel of the place and besides, is supposed to have made Mrs. Rouncewell's will. The old lady relaxes, consents to the admission of the visitors as a favour, and dismisses Rosa. The grandson, however, being smitten by a sudden wish to see the house himself, proposes to join the party. The grandmother accompanies him—though to do him justice, he is exceedingly unwilling to trouble her.

"Much obliged to you, ma'am!" says Mr. Guppy, divesting himself of his wet dreadnought in the hall. "Us London lawyers don't often get an out, and when we do, we like to make the most of it, you know."

The old housekeeper, with a gracious severity of deportment, waves her hand toward the great staircase. Mr. Guppy and his friend follow Rosa, Mrs. Rouncewell and her grandson follow them, a young gardener goes before to open the shutters.

As is usually the case with people who go over houses, Mr. Guppy and his friend are deadbeat before they have well begun. They straggle about in wrong places, look at wrong things, don't care for right things, gape when more rooms are opened, exhibit profound depression of spirits, and are clearly knocked-up. Thus they pass on from room to room, raising the pictured Dedlocks for a few brief minutes as the young gardener admits the light, and reconsigning them to their graves as he shuts it out again. . . .

Even the long drawing-room of Chesney Wold cannot revive Mr. Guppy's spirits. He is so low he droops on the threshold, and has hardly strength of mind to enter. But a portrait over the chimney-piece, painted by the fashionable artist of the day, acts upon him like a charm. . . .

"Dear me!" says Mr. Guppy. "Who's that?"

"The picture over the fire-place," says Rosa, "is the portrait of the present Lady Dedlock. It is considered a perfect likeness, and the best work of the master." . . .

He sees no more of her. He sees her rooms, which are the last shown, as being very elegant, and he looks out of the windows from which she looked out, not long ago, upon the weather that bored her to death. He has come to the end of the sight, and the fresh village beauty to the end of her description, which is always this:

"The terrace below is much admired. It is called, from an old story in the family, the Ghost's Walk."

"No," says Mr. Guppy, greedily curious. "What's the story, miss. Is it anything about a picture?"

"I don't know sir." Rose is shyer than ever. . . .

The story has nothing to do with a picture; the housekeeper can guarantee that. Mr. Guppy retires with his friend, and presently is heard to drive away. It is now dusk.

On the basis of two descriptions and two brief references it would be rash to draw up a set of "rules" that governed these visits; still some generalizations can be made. For example, it must have been a very common custom. In *Pride and Prejudice* we are told that the visitors are making a three weeks' vacation tour through Derbyshire and that they have been gone from their homes only about a week. Nonetheless, when Mr. and Mrs. Gardiner propose a visit to Pemberley which is only a mile or two out of their way, their niece, Elizabeth Bennett, at first demurs. "She must own that she was tired of great houses; after going over so many, she really had no pleasure in fine carpets or satin curtains." In *Mansfield Park,* Mary Crawford, who is about twenty years old, "had seen scores of great houses," while Sir John Middleton in *Sense and Sensibility,* who has proposed an excursion to visit a fine house and its grounds about twelve miles away, "had formed parties to visit them, at least, twice every summer for the past ten years."

As to the tour itself, the house and the grounds are normally visited. Since we are interested in the tour of the house wherein the handiwork of craftsmen is displayed, we can ignore the grounds. The housekeeper normally conducts the tour, though in *Bleak House* the housekeeper, because of her advanced years, has trained a maid to conduct tours. The housekeeper or her appointee seems to have developed a running lecture comparable to that delivered by docents in twentieth century restored house museums. The lecture emphasizes the history of the house and of the family, the outstanding features of the house and its furnishings, and most noteworthy from our standpoint, the cost of many of the furnishings. The guide dwells on the portraits which hang in great profusion. The subjects and their relationship to the present owner are described. If there are other kinds of paintings such as landscapes, they are not mentioned. The parts of the house that are shown comprise what may be called the living quarters. These include bedrooms. The servants' quarters, kitchen, and so on are not included in the tour, however. The tour lasts well over an hour. The sightseers converse with the guide, ask her questions, and are told about the character and habits of the owners.

In *Bleak House* we find that there are certain days and certain hours when the house in question may be viewed, though exceptions are made, for the visitors in this instance are shown through the house even though they arrive at an unscheduled time. In *Pride and Prejudice* it would appear that visitors are admitted at any time. It even seems that visitors would have been shown through the house even if the owner of the house and his family had been living there at the time of the visit. It is clear that Mr. and Mrs. Gardiner, the heroine's uncle and aunt, are eager to be shown the house but not in the least concerned whether or not the owner and his family are in residence. One can only assume that visitors were expected to have the good taste not to ask to be admitted to a house during mealtimes, perhaps, and that visitors would not have been shown into rooms that were actually being used by the family. One gets the distinct impression that many of the rooms in a great house were used only on special occasions such as banquets and balls.

A twentieth-century reader is naturally curious as to who would be admitted to a house. How far down the social scale could a person be and still be admitted? Unfortunately, there is not enough information in the accounts to give a satisfactory answer. A drover passing an estate with a herd of cattle destined for a market town would hardly have expected to view the mansion. In both *Bleak House* and *Pride and Prejudice,* however, it is clear that the social status of the visitors is considerably below that of the owners. In *Pride and Prejudice* Mr. Darcy, owner of Pemberley, has already proposed to Elizabeth Bennett and has been refused. He had experienced great difficulty in overcoming his repugnance for Elizabeth's "low connections," that is, her relatives. His supercilious friends have specifically twitted him on the fact that Elizabeth's uncle is a businessman "who lives somewhere near Cheapside," London's commercial district. Yet it is this uncle, with wife and niece, who asks to be shown through Darcy's mansion and they are admitted. In *Bleak House* the disparity in social status between the viewers and the owner is far greater; the viewers are clerks to London attorneys while the owner is "the most powerful baronet in the land." Yet the two clerks persist in requesting admittance to the house even though told that they have not arrived during regular visiting hours, and they are admitted.

Parallels to this earlier custom may be found in modern times. Some of the great mansions of England are regularly open to sightseers who pay a fee which helps the owners retain the houses in these days of rising costs and heavy taxes. In the United States house tours are not uncommon; they are often arranged by charitable organizations to raise funds for worthy causes. These modern parallels do not, however, have the same function as the earlier custom. The fact that the owners of mansions in the earlier period had to expect that members of the upper social classes would continually be shown through their houses exerted a powerful influence. To the desire to appear to live in a manner worthy of their position and income and to have proper tastes was added pride in their families and their histories. Small wonder that the noble and the wealthy patronized craftsmen and encouraged them to employ their greatest skills and the finest materials. Small wonder, too, that a great quantity of beautiful objects has survived from this period to delight the lover of antiques and to amaze the student of the history of crafts.

8

Tools on Tombstones: Some Indiana Examples

For many years I avoided concerns with folk art because I had encountered so little of it in my fieldwork. Eventually, however, I became so enamored of the remarkable limestone monuments in the Bloomington area, especially the tree-stump tombstones, that I began to write about them. My original interest was aroused by the fact that tools were used in a symbolic way to indicate the craft a person had followed and it is for that reason that I published the following essay and photographs.

*   *   *

Early tombstones—those from the Colonial Era especially—have attracted most attention. Later stones, however, should not be neglected for they, too, can display elements of interest to the student of folklife.

In southern Indiana, tombstones made between about 1875 and 1945 are usually of local stones, mostly limestone. Many seem to have been made by the stone carvers who worked at the stonemills in the area. These were men who, through a long apprenticeship and daily practice at the mills producing architectural stone—capitals, cornices, and the like—developed great skills that they occasionally devoted to tombstones. Inspired in some cases by the death of a relative or of a comrade, they could produce gravestones of striking originality that take a high place in the folk art of southern Indiana.

Among the gravestones of this period in southern Indiana, some will fascinate anyone interested in folk or traditional crafts; these stones mark the graves of deceased craftsmen and show the tools and, sometimes, the products of the craftsmen. Not only have we the skill of the carver, himself a traditional craftsman, but these stones also testify to the esteem in which the craftsman, his family, or his associates held the craft. This practice is, of

This article originally appeared in *Pioneer America* 10, no. 1 (June 1978): 106–11.

course, not restricted to southern Indiana. There is, for instance, an eighteenth-century English example:

> The hollow-grasp handsaw is shown with other carpenter's tools on a foot-stone in the church yard of St. John, sub Castro, Lewis, Suzzex. The head-stone inscription—"In memory of Mark Sharp, Carpenter, Late of the Parish who died 26th November 1741 aged 64 years."[1]

The earliest among my casual list of tools on tombstones is the gravestone of a cooper, Henry J. Hymen, who died July 1, 1898, and who is buried at Loogootee. The memorial consists of two barrels of different sizes, one atop the other, with a cooper's adze on the top barrel, all carved from limestone, in great detail, and of natural size. The staves and the wooden hoops appear in especially clear detail. Carved on the lower barrel is the legend "A cooper by trade," plus the name, dates, and another legend (fig. 8.1).

The next chronologically is perhaps the most remarkable of all. Located in the cemetery at Bedford, it is a monument, a footstone rather than a headstone, to Louis J. Baker who died August 29, 1917, at the age of twenty-three. A stone carver at a local stonemill, he left his work in progress at the mill at the end of that fatal day, went home, and was killed by lightning. His fellow carvers made an exact replica of his workbench, or "banker" as stone carvers call it (fig. 8.2; fig. 8.3 is detail). On the banker is the piece of architectural stone, unfurnished, exactly as he left it; it is even said that this is the exact piece of stone that he was working on. Atop this stone appear his tools; a mallet, a hammer, a pitching tool, chisels, a square, a head of a broom, and his apron. The fidelity of this work is amazing; the woodgrain of the bench is clearly shown, as are the bent-over nails holding the bench together, and the straws in the broom. There is no attempt to tidy things up or to make it finer than it was. These stone carvers, who normally executed the designs of architects, draughtsmen, and others, produced a striking and poignant memorial of their own design and one that speaks to a craftsman far more movingly than a classical urn or some similar ornament.

Nearby in the same cemetery at Bedford stands a monument to the Bedford Stonecutters Association (fig. 8.4). It reminds us that Bedford is a leading producer of the high quality Bedford limestone, which all comes from an area about thirty miles long and a few miles wide with Bedford near its southern end and Bloomington near its northern. Quarrying and stonecutting became important by about 1875 and flourished mightily until about World War II. Limestone in great amounts was shipped far and near. (All of the limestone for the entire Empire State Building, for example, was taken from a single quarry near Bloomington. The quarry was opened to

Figure 8.1. Gravestone of Henry Hymen, Cooper (d. 1898), at Loogootee

Figure 8.2.   Monument to Louis J. Baker, Stone Carver (d. 1917), at Bedford

Figure 8.3.   Detail of Baker Monument

Figure 8.4. Monument to Bedford Stonecutters Association

Figure 8.5.   Detail of Bedford Stonecutters Association Monument

Figure 8.6. Monument to Michael F. Durlauf, Stone Carver (d. 1931), in St. Joseph's Cemetery, Jasper
This monument is believed to have been carved by Durlauf's son, Leo F. Durlauf.

Figure 8.7. Detail of Durlauf Monument

Figure 8.8   Tombstone of W. E. Douthitt, Blacksmith (d. 1947)

Figure 8.9. Tombstone of E. C. Douthitt, Blacksmith (d. 1949)

supply the stone for that one job and has not been worked since. One might say that one can see there the hole in the ground from which the Empire State Building came.) Great numbers of stone carvers worked in local mills to produce the carved work to adorn buildings, and it is certainly appropriate that there should be a monument to these carvers. One only wonders why it was placed in a cemetery instead of some more prominent place.

At any rate, the monument consists of a shaft, atop which stands the figure of a stone carver dressed in the workclothes of the turn of the century. At his left side is the corner of a workbench (banker), with the capital of a pillar atop it on which his left hand rests. In his right hand is a stone carver's mallet. Near the top of the pillar on the front side are two clasped hands. On the back are two hands, one holding a chisel and the other a mallet. On the left side is a "trophy" composed of carvers' tools: a hammer, a mallet, a stone axe, a rule, a pin, a pitching tool, and a number of chisels. On the right side are a square and a pair of dividers (see also fig. 8.5, detail of fig. 8.4).

In St. Joseph's Cemetery in Jasper is a monument to a stone carver made by his son, likewise a stone carver (fig. 8.6). The father, Michael F. Durlauf, died in 1931, and the monument must have been carved at that time by the son, Leo F. Durlauf, who died in 1954. The monument, actually a footstone, consists of a limestone log lying on the ground. It is about six feet long and two feet in diameter with several stubs of branches. Along the bottom of the log, among ferns, ivy leaves, oak leaves, and acorns, appear the carver's stone tools: a tooth axe, a pair of dividers, a mallet, chisels, a pitching tool, a hammer, and a double-pointed sledge or scabbling hammer (fig. 8.7). Carved on the log also is a banner sporting a lyre; the father and the son were both musicians in the community band. On the back of the log is the legend "Carved by request of our dear father by Leo F. Durlauf."

In the Clear Creek cemetery a few miles south of Bloomington are three tombstones shaped like anvils, each with a blacksmith's hammer atop the anvil. Two of these, next to one another, are for brothers, W. E. Douthitt (1900–1947) and E. C. Douthitt (1885–1949) (fig. 8.8). The third, some distance away, is for W. Reynolds (1864–1944) (fig. 8.9). In the Bloomington area, a number of blacksmiths were employed in the stone quarries and mills to make special tools and equipment and to sharpen the many tools used in working the stone.

Note

1. Henry C. Mercer, *Ancient Carpenters' Tools*. The Bucks County Historical Society, Doylestown, Pennsylvania, 3rd edition, 1960.

9

The Sincerest Form of Flattery:
Originals and Imitations in "Rustic Monuments" of the Limestone Belt of Indiana

In the study of folk art I believe that it is of great importance to determine whether or not the art in question is accepted and admired by the community of which the artist is a member or whether it is rejected by the community. To show that the art of the carvers of tree-stump tombstones was both accepted and admired I have written this discussion which is to be presented at a conference on gravestones but which is printed here for the first time.

*   *   *

It is customary to assume that artists are generally representative of the communities of which they are a part so that their art speaks for the community and represents the values of the community. Such, at least, is the assumption seemingly underlying the approach of art historians and others who study the art of the past. At the same time, it has always been recognized that there are some artists with intensely private visions which do not appeal to the community as a whole but appeal only to a small number of individuals who, because of a special interest, strive to understand the artist and his work.

This division between two types of artists is obviously vastly oversimplified. Nonetheless, it proves to be of value in dealing with folk art. Many writers have adopted the requirement that folk art speak for the community as an important part of their definition of folk art. In other words, if one is to add the qualifier "folk" to the word "art," then that art must appeal to and speak for a wide segment of people—in short, the community. If, however, the art appeals to only a small number of people with especially developed tastes, or if the community rejects the art, then that art should not be termed "folk." Otherwise, "folk" becomes meaningless

This article is a revision of a paper originally delivered at the conference of the American Gravestone Society, held in Amherst, Massachusetts, June 1987.

and some more apt term should be used. I have been accustomed to consider folktales, as an example, to be tales that have been widely told so that they must have appealed to many people in order to survive over generations and to spread from one area to another. I find it hard to conceive of a story that no one except the teller liked being considered a folktale. Such a tale could hardly be repeated by other people and become a "traditional narrative." For these reasons I feel that to use the qualifier "folk" with "art" requires community acceptance of that art, at least. If one is to analyze the art and look for community values, certainly the art should appeal to the community and not be rejected.

The artist with a private vision who appeals only to small numbers of people and may well not appeal to the community as a whole seems to have become more common in this and the preceding century. For convenience sake I have previously used the term "romantic" for this art which appeals to the few or is rejected by the community and the term "medieval" for that art which does appeal to the community.[1] I realize the shortcomings of these terms and propose now "private" and "community" as more acceptable substitutes.

I have previously described an innovation in gravestone design which occurred in the late nineteenth century and persisted well into the twentieth century. I have called these innovative monuments "tree-stump tombstones" because they were so called by the carvers who made them and their patrons.[2] In advertisements and more formal circumstances, however, they were referred to as "rustic monuments." These gravestones were widely accepted and many more-or-less stock designs were carved and used in various parts of the United States. In the limestone belt of southern Indiana some special tree-stump tombstones were made.

In the stone mills of Lawrence and Monroe Counties especially there were many stone carvers who labored daily at their benches (or bunkers as the benches are called) producing architectural moldings and monumental details. In their day-to-day work they followed the designs of architects and others. On occasion, however, individual carvers were called upon to create gravestones for relatives or friends and in the process they produced their own designs, designs that were symbolic of the life and interests of the deceased, of religious beliefs, and of the feelings of bereavement of the family and friends. Were these symbols recognizable to a wider circle than the friends and family? Did they appeal to the community? There are several examples which can be cited which demonstrate clearly that these special gravestones were accepted and admired because the original designs were copied or imitated.

One of these examples is a group whose oldest member stands in what is today a remote country cemetery about ten miles east of Mitchell, Indiana. The monument was carved for David Huston (fig. 9.1). He was a

Figure 9.1. Monument to David Huston (d. 1884)
Probably carved by George Eisele.

bachelor farmer who died on December 4, 1884. It appears that before his death he arranged with George Eisele, a Bedford stone carver, for his own monument. It consists of a beautifully detailed tree trunk at least ten feet tall against which leans a full-sized muzzle-loading rifle. From the stub of a branch hang a powder horn and a shot bag. The base of the monument is a rocky hillside in miniature across which streak three miniature hounds in determined pursuit of a jaunty, bounding fox (figs. 9.2 and 9.3).

At some time after 1891 another treatment of the same themes was carved for a grave marker in the municipal cemetery in Mitchell. The person memorialized is another old fox hunter, Eberle Martin. The carver of this monument, Charles Underwood of Bedford, used the same motifs but developed them in his own individualistic way. He also added a portrait of Eberle Martin. While the date at which Martin moved to Mitchell is given on the grave marker, the date of his death is not. We can interpret this as meaning that Martin came to Mitchell in 1891, soon saw the Huston monument, and admired it so much that he wanted one for himself. He ordered it from the carver Charles Underwood rather than from George Eisele. The monument was erected at Martin's grave plot while Martin was still alive (fig. 9.4). After his death, however, no carver went out to the cemetery to properly inscribe the date of death. What is clear, however, is that while each carver must have been told what his patron wanted, it was left up to the carver to follow his own talents and abilities in the specific details.

Much later yet, in 1961, a third monument was carved, inspired by one or both of the preceding. This monument is not a grave marker. It seems to have been commissioned by a couple, L. H. and Maude Rohrer, who donated it to a small municipal park in Bedford (fig. 9.5). I can only assume that the Rohrers deeply admired the Huston and/or the Martin gravestones, probably considering them to be masterpieces of design, and wanted a similar one to stand in Bedford, the home of the other two carvers. It is a sad reflection on the difficulty of finding information about the recent past that I have been unable to find anything about the Rohrers or the identity of the carver. Again, this carver, although told what the overall design should be, worked out specific details for himself.

In another case, two brothers, highly skilled carvers, who lived in Gosport, Indiana, were asked in 1898 to create a tree-stump monument for Marcus C. and Malinda Smith (fig. 9.6). The Smiths had been among the earliest settlers in the area and were known both for their piety and their generosity. This reputation is testified to by passages in a biographical notice for Marcus Smith. In 1863 he was ordained a minister in the Christian Church at the age of 48 "and since that time has been preaching the Gospel to the people in his immediate vicinity.... [He is] a good, kind-hearted gentleman, always liberal in any public enterprise, and ever ready to assist the needy."[3]

According to a great-nephew interviewed in 1971, the two carvers, Silvester and Claude Hoadley, rose to the challenge when asked to create a monument which would symbolize these important traits of the Smiths. On one side of the tree trunk they carved an ax, a maul, and a splitting wedge, not because Marcus Smith devoted most of his time to splitting rails but because these symbols were appropriate for a male pioneer. On the opposite side the brothers carved a small spinning wheel, the symbol of the industry and domesticity of pioneer women in the age of homespun.

At another side of the tree trunk sits a pile of books (fig. 9.7). A hand reaches for the topmost book, the Bible, thus indicating that the couple put the Bible above all other books and read it often. Finally, near the top of the trunk of the tree is a vignette showing one hand passing an object to another hand. According to the aforementioned great-nephew of the carvers, the object is a biscuit and it is thus that the Hoadleys symbolized generosity.

A couple living on a farm not far away from Gosport must have seen the Smith monument and admired it, for they ordered an identical one for themselves while they were still very much alive. John Q. and Highland Patrick died in 1933 and 1935 respectively and are buried in a plot in the Paragon, Indiana, cemetery. At the head of the plot sits the replica of the Smith stone similar in every detail to the Smith stone except, of course, for the names and dates (fig. 9.8). There are also, however, separate headstones for the husband and wife which appear to be considerably newer than the tree-stump stone. It would appear, therefore, that the Patricks before their deaths ordered a replica of the Smith stone from Silvester and Claude Hoadley. The brothers obliged and this monument was set up in the Patrick plot. When the Patricks died at later dates they were provided with separate headstones.

The same carver brothers created in 1893 another striking monument for a married couple, Orris B. and Mary E. Dickerson (fig. 9.9). This monument uses double tree trunks joined at the base and with intertwined branches, a fitting symbol for a loving couple. The monument incorporates many of the motifs of the previously mentioned one such as the pile of books and the miniature spinning wheel carved in low relief. It adds a rifle to the tools for the husband (fig. 9.10.). The monument stands in Riverside Cemetery in Spencer, Indiana, about ten miles from Gosport where the Hoadleys lived, but on the basis of stylistic as well as other grounds there can be no doubt that the Hoadley brothers were the carvers.

In 1902 the children of Joel and Ruth Philbert saw the Dickerson

Figure 9.2.   Detail of Huston Monument

Figure 9.3. Detail of Huston Monument

Figure 9.4. Monument to Eberle Martin
The date of Martin's death is not known, but the
monument, by Charles Underwood, was carved after 1891.

Figure 9.5.   Monument in Bedford Park, Donated by L. H. and
              Maude Rohrer, 1961
              Carver is unknown.

Figure 9.6.   Monument to Marcus and Malinda Smith (d. 1898 and
              1897, respectively)
              Carved by Silvester and Claude Hoadley (see also fig. 9.8).

Figure 9.7.   Detail of Smith Monument

Figure 9.8.   Monument to John Q. and Highland Patrick (d. 1933
                and 1935, respectively)
                Carved by Silvester and Claude Hoadley (see also fig. 9.6).

monument, admired it, and wanted one like it for their parents. They ordered a copy from a monument works in Bloomfield, Indiana, who in turn commissioned a carver, probably Ferdinand O. Cross of Bedford, to produce the stone. This carver copied many of the features of the Dickerson stone, for the Philbert stone, too, is a double tree trunk with intertwined branches (Fig. 9.11). A rifle and an ax lean against the father's side of the monument, but the most remarkable feature is a life-sized, virtually free-standing spinning wheel on the wife's side instead of the miniature wheel in low relief featured on the stones created by the Hoadley brothers (fig. 9.12). In this instance it is safe to say that the later Philbert stone is more striking than its inspiration, the Dickerson stone.[4]

We have, therefore, in three groups of related stones three possibilities. In one case (Smith-Patrick) the same carvers made two identical stones. In one case (Huston-Martin-Rohrer) two different carvers were inspired to copy a third stone. All three stones are of equal effectiveness, to my mind. In the third case (Dickerson-Philbert) one carver was inspired by the work of another but produced a more interesting monument than his model. Thus in three different ways is borne out the old adage: "Imitation is the sincerest form of flattery."

In the case of the tree-stump tombstones of the limestone belt, I feel it is safe to answer "Yes" to these questions: "Were the symbols used by the artist recognizable to the community and did the symbols appeal to the community? Did the artist speak for his community? Did the artist articulate deeply felt concerns for the community?"

Since these questions can all be answered in the affirmative, these tree-stump monuments may unhesitatingly be labeled "folk" or "community" art.

Notes

1. Warren E. Roberts, "Investigating the Tree-Stump Tombstone in Indiana" in Simon Bronner, ed. *American Material Culture and Folklife* (Ann Arbor, Michigan: UMI Research Press, 1985), pp. 136–37.

2. Ibid., p. 141. Other articles I have published describing these monuments are "Tools on Tombstones: Some Indiana Examples," *Pioneer America* 10, no. 1 (June 1978): 106–11; "Traditional Tools as Symbols: Some Examples from Indiana Tombstones," *Pioneer America* 12, no. 1 (February 1980): 54–63; "Tombstones in Scotland and Indiana," *Folk Life* 23 (1984–85): 97–104.

3. Charles Blanchard, ed., *History of Owen County* (1884. 2nd by Owen County Historical Society, 1977), p. 884.

4. I acknowledge with gratitude that the Philbert stone was called to my attention by Gary L. Bogden, a student in my Indiana Folklife class in 1986.

Figure 9.9.   Monument to Orris B. and Mary E. Dickerson (d. 1900
and 1893, respectively)
Carved by Silvester and Claude Hoadley.

Figure 9.10.   Detail of Dickerson Monument

Figure 9.11.   Monument of Joel and Ruth Philbert (d. 1902 and
1867, respectively)
Carved probably by Ferdinand O. Cross.

Figure 9.12. Detail of Philbert Monument

Tools of the Trades

10

Word Origins and Tools

Over the years I have written a number of notes, mostly on rather technical subjects, that I felt would be of little interest to students of traditional culture in general. Rather, I felt they would appeal to collectors who specialized in tools and could be expected to appreciate information on small details. Consequently, these contributions were sent to the *Chronicle* of the Early American Industries Association and published there. The first of these was prompted by an earlier note on the attempts of dictionary compilers to explain why the word "rabbet" is used for a groove in the edge of a board and for the plane used to make such a groove.

*   *   *

John S. Kebabian's article "Bunny-Rabot" in a recent issue of the *Chronicle* showed all too clearly that etymology is not an exact science and that etymologists sometimes make some pretty wild guesses. This reminded me that dictionary makers are hampered because they often lack familiarity with tools, their characteristics, and the way they are used. Following are a couple of examples which have recently caught my attention.

The word "fillister" appears in a number of dictionaries, usually with a reasonably adequate definition. The *Oxford English Dictionary*[1] (hereinafter abbreviated O.E.D.) gives the meaning of the word as "a rabbeting plane used in making windowsashes, etc." while *Webster's New World Dictionary of the American Language*[2] (hereinafter abbreviated N.W.D.) describes it as "a plane for cutting grooves."

It has already been pointed out that the word was spelled "filletster" in America in the nineteenth century at least.[3] Tool catalogs from the last century which have been reprinted used that spelling fairly consistently,[4] and Stanley Tools was still using it as recently as 1952.[5] It is noteworthy that no dictionary I have been able to consult gives the spelling "filletster." This

---

This article originally appeared in the EAIA *Chronicle* 32, no. 3 (September 1979): 46–47.

includes dictionaries devoted to American English such as the N.W.D. and W. A. Craigie and J. R. Hulbert, *A Dictionary of American English on Historical Principles.*[6]

What is even more noteworthy is that the dictionaries I have consulted have either found the origin of the word a mystery or have made a wild guess. The O.E.D. and most other dictionaries simply state "of unknown origin." The N.W.D., however, states that fillister "corresponds in form with German *filister* (Danish *filister*), lit. Philistine, first recorded in sense 'pikeman, member of the town watch'; modified by some such word as *fenester* (cf. FENESTRATE)." Why, one may wonder, did a plane get its name from a Philistine?

The key to the origin of the word lies in the American spelling. The O.E.D. gives the word "fillet" and cites as one of its meanings "A narrow flat band used for the separation of one molding from another," while the N.W.D. gives as one definition, "In *architecture,* a flat, square molding separating other moldings." Is it not certain that a "filletster" was so called because it was used to make a "fillet"? This special type of plane is designed to cut rabbets of varying widths and hence could be used to cut the narrow, flat bands which are often parts of complex moldings. Had the etymologists known of the American spelling, they would not have needed to resort to "Philistine" in attempting to explain the origin of the word.

One must assume that the word originated in Great Britain at an early date as "filletster" and that is was brought to America in that form. Later, the spelling changed in England to correspond more closely to the pronunciation, but Americans clung to the older spelling. Indeed R.A. Salaman points out that in Scotland the plane is called a "filletster."[7] This Scottish use would prove that this form of the word is not an American "corruption" but is the original form in Great Britain.

This raises another interesting question, though. Why did Americans retain a spelling which no dictionaries supported? Noah Webster's *An American Dictionary of the English Language* (1828) would have given them no support, for instance. They must have felt that they knew how to spell the word and did not need to look the spelling up in a dictionary.

Another term that should interest the student of tools is "beetle-browed," defined by the N.W.D. as "having bushy or overhanging eyebrows." All the dictionaries consulted state that the term is derived from the insect. Ernest Klein, *A Comprehensive Etymological Dictionary of the English Language,* says of the term, "Of uncertain origin; possibly related to beetle, 'insect.'"[8] The hesitation of etymologists to ascribe the term to the insect with certainty is understandable. Beetles (the insects, that is) just do not have bushy, overhanging eyebrows.

The source of the term is not far away in a dictionary. Just a few entries away in the N.W.D. one finds "beetle—1. a heavy mallet, usually wooden, for driving wedges, tamping earth, etc." What connection does the tool have with bushy eyebrows? It was customary to affix an iron ring around each end of the head of a beetle. In Craigie and Hulbert's *A Dictionary of American English on Historical Principles*[9] the term "beetle-ring," defined as "a ring placed around the end of a beetle or mallet to prevent splitting," was found in references dating from 1641 to 1881. After the beetle was used for some time, the wood fibres separated and spread back over the beetle-ring. Here are your bushy, overhanging eyebrows! If one has ever seen a well-used beetle, he will recognize the similarity at once. Mercer shows a good example of a beetle with well-defined "beetle-brows."[10]

I would suggest that, in this instance, the origins of the term were not recognized by the etymologists because they had never used a beetle. Dictionary makers toil in the study, not in the woods; the pen is more familiar to their hands than the handle of a beetle. Had it been otherwise, they would not have sought the origins of "beetle-browed" in the insect kingdom.

While I am on the subject of words connected with tools, let me make a few more suggestions. One concerns the word "try" as used in "try-plane" or "trying-plane" and "try-square." The try-plane undoubtedly gets its name from the verb "to try" defined in the O.E.D. as "To bring (a piece of timber) to a perfectly flat surface by repeatedly testing it and planing off the projecting parts." I would suggest that the verb "to try" in this sense is actually a variant pronunciation of the verb "to true." There are certainly English dialects wherein the word "true" would be pronounced as "try." If my supposition be correct, then "to bring a piece of timber to a perfectly flat surface" would be "to true" it, and the plane used especially for this purpose would be a "true-plane" or a "truing-plane." The try-square may be so called because it is a "true-square." It would have been called a "true-square" either because it is perfectly square or because it is used in truing a board. In truing a board, the craftsman needs to constantly check to make sure that the various surfaces are square with one another, and this small square is useful for that purpose.

My final suggestion concerns the word "dido" as used in the phrase "to cut didoes." The O.E.D. defines the word as meaning "A prank, a caper, especially in the phrase 'to cut (up) didoes,'" and calls it "U.S. slang (Origin uncertain)." The O.E.D. cites the earliest appearance in print for the word as 1843. In my youth—let us say about forty-five years ago—in southeastern Maine I heard the phrase used especially by older people to describe the antics of children: "They were really cutting didoes."

Is it possible that the work "dido" in this sense is connected with "dado"? No dictionary that I have been able to consult makes this connection. But then, no dictionary that I have been able to consult defines "dado" as "a groove cut across the grain in a board" or mentions a dado plane. Hence it never occurred to a dictionary compiler that woodworkers cut dadoes. Again it is a matter of pronunciation. Many speakers in America and Great Britain would pronounce "dado" to sound like "dido." I may remind the reader that American servicemen in World War II mimicked their English counterparts by claiming that when an English soldier said, "I say, mate" it sounded like "I sigh, mite." But why would "cutting a dado" come to mean "playing a prank?" There, I must confess, I have no suggestion to offer. But perhaps it would be better to be able to say that "cutting a dido" may be derived from "cutting a dado" than to say that its origin is unknown.

Notes

1. (Oxford University Press: 1933), 12 volumes.

2. (Cleveland, Ohio: The World Publishing Company, 1964), College Edition.

3. Kenneth D. Roberts, *Wooden Planes in 19th Century America* (Fitzwilliam, N.H.: Ken Roberts Publishing Co., 1975), p. 4.

4. See, for example, the J. B. Shannon catalogue of 1873, p. 17, and the Hammacher-Schlemmer and Co. Catalog, *Tools for All Trades,* 1896, p. 40.

5. In a copy of Stanley Tools Catalog No. 34, 1952 edition which I have, one of the blades for their No. 45 plane is called a "filletster."

6. (Chicago: University of Chicago Press. 1938).

7. R. A. Salaman, *Dictionary of Tools Used in the Woodworking and Allied Trades,* ca, 1700–1970. (New York: Scribner's, 1975), p. 327.

8. (Amsterdam: Elsevier Publishing Co., 1966).

9. See n. 6.

10. Henry C. Mercer, *Ancient Carpenters' Tools* (Doylestown, Pa.: 1929). p. 19.

11

Wood Screws as an Aid
in Dating Wooden Artifacts

This note must have aroused a considerable interest because a number of readers in the *Chronicle,* members of the Early American Industries Association, wrote directly to me in reply to the note.

*   *   *

A close examination of any wood screws used is of great importance in attempting to discover the date at which a wooden artifact was made. The artifact in question may be a house, a piece of furniture, a tool, or anything else of wood. If one can remove wood screws from it and has reason to believe they were used when the artifact was originally made, the screws may provide valuable evidence as to the date of construction.

Henry G. Mercer, that remarkable scholar whose wide-ranging interests made him an authority in many fields, dealt frequently with wooden artifacts made in the eighteenth and nineteenth centuries. His early interest in prehistoric archaeology led him to apply some of the approaches of the archaeologist to artifacts from the much more recent past. Consequently, he realized the importance of the wood screw for dating purposes. He showed that early wood screws were laboriously made by hand and that they tapered to a point. By the early 1800s, however, screws were being made in large numbers by "a continuous-motion mandrel lathe, axled on a guide screw. This lathe, therefore, advancing as it revolved and clasping at one end the screw shank, threaded the shank by twisting it through a knife-edged hole, or, more exactly, between two steel cutting points compressible by a lever." Mercer continues:

> Nevertheless, the screw so produced was conspicuously deficient in a very important feature, namely, that it lacked a point. In other words, those nineteenth-century screws, so much more rapidly machine-made, though often somewhat tapered in the shank,

---

This article originally appeared in the EAIA *Chronicle* 31, no. 1 (March 1978): 14–16.

unless retouched by hand, were invariably blunt-ended, and would not, before 1846, penetrate wood without a previously bored or punched hole. Then, by United States Patent No. 4704, August 20, 1846, T.J. Sloan of New York, patented a machine to point them, after which, because when thus pointed, they would more easily grasp the wood and would screw into it after a hammer tap, they so universally superseded the pointless screw, that their sudden and novel presence, as part of its construction, would very closely date a house, as built after 1846.[1]

To summarize then, it may be said that a screw may be dated with fair precision as follows: if it is pointed but uneven in shape, it is from before about 1800, if it is blunt-ended, it is from between 1800–46; if it is pointed but even in shape, it is from after 1846. It should be noted that Mercer used this type of evidence in dating carpenter's tools. In describing a spokeshave, for instance, he says, "In No. 9053, made after 1846, as proved by its pointed wood screws. . . ." In describing a level, he says, "Pointed wood screws used in its construction date it after 1846."[2]

Finding the date of construction of old houses presents many problems. In my experience, it is rare to find reliable written records. The records maintained at county courthouses in Indiana, at least, deal only with land and not with the buildings on the land. In the absence of written records, a close examination of the fabric of a house is about the only way to arrive at an approximate date of construction. If written records are available, it is still important to scrutinize the fabric of a house as a supplement to or a check on the records. Many of the pieces of evidence found in a house give only rather general indications as to date. For example, if we find the marks left by a water-powered "up-and-down" sawmill on the undersides of floorboards or on floor joists, about all we can say is that the house was built before steam-powered circular saws came into use in the area. For southern Indiana that would mean before about 1875.

We can usually ascertain whether or not the hardware used in a house is original. While the hinges, door latches, and the like may have been changed in the front part of a house where visitors are usually entertained, it is generally possible to find original hardware on closet doors, cellar doors, and other more hidden spots. While the hardware itself may give reliable dating information, in my experience it is the wood screws that hold the hardware in place that are most frequently useful.

In my efforts to date old houses in southern Indiana, I have often relied on the evidence from wood screws, for the period between the time of first settlement around 1820 and the Civil War is often important. As far as I know, no one has challenged Mercer's dictum that the machine-made pointed wood screw suddenly superseded the machine-made blunt wood screw in 1846 (fig. 11.1). Recently, however, in investigating two old houses, I have found screws in each house that I am convinced are part of

Figure 11.1.   Blunt Wood Screws
These screws were removed from hinges of a house
that was torn down near Oldenburg, Indiana, in 1976.
On the underside of a floorboard, the date of 1850
was written with a pencil.

the original fabric, some of which are pointed while some are blunt. In such a situation, it is clear at once that the house in question cannot be older than 1846. The puzzling question, though, is how long after 1846 were blunt screws in general use?

Among a small number of woodworking tools that I have collected is a heavy rosewood spirit level and plumb. The screws in the brass end plates are number 8, ¾ inch long, and are blunt ended: those in the brass top plate are number 4, ½ inch long, and are pointed. On the brass top plate is a touchmark of an eagle with a shield and the makers' names: Lambert, Mulliken and Stackpole. Boston, Mass. (fig. 11.2).[3] My experience with the houses, each of which had both blunt and pointed screws, motivated me to try to determine when this level was made. A survey of Boston city directories, which were available to me on microfiche, showed that the company is first listed in 1852 as "manufacturers of plumbs and Levels" at 6 Haverhill,[4] while in 1856 the company name is listed as "Mulliken and Stackpole." Since the company may have been founded in 1851 and not listed in the directory until 1852, we can say that the level must have been made between 1851 and 1856.

Figure 11.2. Inscription on the Top Plate of a Spirit Level and Plumb, Made between 1851 and 1856

In this case, it is clear that blunt screws were being used some years after 1846. What is needed is more evidence to aid in the dating of a wide range of artifacts made of wood. It would seem that tool collectors are in a very favorable position to compile this useful evidence. There is obvious difficulty in locating and visiting large numbers of houses whose dates of construction are reliably ascertained, and the same would hold true for accurately dated pieces of furniture. In the hands of tool collectors, however, there must be a reasonably large number of examples of tools that can be dated with fair accuracy on the basis of patent dates, dates carved by the owner or maker, or by other means. Collectors would not only assist their fellow collectors but also would aid research in other fields if they would share the information they have or could acquire in this connection. I would propose that those who have information or who can obtain it by removing and examining screws from the tools in their collections send it to the editor of *The Chronicle* so it can be published and made generally available. It might then be possible to amass firm data or corroborative data on the following questions:

1. When were machine-made blunt-ended screws first used? Mercer was unable to supply a firm date, using only the phrase "towards the end of the 18th century."[5]

2. When were machine-made pointed screws first used? Even though a patent was granted in 1846 for a machine to make them, it may have been some time before they were produced in any quantity. Moreover, there may be a difference between British and American manufacturers, and many tools used in the United States in the first half of the nineteenth century were made in England.

3. How long were machine-made blunt-ended screws used after 1846? It is, of course, possible that stocks of blunt-ended screws on hand were used up even though pointed screws had become available.

4. Were screws in smaller sizes made with points before the larger sizes of screws were made? The evidence I have would indicate that they were, but much more evidence is needed.

While on the subject, I may venture to request information on another matter concerning wood screws that may also help in dating artifacts. Most of the old screwdrivers I have seen have tips that taper like a wedge, no matter whether the screwdriver is large or small. Modern screwdrivers, on the other hand, have a blunter end and parallel sides for a short distance from the end (figs. 11.3, 11.4). My first impression was that the old screwdrivers had been reground carelessly, but as I saw more of them it

Figure 11.3.   Shapes of Screwdrivers
Modern screwdriver (left)
and nineteenth-century screwdriver (right).

Figure 11.4.   Tips of Screwdrivers
Nineteenth-century screwdriver (left) and modern
screwdriver (right).

became apparent that there was too much consistency in this respect to be the result of accident. The slots in the heads of the blunt-ended screws I have been able to examine also seem to taper, being wider at the top than at the bottom. Unfortunately, I own only a few tools from the first half of the nineteenth century and the heads of the screws in these tools are mostly so rusty as to make it impossible to tell about the slots. Moreover, while I have been able to remove a number of screws from old houses, the heads have usually been either rusty or covered with layers of paint.

More evidence from examples of screws in good condition would be useful in this connection: dated screwdrivers with wedge-shaped tips would likewise give valuable evidence. It would seem that if there was a change in the shape of the slot in screw heads, the makers of screwdrivers would have to likewise change the shape of the tips of their screwdrivers. A wedge-shaped screwdriver tip in a screw slot with parallel sides does not work at all well. Information on this question would help date screwdrivers, screws, and artifacts with screws in them.

It is entirely conceivable that there are written records available that would throw light on the questions raised in this paper. There may be catalogs, manufacturing records, advertisements, inventories, and the like that show with great accuracy when the change from blunt screws to pointed screws occurred. For example, if such written records can be found, information should likewise be published, but it still would be valuable to have corroborative evidence from specific datable tools.

Since writing the above, I have acquired a plane that can serve as an illustration of the importance of knowing when pointed screws superseded blunt screws. The plane is an iron plow plane with a wooden handle. It is designed to take cutters of different widths and is basically a metallic version of the common wooden-handled plow plane (fig. 11.5). I acquired only the main stock of the plane; the arm, the fence, and the cutters are all missing. The cutter in the stock is made from a broken chisel.

The only marking on the stock is the word "PATENT" cast in the metal in large letters. A search through patent records failed to unearth any information. The plane's wooden handle, however, is fastened to the metal stock with two blunt wood screws. The screws would seem to indicate a date of manufacture not much later than 1850.

In a brief article entitled "Patent Plow and Combination Planes, 1850–1900," John Juby implies that the first iron plow plane was patented in 1867. He cites an example patented in that year and calls it a "solid first step in the evolution."[6] The question at once arises, is it safe to assume that the plane described above is earlier than 1867 on the basis of the screws used in it? If we had a substantial amount of data from well documented sources, it would be possible to answer this question.

Figure 11.5.   Iron Plow Plane, Mid-Nineteenth Century

Notes

1. Henry C. Mercer, *Ancient Carpenters' Tools*, 3rd ed. (Doylestown, Pa.: The Bucks County Historical Society, 1960), p. 256. Essentially the same information is given in Mercer's *The Dating of Old Houses* (Doylestown, Pa.: The Bucks County Historical Society, 1923), pp. 24–25.

2. *Ancient Carpenters' Tools*, p. 104, fig. 98 and p. 66, fig. 64.

3. The level is 25½ inches long by 3⅜ inches by 1⅜ inches. The top plate is 8³⁄₁₆ inches long with semi-circular indentations at each end. The side plates forming the "brass lipped side views," as they are called in older catalogs, are rectangular. The small plates over the hold in which the plumb glass is inserted are round and of brass. The end plates of brass are so constructed that they wrap around the body of the level and are held in place by two screws at the top and two at the bottom.

4. *The Boston Directory for 1852* (Boston: George Adams, No. 91 Washington St. 1852).

5. *Ancient Carpenters' Tools*, p. 256.

6. Iron Horse Antiques, Inc., 1976. Catalog Number 12, p. 7. Juby includes a photograph of another example of the plane described above (fig. A25) but is unable to give any information as to the date of manufacture or patent.

12

Another American Example of a Turner's Tool

I had collected a special tool at an auction sale not too far from my home and had recognized it as the American counterpart of an English chairmaker's tool. I had not known of another single American example until a note on one was published in the *Chronicle* to which I replied with this note on my example.

* * *

In the *Chronicle* (38, no. 4), Gus Stahl questions whether a special short-handled ax, or perhaps hatchet, is a bodger's ax, a turner's tool. He found his example in an old tool chest rescued from a western Massachusetts cellar.

I bought an unusual hatchet at a farm auction in eastern Owen County, Indiana, ten years ago (fig. 12.1). In this general area a number of folk craftsmen made traditional slat-back or ladder-back chairs. At least four were active here as late as the 1930s. (See chapter 6, "Turpin Chairs and the Turpin Family: Chairmaking in Southern Indiana" in this volume.) As seen from the side, my example resembles closely that shown in Salaman, *Dictionary of Tools* (New York: Scribner's, 1975), p. 127. This tool was used in England especially by the bodgers who made chair legs and rungs in the forests and supplied them to factories where the chairs were assembled. The bodgers worked in the woods, felling trees, cutting them into lengths, splitting them into billets, trimming them roughly to shape, and then turning them into the final shape in foot-powered lathes. It would not be surprising if American chairmakers used similar tools. The chairmakers in Owen County were farmers who made chairs whenever time and the weather permitted. They, too, started by cutting down a suitable tree and needed a convenient splitting tool. Perhaps because the length of the pieces they split for rungs was not great, they found a splitting-out hatchet worked better than the other great splitting tool, the froe, used by many craftsmen who split wood for other purposes.

This article originally appeared in the EAIA *Chronicle* 39, no. 2 (June 1986): 28.

Figure 12.1.   Hatchet, or Bodger's Ax

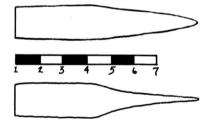

Figure 12.2.
Comparative Blade Shapes of
Chopping Hatchet (above) and
Splitting-Out Hatchet (below)

I assume my example was made by some blacksmith to the specifications of a chairmaker. There is an unusually long poll and there is plenty of metal on either side of the eye through which the handle passes. This design feature helps keep the metal from buckling at that otherwise potentially weak point. (An old hardware catalogue I own shows a drawing of an ax head that has buckled at the eye and warns sternly that warranted axes will not be replaced if they have been used as wedges and hammered on the polls.) But the feature that persuades me that my example is a hatchet intended for splitting rather than chopping is the shape of the head as viewed from above (fig. 12.2). This hatchet would never cut effectively, no matter how well sharpened, but its wedge shape would make for efficient splitting.

It is not surprising that the transfer of the chairmaker's craft from England to the new world involved likewise the transfer of the special tools used by the chairmaker. The splitting-out hatchet appears to be a case in point even though it has not been reported frequently from this side of the water.

13

German People—German Tools?

This article and query is an attempt to gain information which otherwise would be unobtainable. The article and the photos also help to alert folklife researchers to the fact that some artifacts have "ethnic" forms in the United States that differ from the more common British-American forms. This knowledge should help folklife researchers to gauge the amount of ethnic influence and presence in areas where they are doing fieldwork.

*   *   *

Large numbers of German people came to what is now the United States at various periods in the past. We celebrated in 1984 the tricentennial of the arrival of the first German immigrants who came to Pennsylvania, the first contingent of the well-known Pennsylvania Germans or Pennsylvania Dutch as they are sometimes called. In the early 1800s the number of German people entering this country swelled immensely and great waves reached the Midwest, settling in Wisconsin, Ohio, Indiana, Missouri, Texas, and other states.

When one looks closely at where these people settled, one may think at first that they chose parts of the United States that resembled their homeland—until one looks at Texas. Closer examination reveals a much more pragmatic factor. These people understandably went where lots of cheap land was available, just as other immigrants did. They did not choose to settle on the true frontier, that is, on the western edge of settlement at the time they arrived. Nor, on the other hand, did many of them locate themselves in the long-settled areas of the east coast, for there was very little land available there. Instead, these people came mostly to areas that had been thinly settled previously by people of British ancestry. In many regions, therefore, there soon developed a mixture of German-Americans and British-Americans. Some of the subjects of perennial interest to students

---

This article is also set to appear in an upcoming issue of the EAIA *Chronicle*.

of our past are the questions, what did the German immigrants retain of their old world culture and what did they take from their British-American neighbors? It is only through answering questions such as these that we can ever hope to understand the immigrant experience in this great land of ours.

Many cultural items of the German-Americans cannot be clearly identified as German or British in origin for a variety of reasons. Fortunately, enough research has been done with woodworking tools so that it is possible to state with reasonable accuracy which tools have distinctive German forms and which have British. In areas where there were substantial numbers of German settlers one would expect to find tools of German form.

It should be stated that to speak of "German tool forms" is probably oversimplifying a complex situation. It is probable that many of these tool forms are more likely continental rather than simply German. However, in most cases it was the German immigrants who brought these continental forms to the United States.

Following are a few examples of German-type tools found in southern Indiana. In the southern half of Indiana, there was a fair number of Pennsylvania Germans among the early settlers. In the 1840s and 1850s large numbers of immigrants came to the area directly from Germany. The largest concentrations of German immigrants were in the vicinity of Evansville, Jasper, and Oldenberg. I have visited these areas only sporadically over a period of about two decades and have sought tools mainly at farm auction sales and at antique stores.

Bench Planes

The accompanying photos show three "horned" smoothing planes of the type used in Germany. The conspicuous front handle or "horn" can be seen in three variations. There are clearly differences in the shape of the horn and in the way in which it is attached to the body of the plane (figs. 13.1, 13.2).

Other ways in which these three examples differ from British-American planes include the following:

1. The average length is 11 inches, mid-way between the lengths of the British-American smooth and jack planes.

2. They are not made of beechwood as are most British-American planes. One is made of a wood resembling cherrywood or apple-wood while two are made of what appears to be pearwood.

3. All three of these planes have irons which were made in Germany.

Figure 13.1.   Three German-Type "Horned" Smoothing Planes
Average length: 11 inches. The center example is
dated 1837.

Figure 13.2.   Frontal View of Planes in Figure 13.1
Average height: 4¾ inches.

This last fact at once raises the question, were the planes made in Germany? This is a distinct possibility and they may have been brought to this country by the immigrants. It is also possible, however, that immigrant carpenters brought plane irons with them and made the wooden bodies in this country. All three planes give the indefinable impression that they were made by really competent woodworkers but men who were not specialized planemakers. Finally, one of the planes has the date 1837 carved into its side together with a name, presumably that of the maker. Most of the German immigrants to Indiana came after that date so this particular plane probably was made in Germany and brought to the United States.

Some horned planes were made in England but, according to Salaman, they are identified in catalogues as German or continental planes.[1] Some horned planes were apparently made by large American companies also but in comparatively small numbers.

Other Planes

The photos show a round plane and a rabbet plane of German type with a British-American bead plane for comparison (figs. 13.3, 13.4). Differences that are immediately apparent are:

1. Length: the three German-type examples measured averaged 11 inches in length. (One was measured which is not in the photo.)

2. Height: the three examples average $2^{11}/_{16}$ inches in height.

3. Configuration: each plane has deep moldings on the right side (right from the point of view of the user) while the left side is plain.

These three examples appear to be made of beechwood. As with the bench planes, these planes could have been brought from Europe or they could have been made in this country by an immigrant who brought plane irons with him.

Saws

The saw pictured could perhaps be taken for a turning saw except for one feature: the width of the blade would make it impossible to cut a very sharp curve (fig. 13.5). It is, actually, a German-type saw used for cutting across boards. It is made so that the blade can be turned 90° to cut across a wide board (near the end). This particular saw is 39¼ inches from tip to tip and the blade was 1¾ inches wide before it was reduced by many sharpenings. Rip saws look very much the same except for the way the teeth are shaped.

Figure 13.3. Two German-Type Molding Planes
Rabbet plane (left) and round plane (center). Average
length: 11 inches. The right-most plane is a
British-American bead plane, presented for
comparison.

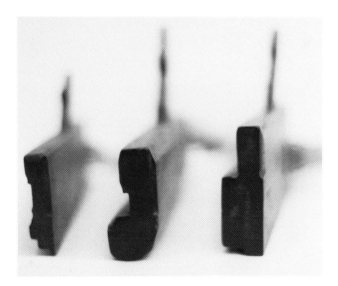

Figure 13.4. Frontal View of Planes in Figure 13.3
Average height of the German-type planes: $2^{11}/_{16}$ inches.

Figure 13.5.   German-Type Saw
Length: 39¼ inches (app. 1 meter); height: 19 inches.

It is likely that a well-supplied German carpentry shop would have a few saws of the British type on hand to take care of the occasional cutting task where the central brace of these German-type saws would get in the way.

Marking Gauges

A common type of marking gauge used in Germany has two arms held in place in a block with wedges. In the illustrated example the body of the gauge has some decorative steps cut into it (fig. 13.6). American factories made gauges of this general type, sometimes with arms and bodies of metal, but Anglo-American craftsman-made wooden gauges generally have a single arm.

These are but a very few examples where there are easily recognizable differences between German and British-American woodworking tools. Other well-known examples would include the so-called goosewing ax and certain twibils.[2]

Figure 13.6. German-Type Marking or Mortise Gauge
Length: 8¾ inches; width: 4⅝ inches.

It is of considerable importance for students of American material culture to be able to identify ethnic differences in artifacts so as to be able to make more valid appraisals of the history of this country with its rich mix of immigrants from many parts of the world. Yet I cannot think of a single detailed discussion on the topic of ethnic differences in artifacts. (If anyone knows of such a discussion I would be very pleased to learn of it.) Some faltering first steps have been made in the direction of identifying German forms in folk architecture.[3] This present note is a small and feeble attempt to start a discussion of ethnic characteristics in woodworking tools. What a contribution tool collectors could make to the advancement of scientific research by sharing their knowledge and experience on this subject! If only collectors who have attended farm auction sales in strongly German-American areas could tell of their experiences, for example! Were there large numbers of German-type planes, "goosewing" axes, and the like, or were there only British-American planes and broad axes? I could go on with other similar questions but, in hopes of starting the ball rolling, I will give a brief statement of some of my experiences.

Over a period of nearly 20 years I have visited many times in areas where there are many people of German ancestry. I have attended at least a score of farm auctions in the vicinity of Jasper. I have visited many antique stores and have interviewed many collectors and local historians. I must report that German-type planes are extremely rare. For every hundred British-American planes, I have seen no more than one of German type. German-type saws and marking gauges are even scarcer. In 20 years of looking I have seen two goosewing axes in southern Indiana. One was at an auction sale in Evansville. One is owned by a man living near Bloomington who is of Pennsylvania-German descent and maintains that his ax was brought to Indiana by his Pennsylvania-German great-grandfather around 1835. He inherited no other German-type tools.

The overwhelming impression, therefore, is that German immigrants to southern Indiana brought very few woodworking tools from Germany. Or if they did, they discarded them early on and acquired tools of British-American types. It would be very valuable to learn whether a similar generalization could be made for other areas in the country.

Notes

1.   R. A. Salaman, *Dictionary of Tools* (New York: Charles Scribner's Sons, 1975), pp. 316–17, 350.

2.   See Dean Straffin, "Axe Handle Twibils," EAIA *Chronicle* (June 1985): 28 ff.

3.   See Warren E. Roberts, "The Green Tree Hotel: A Problem in the Study of Ethnic Architecture," *Pioneer America* 15, no. 3 (1983): 105–21.

14

Early Tool Inventories:
Opportunities and Challenges

I consider this essay my major contribution to the question I have frequently raised: Are written records or folklife research more reliable in dealing with traditional material culture? In this case it is clear that the written records need to be corrected and supplemented by fieldwork. I am sorry to report that I once heard a curator at a leading museum devoted to early nineteenth-century rural life state that folklife studies could contribute nothing to his museum's research. I feel, obviously, that he was sadly mistaken and this essay supports my contention.

*   *   *

In trying to discover the history of woodworking tools, most writers have turned to records of various kinds that show what tools were made in earlier times, who made them, and when. Such information is certainly of the highest value and those writers who have used this method are to be thanked for their research and the light it has thrown on the history of tools.[1]

Such research, however, can only partly illuminate the history of tools because it must ignore a very vital question. The records of tool manufacturers and dealers can answer the question, "What tools were, theoretically, available for craftsmen to purchase at such and such a date?" They cannot, however, answer the question, "What tools did craftsmen at a certain time in the past actually use?" The answers to these two questions are not, unfortunately, exactly the same for a number of reasons. For example, the craftsmen may have consistently made some tools and equipment themselves rather than buying them. An example would be a workbench. I doubt very much that anyone could find manufacturers of woodworkers' workbenches or dealers who sold them in the eighteenth century yet carpenters and cabinetmakers certainly had workbenches. The records of tool manu-

This article originally appeared in the EAIA *Chronicle* 39, no. 3 (September 1986): 40–44.

facturers and dealers also cannot tell us what quantities of tools craftsmen actually owned, that is, how many planes, how many saws, how many chisels?

There is, however, a source which has the potential of answering the question, "What tools and how many of each kind did early craftsmen actually own?" This potential source is inventories made in the past. While there are other kinds, far and away the most common inventory is that made at the time of a person's death or shortly thereafter. These inventories were required by law and by custom in most parts of America to determine the estate of the deceased. This was necessary partly for inheritance purposes and partly tax purposes. After all, most people had relatively little money. Their "worldly goods" consisted largely of real estate and artifacts, "real and personal property." Appraisers or "viewers" were appointed by the courts and copies of the inventories and appraisals were filed at the courthouse. Sometimes when an auction sale of the goods was held, the items sold and the prices realized were also listed and filed. In the following I will list some of the strong and some of the weak points of such inventories as a source of data for the history of tools, the opportunities and the challenges they present.[2]

Opportunities

1.   The court was required to appoint competent people to make the inventories. A cabinetmaker for example was often chosen to inventory and appraise a deceased cabinetmaker's tools. In a few cases where I have been able to discover the identity of the appraiser, such has been the case.[3] This fact means that the inventories have special value. One cabinetmaker looking at the tools of another would know what the tools were, the names actually in use for them in the area, and their value. Conversely, the appraiser would also know what tools were of little value so that they were silently omitted from the inventory or lumped together with other valueless items.
2.   Tools are presented in some sort of context.
     a.   Many of the inventories are so detailed that we can reconstruct the workshop of the deceased with some accuracy and place many of the tools in it. For example, an inventory may list a stove in the workshop, may use a phrase such as "scrap lumber in the loft [of the workshop]," or "in the rack by the window [not *a* window but *the* window]," or list a workbench and then list tools "in the drawer."
     b.   We can tell sometimes which tools were used with which other tools. As an example, pit saws tend to appear in context with other tools that we recognize as wagonmakers' tools. They do not appear usually with carpenters' or cabinetmakers' tools. It

would appear that carpenters and cabinetmakers got nearly all their lumber from sawmills, at least in the eighteenth and nineteenth centuries. Wagonmakers undoubtedly got a great deal of their lumber from sawmills, too, but they probably needed odd sizes of heavy lumber or special shapes such as a long tapering shaft that could be cut out from a squared log with a pit saw but which a sawmill would not normally provide.

    c.   In some instances the context provided gives some indication how a tool was used. For instance, a cabinetmaker might well own an ax, but if it was listed in his inventory as being in the woodshed rather than in the workshop, we could assume it was used primarily for chopping and splitting firewood rather than for building furniture.

3.   Inventories can ideally answer such questions as, "Did a typical nineteenth-century carpenter own more tools in general or more tools of one type (i.e., planes) than an eighteenth-century carpenter?" or, "Did a craftsman in a city own more tools or more tools of a certain type than a craftsman in the countryside?" or, "Did a pioneer cabinetmaker in the backwoods of Indiana in the early years of settlement own fewer tools than a cabinetmaker 'back East'?"

4.   Values are assigned tools or groups of tools (i.e., "1 set bench planes . . . $3.50") in the inventories. Moreover, when an auction sale was held, the prices actually reached at the sale are listed and can be compared with the appraisers' estimates. One can, therefore, determine which tools were expensive and which cheap. A final advantage here is that other goods are likewise appraised so that one can compare the value of a saw, let us say, with that of a chair.

5.   Perhaps even more important is the larger, or more general, context. The inventories also show us what is so often overlooked; that is, that the cabinetmakers in Pennsylvania and the Midwest were also farmers. The inventories consistently list in addition to woodworking tools the tools and implements needed in farming. Individual inventories also sometimes specify as property such things as "About one acre of wheat, 4 acres of grass @ $4 per acre, and 4 acres of oats."

Indeed, a detailed examination of all the goods listed in inventories would make it possible to say a good deal about the daily lives of the craftsmen and their families. Spinning wheels, looms, churns, lard rendering kettles and such possessions show what tasks were carried out in or near a person's dwelling; while the names used in inventories for rooms in a house and for outbuildings such as smokehouses tell us a great deal about a person's architecture; and a person's level of wealth and standing in a community can be assessed by analyzing inventories and comparing one with another.

Challenges

1. Inventories of the type described are not easy to find.
   a. In some counties the records of this sort have not survived due to fire, accident, or negligence.
   b. In any county it is difficult to know who were the woodworking craftsmen and when they died. Some craftsmen get listed in compilations such as Betty Larson Walters, *Furniture Makers of Indiana, 1793 to 1850* (Indianapolis: Indiana Historical Society, 1972). These are generally the ones who lived in towns and cities and advertised their wares. On the other hand, craftsmen who lived in the countryside often farmed as well as worked at their crafts. Such men usually appear in records such as censuses as "farmer" rather than as "carpenter" or whatever.

   A case in point is Thomas Lincoln, father of Abraham. Because of the great interest in the son, some attention has been paid the father and many people, relatives and neighbors, have been interviewed and their reminiscences recorded. We know, therefore that Thomas Lincoln was a cabinetmaker and joiner and quite a number of his pieces of furniture have survived.[4] Yet he did not advertise in any newspapers or the like nor is he listed in records as a cabinetmaker. He does not appear at all in the 1820 Census of Manufacturers, for instance, even though many other cabinetmakers do.

   At any rate, if one wished to do research in any specific county, he would probably have no other recourse than to read through inventories hoping to find some for woodworking craftsmen. This is, unfortunately, somewhat akin to looking for a needle in a haystack.

2. Should one find an inventory with a large number of tools listed, can one be sure he has found a specialized craftsman? He may have found a farmer who just happened to own a number of woodworking tools which he used very little. In the research I will be reporting on, I was looking for cabinetmakers specifically. If I found an inventory with a large number of woodworking tools, it could be that of a carpenter, a wagon2-maker/wheelwright, a chairmaker, a cooper, or perhaps others. I finally decided that if the inventory listed ten or more molding planes, I would consider that man a cabinetmaker. While this is certainly arbitrary, it is nonetheless logical. A wagonmaker/wheelwright would need and use very few molding planes.[5] (A coachmaker would certainly use molding planes, but coachmakers are pretty rare birds.) Chairmakers and coopers also used very few molding planes because the chairs made by most chairmakers and the barrels made by coopers have virtually no moldings. If a carpenter also did "finish work" such as

staircases and mantelpieces, he would certainly require many planes. It was, however, a common practice for the finish work to be done by a "joiner" who was very often also a cabinetmaker so that the presence of a number of molding planes in an inventory still seemed to be a reasonably reliable criterion in deciding which inventories belonged to cabinetmakers. Similar criteria could probably be developed for other types of craftsmen such as coopers.

3. It is true that great numbers of tools are listed in the inventories and that specific values are assigned individual tools or groups of tools (i.e., "Brace and set of bits ... $1.50"). It is also true, however, that some tools are consistently not listed in inventories. There are two possible explanations. One is that craftsmen did not generally own or use certain tools in the era under investigation. If we know that a certain tool was manufactured in 1800, and that it cost a significant amount of money, yet that this same tool does not appear in craftsmen's inventories, then we must look for some explanation.

It is also possible, however, that the appraiser saw a certain tool in the workshop of the deceased but knew that it had little or no value. If it had no value, he might have omitted it from the inventory. If it had little value, he might have lumped it together with others such as "box of sundries ... 10¢." We must always try to remember that items we value today or which we consider worthless were not necessarily considered so in earlier times. While we consider worn-out files to have no value, they must have had some two hundred years ago for they are consistently listed in inventories.

In individual cases an appraiser may have silently omitted a tool because it was so worn or so old as to be valueless, but if we can examine a number of inventories, we can make allowances for individual discrepancies.

Using Tool Inventories: An Example

I was faced with the challenge of estimating what tools would have been in a cabinetmaker's workshop in a rural area in southern Indiana about 1825.[6] I decided to find as many cabinetmakers' inventories from the period around 1800–1850 as I could and take as much of an average as possible. I was indeed fortunate to be able to use the inventories copied out and published by Mrs. Margaret Schiffer.[7] Because she carried out research in Chester County, Pennsylvania records over a period of many years, she was able not only to locate and copy at least a hundred inventories but also was able to find in obscure records of many kinds references to the deceased men as cabinetmakers. An example would be James Henderson. His inventory shows a number of woodworking tools and Mrs. Schiffer was able to find a document which stated that in 1792 "James Henderson, cabinet-maker" bought a piece of property in West Chester. In this instance we need not bemoan the fact that a hurried appraiser lumped together "A lot of planes" and "4 axes" for a total of $18.75 so that we can't tell if Henderson owned molding planes. The document cited proves that he was a cabinetmaker.

Since I was able to find 55 inventories of cabinetmakers' tools for the era I was concerned with in Mrs. Schiffer's book, it is this monumental tome that really made my research possible. I also located a few other inventories from other eastern localities besides Chester County, Pennsylvania and a few from Kentucky and Indiana. While I wish I could have found more from other localities besides Chester County, the ones I did find (a total of 11) did show that the inventories from Chester County were surprisingly representative of all inventories from the 1800–1850 era.

In justice to the richness of Mrs. Schiffer's book and to her dedication to her task, I should note that there are about 60 inventories in her book I did not use for a variety of reasons. Some are from years too early for my purposes and some were done by hurried appraisers who did not give adequate detail. In addition, there are inventories and other documents reproduced for clockmakers, for example, while also many other documents besides inventories are reproduced. In general, a wide variety of information is given for a wide variety of craftsmen. Small wonder that the author of the Foreword, Charles F. Montgomery, said of the book, "The wealth of information is incredible." (p. 7)

Table 14.1 is a geographical comparison of tool inventories. The first four columns list the results from 55 inventories from Chester County, Pennsylvania; the middle four columns give the parallel results from 4 inventories from other localities in the Eastern United States.[8] The final four columns present the comparable information from 7 inventories from Kentucky and Indiana, areas that had not been settled long at the time the inventories were taken.[9] Each of these geographical groupings presents the information for, respectively, the average number of each tool owned, the number of owners, the number from the total of that inventory *not* owning any of that tool, and the number owning several.

Is It True That the Pioneer Had Only His Ax?

Even a hasty glance at the table will show that some interesting and valuable comparisons can be made. The first is that the cabinetmakers in Kentucky and Indiana whose inventories were taken in the early decades of settlement—the pioneer era—had as many tools, if not more, than their Eastern counterparts. If we add the inventories from Chester County, Pennsylvania and the other representative Eastern inventories—a total of

59—and the average thus obtained is compared with the Midwestern pioneer cabinetmakers, the results are instructive. Table 14.2 gives the results for some of the most common tools.

Let us look at another statistic: the total number of planes owned by any one cabinetmaker (bear in mind that the dates of the inventories are 1800–1850):

84 planes the largest number owned as shown in any inventory—owned by Absalom Wells of Woodford County, Kentucky, who died in 1827.[10]

66 planes owned by James Williamson, London Grove Township, Chester County, Pennsylvania. Inventory taken May 16, 1848.[11]

58 planes owned by John G. Henderson of Salem, Indiana. Inventory taken in 1820.[12]

So much for the supposition that Midwestern pioneer cabinetmakers had fewer tools than their Eastern brethren! It is possible that the men who moved to the newly settled frontier intending to make cabinetware brought extra tools with them because it would be more difficult to obtain them in their new homes. In a recently published series of articles, however, I have shown that specialized craftsmen who made wooden planes were working in towns such as New Albany and Richmond, Indiana, well before 1850.[13]

This survey of cabinetmakers' inventories reinforces the conclusion I reached in my article, "The Tools Used in Building Log Houses in Indiana."[14] I concluded that at least 75 tools were needed to build the typical log house associated in the minds of most people with the frontier. I further suggested that pioneers were better provided with tools than is generally assumed. This conclusion certainly seems to hold true for pioneer cabinetmakers as well.

Comments on Specific Tools and Other Matters of Interest

Planes: Quantities and Varieties

In order to show the wide variety of planes named in the inventories and the comparative popularity of each, a list is herewith given of each named type of plane in the inventories with the total number listed. For this purpose I have lumped all the inventories together: 55 from Chester

Table 14.1 Geographical Comparison of Tool Inventories, 1800–1850

	Chester County, Pennsylvania				Eastern United States				Kentucky and Indiana			
	Average Number Owned	Number of Owners	Number not Owning	Number Owning Several	Average Number Owned	Number of Owners	Number not Owning	Number Owning Several	Average Number Owned	Number of Owners	Number not Owning	Number Owning Several
Planes	27	55	0	28	50	4	0	0	53	7	0	4
Adze	1	33	22	4	1½	2	2	0	1	1	6	0
Augers	4½	43	12	14	5	1	3	0	2	4	3	0
Broad Ax	1¼	32	23	0	1½	2	2	0	0	0	7	0
Other Axes	1¼	22	33	0	0	0	4	0	2	1	6	0
Bevel	1¼	8	47	1	2	3	1	1	2	1	6	0
Brace	1	34	21	1	1	4	0	0	1	5	2	0
Bits-One Set	1	27	28	0	1	1	3	0	1	1	6	0
Chisels	10¼	55	0	24	16¾	4	0	0	15¾	5	2	1
Clamps	3¼	17	38	5	7	4	0	0	1	3	4	0
Compasses	2	19	36	3	1	1	3	0	1½	3	4	0
Draw Knife	2	39	16	4	1	1	3	0	1	2	5	0
Files	5½	30	25	15	0	0	4	0	4½	6	1	2
Froe	1	21	34	0	0	0	4	0	0	0	7	0
Gauge	3½	21	34	12	6½	3	1	1	4	6	1	0
Gimlet	2	14	41	6	0	0	4	0	3½	2	5	0
Glue Pot	1	34	21	1	1	1	3	0	1	2	5	0
Gouge	7	29	26	9	15½	2	2	0	14½	3	4	0
Grindstone	1¼	20	35	1	2	1	3	0	1	2	5	0
Hand Screws	9	14	41	5	0	0	4	0	15	2	5	0

Hammer	2	33	22	2	3½	2	2	2	0	2½	4	3	0
Hatchet	1	21	34	2	1	2	2	2	0	2	2	5	0
Holdfast	1¼	18	37	1	0	4	0	4	0	0	7	0	0
Lathe	1	35	20	0	0	0	4	4	0	1	3	4	0
Lathe Tools, set	1	23	22	1	1	2	4	4	0	1	2	5	0
Oilstone	1	22	33	0	1	0	2	2	0	1¼	3	4	0
Patterns, Lot	1	10	45	3	0	2	0	4	0	1	1	6	0
Pincers	1	16	39	1	1	0	3	1	0	1	2	5	1
Rasp	1	6	49	1	1	1	1	3	0	1	2	5	1
Rule	1	13	42	0	2½	2	3	2	0	2	2	5	0
Saw	2½	49	6	9	8	4	0	0	0	3½	7	0	0
Saw Set	1¼	9	46	2	1	1	3	3	0	1	1	6	0
Screw Driver	2	8	47	2	2½	2	2	2	0	2	2	5	1
Spokeshave	2	8	47	1	1	1	3	3	0	1	2	5	0
Square	1½	51	4	6	3	3	1	1	0	2½	6	1	1
Workbench	2	31	24	1	0	0	4	4	0	5	3	4	0

Table 14.2. Distribution of Other Common Tools

	Eastern Cabinetmakers: Average Number Owned	Midwestern Cabinetmakers of the Pioneer Era: Average Number Owned
Planes	28½	53
Chisels	10½	15½
Gouges	8	14½
Saws	3	3½

County, Pennsylvania; 4 from other Eastern states and localities; and 7 from Indiana and Kentucky, mostly from the 1800–1850 era:

Astragal	4	Match	6 "sets"
Apple Mill	2	Molding	245 and 11 "lots"
Bead	32 & "lot"	Nosing	11
Double Bead	1	Ogee	6
Bench	89 & 5 "sets" & 5 "lots"	Panel	1
Bollection	3	Picture Frame	2
Block	9	Plough	21
Coping	1	Plough & Groove	17 pair & 4 "lots"
Cornice	12	Quarter Round	3
Cove	3	Rabbet	25 & "a few"
Cove & Bead	1	Side Rabbet	1
Fillister	8	Skew Rabbet	1
Fore	37	Raising	11
Gauging	1	Reed	1
Groove	7 & "lot"	Round	(See "Hollow")
Half Round	2	Sack	1
Halving	1	Scraper	1
Hollow	5	Smoothing	63 & "lot"
Hollow & Round	13 pair & "lot"	Snipe Bill	1
Jack	32	Table	5 pair
Jointer	26 & "lot"	Tooth	2

Specific Planes

Jack, smoothing, and bench planes. In the list above it can be seen that there are twice as many smoothing planes as there are jack planes. It is generally believed today that the jack plane did the preliminary leveling of wood and the rough work when considerable amounts of wood were to be removed. It was, therefore, a very important plane and one would expect to find jack planes to be more numerous than other bench planes. Why, then, were there twice as many smoothing planes as there were jack planes? The answer may possibly be found in a confusion of terms. In the era under discussion, the terms "jack" and "fore" were being used interchangeably for the same plane.[15] If one adds the 37 fore planes to the 32 jack planes, the total slightly exceeds the 63 & 1 lot of smoothing planes.

It is worthy of note in this connection that the appraisers listed 89 "bench planes" which could be anything from a small smoothing plane to a long jointer. Many of the appraisers thought of bench planes as coming in "sets" (probably smoothing, jack or fore, and jointer) and perhaps some appraisers used "lot" to mean "set."

Trying plane. Although the term "trying plane" is sometimes used by American scholars writing on American tools,[16] the term does not appear in any of the inventories, suggesting that it is an English term and not an American one.

Plough & groove planes. The wording in the inventories suggests that "a pair of plough & groove planes" was used in the same way we would use "a pair of tongue and groove planes." The term "set of match planes" was also used at the time probably meaning exactly the same thing as "a pair of plough & groove planes."

Dado planes. Since there are no dado planes listed in the inventories, it would seem the term was not used in the 1800–1850 era. The plane itself may have been used and called simply a rabbet plane; there is no way of knowing from the inventories.

Toothing planes. There has been in the pages of EAIA *Chronicle,* at least considerable discussion as to how toothing planes were used.[17] The inventories show that between 1800–50 they were not used much at all by cabinetmakers!

It has been suggested that an important use of the toothing plane is to provide tiny grooves on the surface of a piece of wood that is to have veneer glued to it. The grooves left by the toothing plane, it is alleged, hold more glue thus making the joint stronger. Between 1800–50 furniture styles such as the Empire were popular which made extensive use of veneers. The fact that so few toothing planes were owned by cabinetmakers would raise doubts concerning the need to go over the surface with a toothing plane before gluing.

In this connection it may be worthwhile to note that, of the two toothing planes found in the inventories, one is listed, as "1 Tooth Plane & Scraper ... 50¢."[18] This entry would make it seem that the appraiser assumed that the plane and scraper belonged together. He must have thought the plane was to be used on rough or curly grained wood to be followed by the scraper leaving a smooth surface.

Other Tools Listed in the Inventories

Lathe. Although most inventories that list a lathe give no hint as to what kind of lathe it is, a few do. There are a few phrases used such as "1 lathe, 1 large wheel for turning" which clearly show that the so-called great wheel lathe is being referred to. On the other hand, when J. McCullough's inventory was taken in 1834, the appraiser listed "Turning Lathe & turning tools ... $4.00" but also listed on a separate line "Spring turning lathe ... 25¢." The 25-cent lathe must have been what is more generally called a pole lathe.

The spellings used in the inventories show a complete disregard for consistency. This was in the pre-Noah Webster days and it was taken for granted that if a person could pronounce a word, he could spell it. At any rate, spellings sometimes show that a word was rather different in an earlier era than it is today. At least five appraisers use the spelling "lay" or something very close to it. This older form of the word without the final "th" was once widespread in America and in some areas such as Tennessee has persisted until today among older craftsmen.[19]

Files. In a surprising number of cases, appraisers listed "1 lot of old files" or some similar term. Since old files have little value today, we may wonder at the care taken by the appraisers to list an item of such little value. Actually, in earlier times worn-out files did have value because it was possible to have them retoothed. The following 1861 advertisement is of note:

> Capitol City File Works, Pennsylvania St., one square east of Union Depot, Indianapolis, Ind. . . . Manufacturers of all kinds of Files and Rasps. Old Files Recut and warranted equal to new for use. Letters of inquiry and work from the country will meet with prompt attention.[20]

Glue. Well over half of the cabinetmakers owned glue pots, but it is at first curious to note that almost none of them owned any glue, ostensibly. Actually, the glue was there but it was such that most appraisers did not think that it had any monetary value. The key is in two inventories, one from 1777 and one from 1812, that list together, "Glue pot & pigs foot." The "hide glue" that today is bought in flake form and heated together with water in an electric glue pot has its counterpart in the pigs foot of the inventories. If not a by-word for a nail pry, the pigs foot must have been the hoof of a pig to be put in the pot and boiled for a long time to produce the glue. That pot must have added quite a fragrance to the workshop! I suppose the other cabinetmakers prepared glue in much the same way. Glue was sold in stores, probably in flake form.[21] If the appraisers had seen "store-bought" glue that had a definite monetary value, they would undoubtedly have listed it. It seems most likely, therefore, that they saw only "homemade" glue and thought of it as valueless.

Rules. When we find that a total of 49 cabinetmakers' inventories do not list a rule of any kind while only 17 do, we may well wonder whether the typical cabinetmaker did any measuring! I suggest, however, that the appraisers recognized a "store-bought" folding rule with its boxwood arms and brass joints as something of value and listed it separately when they saw one. The typical cabinetmaker, however, got by with some sort of home-made measuring device which the appraisers thought to be of no value.

When they saw one of these they failed to list it. Because the descendants of early cabinetmakers also thought a homemade rule was of no value, few have survived to the present.

Some time ago I raised the question as to what kind of rule a cabinetmaker would have owned in the first two decades of the nineteenth century. Several students of tools were kind enough to point out that folding rules were being made in England at and before the time.[22] The inventories, however, provide important information that the catalogues of makers and dealers do not: nearly two out of three cabinetmakers in the era and the area discussed did not own manufactured rules.

The terms used for the rules when they are listed in the inventories and the prices given are of some interest. Rules are usually called simply "two-foot," but one is termed "double-joint" while some are called "box." In 1838 and 1839, two appraisers in central Indiana used the term "English" in describing rules. Prices range from 10 cents to 75 cents depending on the date, the area, and, I suppose, the condition of the rule. Sums of money mean nothing without a basis for comparison. The appraiser who in 1838 in Hamilton County, Indiana thought an "english rule" worth 75 cents, thought a jack plane worth $1.00 and a "rabbit" plane worth 50 cents.

Screwdrivers. The fact that so few cabinetmakers owned screwdrivers is puzzling. Even one made by a blacksmith from an old file would have some monetary value, it would seem. Moreover, screws were readily available by these dates as were hinges, locks, and the like,[23] and one would suppose that a cabinetmaker would use these items on a fairly regular basis.

Mallets. At first sight, one who read over the inventories might assume that cabinetmakers owned no mallets. I actually found only three cabinetmakers' inventories that listed mallets and that is 3 out of 66! The reason mallets do not appear in inventories surely is that the mallets were made by the cabinetmakers themselves and the appraisers thought they had no monetary value.

Sandpaper and scrapers. Only two cabinetmakers out of the total 66 had sandpaper listed in their inventories and these two died in 1849 at the very end of the era we are looking at. Since sandpaper was a commodity that could be bought at stores, one would expect appraisers to recognize its monetary value and to list it. Loring McMillen has shown that sandpaper was being sold in New York City as early as 1764.[24] Thomas Lincoln bought some sandpaper at a store in Elizabethtown, Kentucky in 1808.[25] One is left with the conclusion that cabinetmakers in the 1800–1850 era simply did not use much sandpaper. Hummel found no mention of it before 1815 in the reasonably complete account books of the Dominy family of craftsmen.[26]

Today's woodworker typically depends on sandpaper (technically, I suppose, "abrasive sheets" would be a more accurate term, since today's "sandpaper" often contains neither sand nor paper) to obtain a smooth surface on wood in furniture, interior woodwork, and the like. Admirers of antique furniture know that early cabinetmakers did not leave rough surfaces on the pieces they made. How did they do it without sandpaper? It is generally assumed that they depended on razor sharp smoothing planes and that scrapers were used to remove any unevenness left after planing. This would explain why there is such a number of smoothing planes in the inventories, but why are there no scrapers listed? (Only one out of 66 inventories listed a scraper and that in 1848. See the discussion of the toothing plane, above.) I can only assume that woodworkers made their scrapers out of scrap pieces of steel such as bits of old saw blades. Appraisers felt they had no value and so did not list them.

Notes

1. I would like to thank Raymond R. Townsend of Williamsburg, Virginia who was kind enough to send me a great deal of helpful material he had accumulated in his research and David G. Vanderstel, Senior Historian, Conner Prairie Pioneer Settlement, for sending me useful inventories from central Indiana.

2. The two types of research I mention represent an overly-simplified classification. It ignores several other types of research that do not fit neatly into categories. For example, an outstanding example of research starting with the tools actually owned by a family of craftsmen is Charles Hummel's *With Hammer in Hand* (Charlottesville: University Press of Virginia, 1968).

    Some important research has also used handbooks and encyclopedias that tell craftsmen what tools to use or describe the tools that craftsmen theoretically used. These two types of source are also extremely valuable but they still do not answer the question, "What tools did early craftsmen actually use?"

3. See Margaret Berwind Schiffer, *Furniture and Its Makers of Chester County, Pennsylvania.* (Philadelphia: University of Pennsylvania Press, 1966), p.180 where Amos Darlington, cabinetmaker, was named one of the appraisers of Thomas Ogden's property. See also Mrs. W. H. Whitly, *A Checklist of Kentucky Cabinetmakers from 1775 to 1859* (Paris, Ky., 1982, 2nd ed.), p. 84. For the cabinetmaker named Pew who died in 1811, she says, "One of the three appraisers was a cabinetmaker." See further Wallace P. Guslar, *Furniture of Williamsburg and Eastern Virginia, 1710–1790* (Richmond: Virginia Museum, 1979), p.182.

4. See, for instance, R.G. McMurtry, "Furniture Made by Thomas Lincoln," *Lincoln Lore,* no. 1512 (February 1964).

5. George Sturt, *The Wheelwright's Shop* (Cambridge: Cambridge University Press, 1923) mentions decorative chamfers on wagons. The chamfers were made with drawknives. He never mentions moldings made with planes.

6. The research on which this paper is largely based was done while preparing a study for the Lincoln Boyhood National Memorial near Lincoln City, Indiana. The research was supported by the Eastern National Park and Monument Association.

7. See footnote 3.

8. L.B. Romaine, "A Yankee Carpenter and his Tools," EAIA *Chronicle* 6, no. 3 (July 1953): 33–34 [Amana Thompson, 1827. Thompson was also a joiner and cabinetmaker]; Alfred Coxe Prime, *The Arts and Crafts in Philadelphia, Maryland, and South Carolina 1721–1785* (The Walpole Society, 1929), I, 164. [Joseph Cresson, 1779]; John S. Kebabian, "The George W. Cartwright Tool Chest," EAIA *Chronicle* 30, no. 4 (December 1977): 68–69 [G.W. Cartwright, died 1867]; Wallace B. Guslar [see footnote 3], p. 182 [Major Edmund Dickenson, 1778]. Because of the scarcity of inventories I could find in eastern localities outside Chester County, Pennsylvania, I have included some inventories that fall outside the 1800–1850 limits by a few decades.

9. Kentucky inventories: Whitly (see footnote 3), Wm. Thompson, 1792, p. 107; Chas. Wentling, 1799, p. 114; Jas. Pew, 1811, p. 84; Absalom Wells, 1827, p. 114; Indiana: John G. Henderson, 1820, in Betty L. Walters, *Furniture Makers of Indiana* 1793–1850 (Indianapolis: Indiana Historical Society, 1972), p. 110; The following from the archives of the Conner Prairie Pioneer Settlement, Noblesville, Indiana: Charles Davis, 1837; Nathan Hockett, 1839.

10. Absalom Wells, 1827; Whitly (see footnote 3), p. 114.

11. Schiffer, pp. 252–53.

12. Walters, p. 110.

13. *Ohio Tool Box,* 1984, issues 3 and 4.

14. *Pioneer American* 9, no. 1 (July 1977): 32–61.

15. Hummel, p. 106.

16. Ibid., p. 106 and references cited.

17. As an example, see Albert Hubbard, "The Toothing Plane," EAIA *Chronicle* 27, no. 1 (April 1974): 17, and references cited. See also Hummel, p. 125 and R.A. Salaman, *Dictionary of Tools* (New York: Chas. Scribner's Sons, 1975), p. 368.

18. James Williamson, inventory of 1848, in Schiffer, p. 253.

19. Helen Krechniak, *Tennessee Mountain Crafts* (Nashville: Tennessee Division of Information, n.d.), p. 8.

20. James Sutherland, compiler, *Indianapolis Directory and Business Mirror for 1861* (Indianapolis: Bowen, Stewart & Co., 1861).

21. Whitly, p. 103, cites items in an inventory of the contents of a rural store in Adair County, Kentucky, ca. 1840, which includes glue.

22. See *The Fine Tool Journal* 27, no. 2 (October 1983): 23–26.

23. The same rural store mentioned in footnote 21 had seven gross of wood screws in stock in 1840 and large numbers of hinges and locks of various kinds.

24. Loring McMillen, "Sandpaper," EAIA *Chronicle* 8, no. 2 (April 1955): 17.

25. *Lincoln Lore,* no. 1577 (July 1969), p. 4. One wonders if Lincoln bought the sandpaper as a novelty he wanted to try.

26. Hummel, p. 65.

15

Planemaking in the United States:
The Cartography of a Craft

It is possible to study crafts in many ways. I hope I have already made it clear that I feel that fieldwork is of primary importance. In this case, however, I have tried to use all available information from historical records together with fieldwork data, in this instance drawn from the experiences of great numbers of tool collectors, to show where and when wooden planes were made by craftsmen in the United States.

*   *   *

As a student of folklife, I have long been intrigued by the cartographic approach to material culture. The folk atlases produced in several European countries first aroused my admiration. In the United States I have especially envied the work of cultural geographers and those influenced by them such as Henry Glassie. At the same time, however, I have wished that the data which make possible detailed maps of twentieth century phenomena could be available in equivalent detail for historic material culture. This wish is not entirely the result of antiquarianism. It is, instead, bound up with the conviction that, prior to the establishment of an efficient transportation network, folklife, material culture, and geography were more closely bound to one another and that the relationship has significance if only we can discover it.

The relative neglect of areal distribution patterns in historic material folk culture is underlined by two important publications. Henry Glassie's seminal work, *Pattern in the Material Folk Culture of the Eastern United States,* important as it is in most respects, nonetheless fails to present maps showing in detail the distribution of a cultural item. *This Remarkable Continent* represents the attempt of the distinguished editors and their collaborators "to present ... the best possible cartographic statement of

This article originally appeared in *Material Culture* 18, no. 3 (Fall 1986): 167–85.

what is known today . . . about spatial dimensions of North American society and cultures" (Rooney et al., p. vii). Among the hundreds of maps, there are few that can be said to deal directly with the material folk culture of the pre-industrial era. The exceptions are maps dealing with small areas not much larger than a state and a few maps based upon speech patterns.

Presenting appropriate data in the form of maps (the cartographic approach) has many advantages. For one, it makes it possible for the reader to grasp important facts immediately. For example, glance at figure 15.2, and then read over table 15.2. The same important information can be gleaned from each, but it can be obtained more directly, more immediately, more *picturesquely,* if I may say so, from the map. More importantly, the cartographic approach facilitates research on topics important to the understanding of human society such as diffusion, changes over time, regionalization, and ethnicity. To be sure, the cartographic approach has limitations; nonetheless, it is an important research tool in the study of culture and, especially, traditional material culture.

What follows is an attempt to present the areal aspects of wooden planemaking in the United States. There is as well an explanation as to why it is possible to present this data but why at this time comparable data for other folk crafts are unobtainable.

Methodology

Among the many artifacts that were made in the United States or the colonies before the Industrial Era, the wooden planes used by woodworkers hold a special place: nearly every one has stamped on its nose a name and a place, usually the name of the maker and the place where he worked. Most early artifacts, unfortunately, do not bear the names of the makers nor the places they were made. Take as an example the ubiquitous slat-back chair (Roberts 1981). I have never seen a slat-back chair which has been marked by the maker with his name or place of residence. It is true that a person who has had extensive experience in studying one area can often identify the chairs made by one maker because of certain distinguishing characteristics. Nonetheless, the absence of signed examples makes it difficult to generalize about the geographic aspects of chairmaking, because compiling a comprehensive list of chairmakers together with every example of their chairs is difficult or impossible.

One cannot be sure why planemakers were one of the few craftsworkers to consistently identify their products with stamps giving name and place (some of the other craftsworkers who also did are mentioned below). It is clear, however, that planemaking in America was a continuation—almost an imitation—of planemaking in England. Planes were made by specialized craftsmen in England long before they were in the American colonies and English planes were widely sold in the colonies (Pollaks, 12–13). English-made planes were normally stamped with the name and location of the maker, probably as the guarantee of quality when the planes were sold far from the place where they were made. American planemakers simply perpetuated the practice of their English predecessors and counterparts.

There are many reasons why I have chosen to present cartographic aspects of wooden planemaking rather than some other craft. Some of these reasons are as follows:

1. There were relatively few planemaker-craftsmen working in the United States or the colonies so that it has been possible to locate almost all of them. As a simple comparison, there were 11 planemaker-craftsmen working in Indiana in 1850 according to the federal census of that year (Roberts 1985) while there were 430 blacksmiths in the state according to the same source. Such a large number of blacksmiths means that data from other sources to be used to test the accuracy of the census figures would take a lifetime to assemble (as I will later show, it is necessary to test the accuracy of the census figures since they are often wildly inaccurate).

Before proceeding, I want to deal with the term "plane-maker-craftsmen." I use this awkward term to refer to the craftsmen who produced planes in relatively small numbers using mostly hand tools. These people (they were mostly men but, as we will see, there were two or three women planemakers) worked either alone in their own shops or with a few helpers. They are to be distinguished from the factories which began to develop in the mid-nineteenth century and which used machinery and relatively unskilled factory hands to tend that machinery. In the remainder of this paper I will use the term "planemaker" rather than "plane-maker-craftsman" to save space but I will be referring to these highly skilled craftsmen who made planes by hand rather than to factory employees.[1]

2. The sources available for information on planemakers are detailed and reliable. One source is the names of makers and the locations where they worked stamped on planes themselves. Virtually every wooden plane has, stamped on its nose, the name of the maker and the name of the town and often the state where that maker worked. When large factories began producing planes they also stamped their names and locations on the planes they made. If a wooden plane has no name stamped on its nose, it usually means that a

woodworker has made the plane for his own use. Often these "homemade" planes can be recognized because they use a different pattern from that used by the specialized craftsmen or because they are not so well made or carefully finished.

Tool collectors have been avidly collecting wooden planes for many years, and many collectors are both scholarly and curious about their collections. Hence a great deal of effort has gone into compiling lists of planemakers based largely on the names found on planes.

The information thus compiled is, first, accurate and detailed. For example, while some sources tell us only what state craftsmen worked in, the plane imprints often give the name of the town as well as the state. Second, this information can be cross-checked with other sources for authenticity and for further information. The information not normally found on planes is the year of manufacture. These dates, however, can often be provided by other sources.

Another source is city and business directories. The dates at which these are first printed and the accuracy of their coverage vary from place to place. In a few eastern cities, directories were first published shortly after the Revolutionary War while in the Midwest it was at least a half a century later that directories appeared in many states. City and business directories cannot alone, then, give us complete information. Nonetheless, they are important for two reasons. First, they do establish dates for some planemakers. Once the working dates of a substantial number of planemakers have been discovered, it is possible to recognize stylistic criteria useful in dating planes which otherwise could not be dated. Second, they make it possible to cross check information from other sources. For example, while there are some planemakers listed in city directories for whom planes have never been found and some names on planes which have never been found in directories for the cities or towns where the planemakers worked, on the whole the names on planes and the names in directories supplement and validate one another well.

Let us take as a simple illustration the town of Louisville, Kentucky. (In the years we are considering, it was probably a town rather than a city.) Charles J. Ewing has compiled a list of 13 planemakers in Louisville from city directories printed between 1832 and 1866. Every one of these planemakers is also found in a listing compiled from plane imprints (Pollaks).

Another source is census records. One would think that census records would be rich in information about planemakers, especially when one considers that a separate census of manufacturers was compiled nearly each time that a general census (census of population) was taken. The coverage of planemakers, however, turns out to have been incredibly erratic.

Early census material available to today's researcher consists of two types. There are the original returns made out in longhand by the census takers. These originals, of course, are in Washington, D.C., but most large libraries have microfilm copies. Then there are volumes printed by the census bureau a few years after each census was taken. They contain abstracts, summaries, tables, and statistics.

I have just charged that the censuses as a whole have been incredibly erratic as concerns planemakers. Let me document this charge. On one occasion I took many hours to read through the entire 1850 Census of Manufacturers for Indiana. I found three entries on planemakers even though there is clear proof that at least twice that many were working in 1850. Either the census takers were careless or the planemakers did not admit to making $500 worth of goods in a year, the amount of merchandise supposed to be made in order to be listed. (One planemaker, Joseph Gilmer, had gone off to California to dig for gold according to an entry after his name in the general census for 1850.)

At any rate, despite the fact that there are planemakers listed in the census, the summary volume does not mention planemaking anywhere in its charts and tables. It does show in one table that in the entire United States there was one maker of shoulder braces who employed three hands, so the fact that there were not huge numbers of planemakers or that they did not produce huge quantities of planes was not the reason they were excluded. They were probably lumped in with "makers of hardware" or "tool makers" or some other group.

If the summary volume for the 1850 Census of Manufacturers is silent on the subject of planemakers, so also are those for 1840 and 1820. The volume for 1810 lists at least a few planemakers, four for Pennsylvania and two for Maryland.

If the censuses for manufacturers are disappointing, the censuses of population are less so. Unfortunately, none of the general censuses before 1850 asked for any specific information on trade or profession, but the census takers in 1850 were instructed to record the trade or profession of adult males. The summary volume for this census gives a listing of 402 planemakers in 11 states.

But how accurate are these figures from the 1850 general

census? I can only answer for the state of Indiana. Based upon a search for Indiana planemakers I have recently completed (Roberts 1985), I can testify that these census figures are quite reliable. That is to say, the evidence that is available from plane imprints themselves and from other printed sources such as city directories agrees remarkably well with the evidence from the census. There are three planemakers known from imprints who cannot be found in the 1850 census. Perhaps they were not living in the state that year. (As previously mentioned, one planemaker is listed as a resident of the state even though the notation after his name says, "Digging gold Cal"). On the other hand, three men are listed in the census as planemakers for whom no plane imprints have ever been found. They were probably employees in the shops of others.

Comparisons to Other Crafts

To show the importance of planemaking for a cartographic treatment—indeed, why it appears to be the only early craft that can be so treated—comparisons with other crafts are instructive.

Instructive and valuable though it might be to have maps dealing with historic aspects of cabinetmaking in the colonies and the United States, it would be impossible to obtain meaningful and reliable data to make such maps for many reasons. First, the vast majority of cabinetmakers did not put their names on their products. For example, Betty Lawson Walters compiled a list of more than 2,000 names of men who worked as cabinetmakers in Indiana between 1793 and 1850. She was able to find only about twenty-five pieces of furniture which had a name of one of these cabinetmakers on it. For this reason it is impossible to compile a list of cabinetmakers from their products, a list which could be used to check the reliability of lists compiled from other sources.

Second, lists compiled from census records are notoriously inaccurate. Great numbers of cabinetmakers lived and worked in the countryside in the pre-industrial era. They were both farmers and cabinetmakers, yet they tended to tell the census takers that they were farmers (Roberts 1983). Moreover, the general censuses did not record trade or profession before 1850, and, as I have stated above, the census of manufacturers missed large numbers of craftsmen.

Third, lists of the names of cabinetmakers compiled from city directories and from advertisements in city newspapers must be very incomplete because many cabinetmakers lived in the countryside. Consider Ethel Hall Bjerkoe's *The Cabinetmakers of America* compiled from such sources. It contains the names of perhaps 1,750 cabinetmakers of the seventeenth, eighteenth, and early nineteenth centuries. One wonders if Mrs. Bjerkoe realized that her list contained probably less than 10 percent of the cabinetmakers who actually worked in the country in the time period indicated. Walters' list for Indiana alone contains over 2,000 names—none of which appear in Bjerkoe's listing. Such are the pitfalls involved in compiling lists of names of craftsmen when the craft was widely spread, common, and practiced both in countryside and city. Bear in mind that planemakers were relatively few in number—there never was a time when more than 500 worked in the entire country—and that almost all of them worked in towns or cities; at least, most plane imprints give the name of the town or city in or near which the maker worked.

There are many resemblances of a general sort between the makers of planes and of pewterware. Their numbers were small, they worked mostly in towns and cities, and they marked their wares. Moreover, there are ardent collectors who have compiled lists of pewterers. One such is J. B. Kerfoot's *American Pewter.* Cartographic representation of the craft of the pewterer would be rather meaningless, however, despite these resemblances to planemaking. Of the 214 names of pewterers Kerfoot lists, all but 17 worked in Philadelphia, New York, or cities in New England.

Should we draw up a map showing this distribution, we could conclude that people living in the South (i.e., south of Philadelphia) who owned pewter obtained it either from the North or from England and that this fact would support the generalization that the southern United States had fewer crafts than the northern states (Bridenbaugh, 30–32). Such a map would also confirm the fact that pewter making changed from a handicraft to factory production at an early date so that when people began streaming into the Midwest, any pewter they bought had been made in factories and that pewterers did not move with them as did blacksmiths and planemakers.[2]

Again, there are resemblances of a general sort in the case of gunsmithing and planemaking. Most gunsmiths marked their products with name and, often, location; there are ardent collectors; and lists of gunsmiths have been compiled. Historic aspects of gunsmithing could not be mapped with any degree of accuracy, however. There is relatively little information available for the total number of gunsmiths working in the eighteenth century. At a fairly early date in the nineteenth century factories were producing guns in considerable numbers. The 1850 census records, therefore, would present a misleading picture if they were used as the basis for mapping. 3,843 men told the census takers for the General Census of 1850 that they were gunsmiths. Many of these 3,843 were probably repairers of guns which had been made in factories. Any maps drawn would not reliably show whether guns were being produced in the various states where these men lived or whether guns were only repaired there. By contrast, planemakers continued to produce planes by hand well into the 1850s and where a planemaker was working, it is almost certain that he was producing planes rather than repairing them.

Virtually the same generalizations may be made for clock- and watchmakers. That is, although the makers of clocks and watches often put their names and locations on their products, many craftsmen who used the time-honored term "clock- and watchmaker" to describe themselves actually rarely or never produced timepieces. Instead, they repaired them. Moreover, factory production of timepieces also began at an early date.

Many weavers of Jacquard coverlets not only put their names in the corners of their coverlets but sometimes the locality where they worked and the year the coverlet was made. Unfortunately, the lists which have been compiled of the names of Jacquard coverlet weavers are woefully inadequate, the list for Indiana being an honorable exception (Montgomery). As support for this charge of incompleteness let me cite the following statistics. According to the 1850 Census of Population there were in Indiana 157 people who told the census taker they were weavers. The census does not differentiate between weavers who used the Jacquard loom and those who did not, but thanks to Mrs. Montgomery's list, we know that there were 90 weavers of Jacquard coverlets. Mrs. Montgomery may have missed a few weavers of Jacquard coverlets just as some weavers told the census takers they were farmers.[3] Nevertheless, we can assume that just about 60 percent of the professional weavers in Indiana had Jacquard looms.

Now let us look at Pennsylvania's weavers. The 1850 Census of Population reported that 23,340 Pennsylvanians told the census takers they were weavers. (According to the census, seventy-three percent of all the weavers in the country lived in Pennsylvania. Here one has to have some doubts about the reliability of the census, I'm afraid.) If Pennsylvania is comparable to Indiana, there should be somewhere around 14,000 Jacquard coverlet weavers in Pennsylvania. Many Jacquard coverlet weavers elsewhere in the United States were German-Americans so that one would expect there to be a substantial number of them in the German-American areas of Pennsylvania. Yet John W. Heisey's *A Checklist of American Coverlet Weavers* published in 1978 lists only 420 coverlet weavers in Pennsylvania. One can only conclude that the checklist missed a number of coverlet weavers. It would, therefore, be useless to make a map showing the numbers of Jacquard coverlet weavers in various parts of the country using Heisey's checklist, the only one in print.

This discussion of other crafts shows why I feel that planemakers represent an unparalleled opportunity for cartographic representation of a historic craft. The reliability of the information available for them is unmatched by that available for any other craft.

Planemaking

Wooden planes made in the British Isles and the United States resemble one another so closely that it is impossible to distinguish a British wooden plane from an American one unless one looks at the name of the maker on the nose of the planes. American makers even used beechwood for most of their planes as did British makers, and American and British beechwood are so similar to one another that even an expert at wood analysis needs a microscope to tell them apart (Peattie, 181). At the same time, wooden planes made on the European continent differ significantly from planes made in the British Isles and the United States. But German carpenters and cabinetmakers who came to the United States abandoned their German-style tools such as wooden planes and adopted British-American-style planes.

The first craftsman to specialize in planemaking and to imprint his name on planes whose planes have survived was Thomas Granford II who was listed as a planemaker in the London tax records for 1692 (Smith). Planes made by British craftsmen were certainly brought to this country in the tool chests of immigrant woodworkers, but English planes were also imported and sold in this country (Pollaks, 12–13).

Planemaking by specialized craftsmen who imprinted their planes with their names began in this country shortly after it had in England. Francis Nicholson of Wrentham, Massachusetts, is the earliest recorded planemaker in this country. He began about 1728 and worked until about 1753.[4]

What appears to be the "cultural hearth area" for planemaking in what is now the United States is a relatively small area in southeastern Massachusetts and northeastern Rhode Island including the towns of Dedham, Medway, Mendon, Middleboro, Norton, Rehoboth, and Wrentham, Massachusetts, together with Providence, Rhode Island. All are within a radius of 25 miles (see fig. 15.1 and table 15.1).

All the known pre-Revolutionary War American planemakers (10 in all) worked in these towns with the following exceptions: E. Briggs worked in Keene, New Hampshire, but had moved there from Norton, Massachusetts, where he undoubtedly learned planemaking from Henry Wetherel of that town; I. Walton and his two sons worked in Reading, Massachusetts, at an early date (ca. 1730) and Reading is about 25 miles north of the hearth area; John Sleeper worked in Newburyport in northeastern Massachusetts as early as 1775; Samuel Caruthers worked in Philadelphia beginning about 1750 while his apprentice, Benjamin Armitage, Jr., also worked in that city beginning about 1760; Dietrich Heiss made planes in Lancaster, Pennsylvania, between 1769–1814 and Thomas Grant may have worked in New York City before 1770.

Figure 15.1. Geographic Distribution of Planemakers in the American Colonies Active before 1775
Each dot represents one planemaker.

Table 15.1   Towns in Which Planemakers Were Active before
the Revolutionary War

Massachusetts	
Dedham	2
Medway	1
Mendon	1
Middleboro	1
Newburyport	1
Norton	1
Reading	1
Rehoboth	1
Wrentham	1
Total	**12**
Rhode Island	
Providence	2
Total	**2**
New Hampshire	
Keene	1
Total	**1**
Pennsylvania	
Philadelphia	2
Lancaster	1
Total	**3**
Grand Total	**18**

After the Revolutionary War planemaking expanded, but only rather slowly. Wooden planes were still mostly made in Massachusetts and Rhode Island in 1800. By 1810 there were planemakers active in the towns already mentioned plus, in Massachusetts, New Bedford, Beverly, and Boston. In Connecticut planes were being made in Chatham and Hartford. In the state of New York there were planemakers working in Albany and Kingston though none in New York City. Philadelphia had at least nine active makers while two were working in Lancaster, Pennsylvania, and two in the vicinity of Pittsburgh.[5] Two were also active in Baltimore.

It was in the second quarter of the nineteenth century that the making of wooden planes by craftsmen reached its zenith. During that period factories began to appear in New England, New York, and Ohio, but in most parts of the country the hand craftsman still held sway.

For our purposes it is fortunate that census takers and the compilers of data for the Census Bureau did not always ignore planemakers. Although, as mentioned above, the Census of Manufacturers never included data of any use on planemakers, the Census of Population for 1850, the first to list every person by name and the first to give the trade or profession of adult males, is very helpful for our purposes. Not only did the census takers record planemakers as planemakers (they sometimes get obscured by being called "toolmakers" or something similar), but the clerks in Washington, D. C., listed planemakers as planemakers (they did not always do so) in the summary volumes for most states (see fig. 15.2 and table 15.2).

The statistics in table 15.3 have been gleaned from the 1850 census. The cartographic representation in figure 15.2 together with table 15.2 gives a much more detailed representation by showing where in each state the planemakers are concentrated. A glance at the area around Cincinnati, Ohio, for example, shows the large number of planemakers within a radius of about 50 miles. Simply relying upon the census figures in the summary volume as shown in table 15.3, therefore, produces somewhat vague results. It is the name of the maker imprinted on a plane plus the location as well as the lists compiled by tool enthusiasts that make the more detailed and meaningful cartographic representation possible.

But what of the discrepancies in numbers between tables 15.2 and 15.3? There are far more planemakers listed in the census of population than in the list based upon plane imprints and directories, yet the list with fewer people includes states not shown on the longer list. One reason for the discrepancies in numbers is that a planemaker such as William B. Belch of New York City had seven men working in his shop. They would have told the census taker that they were planemakers, yet Belch marked his planes W. B. Belch/New York, so, on the basis of the plane imprint, we would only be justified in assigning one planemaker to his shop (we know about the seven workmen in Belch's shop from other sources, but such information is readily available for only about a dozen planemakers). Nonetheless, I feel that the list based upon plane imprints and city directories is valuable in showing the geographic distribution of planemaking. Undoubtedly, more names of planemakers and their working dates will come to light in the future, but it is unlikely that such additional information will change the picture dramatically.

The fact that the list with fewer people on it nonetheless contains planemakers in states not in the list with more must be attributed to faults in the census. It is possible that census takers in Philadelphia, for instance, wrote down "toolmaker" or something similar when told that a man made planes. It is unlikely, however, that the census takers in Lancaster, Reading, and Washington, Pennsylvania, all failed to use the term "planemaker." What probably happened is that some clerk in the Census Bureau in Washington, D. C., was assigned the boring task of compiling a summary of the different kinds of trades and professions in Pennsylvania and the numbers for each. He probably put planemakers under the heading "Tool Makers." Why his

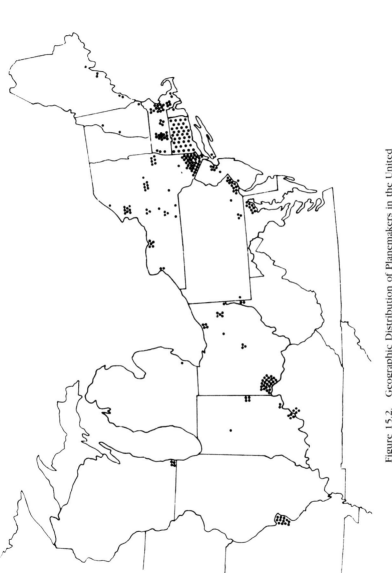

Figure 15.2. Geographic Distribution of Planemakers in the United States, 1850

Each dot represents one planemaker. Dots have been placed as closely as possible to the towns where each planemaker worked. Consult table 15.2 for the names of the towns.

Table 15.2   Names Drawn from Plane Imprints and from City Directories

Connecticut
Derby	8
Glastonbury	2
Hartford	4
Middletown	5
New Hartford	1
New Haven	6
New London	1
Norwich	1
Riverton	1
Salisbury	1
Saybrook	3
Wallingford	2
Winsted	1
Total	**36**

Indiana
Brownville	2
Jeffersonville	1
Lafayette	1
Madison	2
New Albany	3
Richmond	2
Total	**11**

Kentucky
Louisville	4
Total	**4**

Maine
Augusta	1
Bangor	1
Portland	2
Thomaston	1
Waldoboro	1
Total	**6**

Maryland
Baltimore	9
Total	**9**

Massachusetts
Amherst	4
Boston	6
Conway	2
Goshen	1
Hanover	1
Hingham	1
Lowell	3
Middleboro	1
New Bedford	2
Northampton	4
Norton	1
Orange	1
Pittsfield	1
Smithfield	1
Springfield	2
Taunton	2
Westfield	1
Williamsburg	1
Worcester	2
Worthington	1
Total	**38**

Michigan
Detroit	1
Total	**1**

Missouri
St. Louis	12
Total	**12**

New Hampshire
Lebanon	1
Littleton	1
Hudson	1
Total	**3**

New Jersey
Camden	1
Newark	5
New Brunswick	3
Total	**9**

New York
Albany	5
Brooklyn	2
Buffalo	2
Delhi	1
Deposit	1
De Ruyter	1
Elmira	1
Kingston	1
McLean	3
Newport	1
New York City	31
Ogdensburg	1
Poughkeepsie	1
Rochester	5
Salina	1
Syracuse	2
Troy	3
Utica	6
Watertown	8
Total	**75**

Ohio
Cincinnati	24
Cleveland	4
Columbus	3
Lisbon	1
Ravenna	5
Vernon	1
Total	**38**

Pennsylvania
Lancaster	3
Philadelphia	12
Reading	1
Washington	1
Total	**17**

Rhode Island
Providence	3
Warren	1
Total	**4**

West Virginia (Virginia in 1850)
Wheeling	2
Total	**2**

Wisconsin
Milwaukee	4
Total	**4**

Grand Total	**269**

Table 15.3   1850 Census of Population

State	Number of Planemakers	Population of State	Number of Inhabitants to One Planemaker
Connecticut	52	370,792	7,130
Indiana	11	988,416	89,856
Kentucky	8	982,405	122,800
Maryland	18	583,034	32,390
Massachusetts	69	994,514	14,413
New Hampshire	2	317,976	158,988
New Jersey	22	489,555	22,252
New York	94	3,097,394	32,951
Ohio	92	1,980,329	21,525
Pennsylvania[1]	25	2,311,786	92,471
Rhode Island	9	147,545	16,393
Total Planemakers	**402**		
Total U.S. Population		**23,191,876**	
Number of Inhabitants to One Planemaker for the Entire United States			**57,691**

1. The figure for Pennsylvania was omitted from the 1850 census by mistake. This estimate is based on the figure for 1860.

supervisors did not notice and wonder why there were planemakers in nearly every other state near Pennsylvania though none in that state, I cannot say. Such was—and is—the bureaucracy (I have estimated the number of planemakers in Pennsylvania in table 15.3).

To show what happened between 1850 and 1860, we may examine the figures for planemakers as given in the summary volume for the 1860 Census of Population (see table 15.4). These figures for 1860 do show some changes. They show a marked decline in planemakers while the population has increased by nearly a third: one planemaker for 57,691 inhabitants in 1850 but one planemaker per 120,472 inhabitants in 1860. Factories where machines did much of the work were beginning to produce planes in large numbers. Casey, Kitchel & Co. of Auburn, New York, made planes using 40 convicts and a "steam planing mill." They produced $22,000 worth of tools in a year. The Union Tool Co. of Goshen, Massachusetts, between 1852–54 employed 20 men and used both water and steam power. The Ohio Tool Company was incorporated in 1851 and in that year employed 200 convicts.

By contrast, the 1860 census shows a small number of planemakers in states not represented in the 1850 census. From our other sources of information, however, we know that this only means somewhat improved reporting and tabulation in 1860. The disappearance of Rhode Island from

Table 15.4   1860 Census of Population

State	Number of Planemakers	Population of State	Number of Inhabitants to One Planemaker
Connecticut	49	460,147	9,390
Illinois	3	1,711,951	570,650
Indiana	8	1,350,428	168,803
Kentucky	2	1,115,684	557,842
Maine	3	628,279	209,426
Maryland	17	687,049	40,414
Massachusetts	31	1,231,066	39,711
Michigan	3	749,113	249,704
Missouri	4	1,182,012	295,503
New Hampshire	2	320,073	160,036
New Jersey	7	672,035	96,005
New York	70	3,880,735	55,439
Ohio	36	2,399,502	66,652
Pennsylvania	20	2,906,115	145,305
Tennessee	2	1,109,801	554,900
District of Columbia	4	75,080	18,770
Total Planemakers	**261**		
Total U.S. Population		**31,443,322**	
Number of Inhabitants to One Planemaker for the Entire United States			**120,472**

the list of states in 1860 is only another accident. J. E. Child was a planemaker in Providence between 1852 and 1875, for instance, according to other sources.

It should be emphasized that the map of the location of planemakers in figure 15.2 represents the year 1850. It was in that period that the largest number of planemakers was at work. Earlier there were fewer (half as many planemakers were working in Indiana in 1840 as in 1850, for instance). As already shown, the planemakers in the country in 1860 were 35 percent fewer than in 1850. It is for these reasons that the year 1850 was chosen for cartographic representation.

What generalizations can be made from our data? First, there is no direct correlation between the population of the United States and the number of and location of planemakers. True, prior to the Revolutionary War planemaking was confined to a few areas on the east coast, but only in Pennsylvania and northwards. It is nonetheless true that woodworkers flourished in the South and used planes as much as in the North. Southern houses, for example, surely have as many planed floorboards and molded fireplace mantels as northern houses and the floorboards were planed and the moldings for the fireplace made with molding planes at the place where the house was built. They were not made in the North and shipped down nor in England and shipped across the sea.

The pattern persisted right up to the end of the era of the wooden plane. As people migrated westward, planemakers went with them in the North but not in the South. Take the statistics drawn from the 1860 Census of Population. On the East Coast, the District of Columbia is the farthest south that any planemaker worked and there is a total of four there. Farther west, with a few insignificant exceptions, no planemakers worked farther south than the southern bank of the Ohio river in Louisville, Kentucky.

If we add the information on planemakers from all sources together, we can say that, again, with only a few insignificant exceptions, present data show no planemakers ever worked in Alabama, Arkansas, Delaware, Florida, Georgia, Louisiana, Mississippi, North Carolina, South Carolina, Tennessee, Texas, and Virginia.

What are the exceptions? A few planes have been found with imprinted names and locations in southern states: Louisiana, Tennessee, and Virginia. In many cases, probably in most, these names are the names of hardware dealers who purchased planes either from England or the North and had their own names put on them.

Let me cite a specific example. Several years ago I purchased a large, old hand saw that had stamped deeply in the metal of the blade both "W. Butcher/Sheffield" and "P. A. Lanauze/New Orleans." Since these names must have been stamped into the metal while the saw was being made, and since W. Butcher was a well known manufacturer of edge tools, P. A. Lanauze must have been a hardware dealer in New Orleans who arranged to have his name stamped in the blade of the saw while it was being made in Sheffield, England. Wooden planes have been found with the Lanauze imprint on their noses. It would seem likely that Lanauze also bought planes from some factory and had his name stamped on them.

Another generalization is that no planemakers worked more than a few miles west of the Mississippi River save for one. H. G. Stilley was a planemaker active in Oakland and San Francisco, California, as early as 1869. Except for him, the planemakers who worked west of the Mississippi River, mostly on its western bank, included a substantial number in St. Louis, Missouri; a few in Iowa, in Muscatine and Davenport on the river and in Des Moines, some 100 miles west, and in Winterset near Des Moines; and a doubtful few in New Orleans, doubtful because the recorded names may be those of hardware dealers rather than planemakers.

Why did planemaking essentially stop at the Mississippi? Because by the time the population had pushed westward, planes were being mass produced in factories. If planemakers did move westward, they must have found no demand for their planes. Perhaps it was most cost effective to make planes from beechwood in eastern states and ship the planes west than to ship beechwood west to be made into planes (the beech tree grows east of the Mississippi).

A final generalization concerns the concept of "hearth area" or "source area."[6] As has been shown, prior to the Revolutionary War there were 10 planemakers working within a radius of 25 miles in southeastern Massachusetts and northeastern Rhode Island and a few more a few miles away. This would appear to be a classic case of hearth or source area, especially when in 1850 large numbers of planemakers were also working in the New England states.

The problem with this simplified presentation is that it does not explain why there were two planemakers in Philadelphia as early as 1750 and one in Lancaster, Pennsylvania, as early as 1769. There is no way of demonstrating any connection between the men working in these two areas. It might be possible to assume that three planemakers (at least) migrated from England to begin the craft in these areas—except that the man who made planes at an early date in Lancaster, Pennsylvania, was named Dietrich Heiss. As previously mentioned, Heiss, despite his name, made Anglo-American-type planes and not German types. Perhaps he was a planemaker in Germany who emigrated to Lancaster and made Anglo-American planes when he saw what his customers demanded.

A second problem with the hearth or source area concept as applied to planemaking is as follows. The birthplaces of Indiana planemakers were found in the 1850 census and elsewhere and not one of the 15 planemakers so investigated was born in New England (Roberts 1985). One each was born in Germany, England, and Ireland. Three were born in New York, three in Ohio, two in Maryland, and one each in New Jersey, North Carolina, Pennsylvania, and Virginia. So much for Massachusetts and Rhode Island as the source area for the rest of the United States! In other words, the planemakers in Indiana came from the same countries and states, generally speaking, as did the other settlers in Indiana, and those states are the mid-Atlantic states mostly. And this despite the fact that planemaking was normally learned by serving a long apprenticeship. The ages of the planemakers at the time they moved to Indiana show that they probably served apprenticeships learning to be planemakers "back East." The average age at which the 10 whose ages can be found moved to Indiana is 20. When they had completed their apprenticeships they moved out to Indiana looking for places to establish themselves.

A substantial number of Connecticut planemakers did migrate to upstate New York but upstate New York was generally settled by New

Englanders. In other words, the pattern described above held true here also. The planemakers in upstate New York came from the same states as did many of the settlers.

At the moment I can only conjecture that planemaking did not spring up in one section of the United States and spread from there to other parts of the country even though maps would tend to create the impression that that was the process. Instead, it is more likely that planemaking was actually introduced independently from the British Isles to many parts of this country.

Surveying planemakers produced some unexpected sidelights, that is, information that does not help in cartographic considerations but nonetheless helps in understanding something about the craft and about social considerations of the day.

Although one could say that planemaking was a man's world, there were two women planemakers, Charollete White of Philadelphia, active in 1840, and Catherine Seybold of Cincinnati, active between 1853 and 1855. Both these women were the widows of planemakers who had died the year before the ladies themselves were active as planemakers. It is likely, therefore, that the widows did not actually physically labor in the workshops. They probably kept the shops open with some workmen who had worked under their husbands until the shop could be sold to someone.

Although almost all planemakers were white males, a few black men did make planes. The most celebrated is Cesor Chelor who was the slave of America's first planemaker, Francis Nicholson of Wrentham, Massachusetts. When Nicholson died in 1753, his will freed Chelor and granted him 10 acres of land, tools, and other property. Chelor made planes using his own imprint until his death in 1784. Nicholson also had a son named John to whom he left tools and John also became a planemaker. There were two black planemakers working in Newark, New Jersey, between 1835 and 1837, John A. King and John Teasman, while George Bale, another black planemaker, worked in New York City between 1842 and 1860. While there were well over 100 white planemakers for each black one, the fact that blacks living in the North well before the Civil War could become independent craftsmen is nonetheless worthy of note.

And what did a plane cost in 1850? Some statistics are available but they must be used with caution. Factories were manufacturing planes in 1850, but I am dealing with craftsman-made planes. The average plane in Indiana cost $2.25. The average plane in New York City sold for $1.50, but the average plane in upstate New York brought $.70. Why the marked differences? The factors here would appear to be competition from planes produced with convict labor at Auburn, New York, plus the costs of transportation. For example, around 1840 convict labor cost 37½ cents per day while in 1850 planemakers in Indiana paid their "hands" $20 per month. Hence planemakers working near Auburn could only charge a low price for their planes. In New York City the cost of shipping planes from Auburn raised their price to where the city planemakers could charge $1.50 for their planes and still sell them. In Indiana the costs of transportation would have drastically raised the price of Auburn, New York, planes.[7]

The only truly reliable information I have ever found concerning the earnings of a planemaker—other than the wages paid "hands"—relates to three partners in Winthrop, Connecticut, doing business as G. W. Denison & Co. in 1870. The partners told the census taker for the 1870 Census of Manufacturers that each had invested $750 in the firm. Each took $300 in profit for the year plus wages of 27½ cents per hour. At 60 hours a week for 50 weeks, their wages would have amounted to $825 each for the year.

One final sidelight. If the first planemaker in the country began work about 1728, how long did planemaking as a craft continue? Present evidence indicates that Edward Carter of Troy, New York, was the last planemaker. He made planes by hand as late as 1903.

Notes

1. There is probably a third category midway between the planemaker-craftsman and the employee of the factory where planes were made. Two companies were very active in producing planes in the second half of the nineteenth century, the Auburn Tool Company of Auburn, New York, which was founded in 1821 and began large-scale operation in 1834, and the Ohio Tool Company of Columbus, Ohio, founded in 1851 (K. Roberts, 34–37). The locations of these companies are significant: they employed convict labor from the state penitentiaries to make planes. Surely, in the early years the convicts worked mainly by hand, but they are, of course, anonymous and probably worked on some kind of an assembly line basis. In 1850 the Census of Manufacturers showed that the company then using convicts from the New York penitentiary employed 40 convicts and used a "steam planing mill." Hence the convict laborers cannot be called planemaker-craftsmen even if we knew who they were.

2. One minor exception to this generalization is that two pewterers did work in Cincinnati, Ohio, after 1825. These were probably small factories, however, rather than hand craftsmen (Kerfoot, 64).

3. Mrs. Montgomery reported that, "Many weavers listed themselves as farmers in the 1850 census, although coverlets, signed and dated from that period, proved that they were also weaving" (6).

4. Data on specific planemakers throughout this article is drawn from K. Roberts supplemented by data drawn from the Pollaks. Data on Indiana planemakers is taken from W. E. Roberts, 1985. Any exceptions are noted.

5. The two Pittsburgh makers are not listed by K. Roberts or the Pollaks but are cited (not by name, unfortunately) in the summary volume for the 1810 Census of Manufacturers. This

summary volume does not list any planemakers in Massachusetts, Connecticut, or New York, showing again how untrustworthy are many census records.

6. Fred B. Kniffen uses the term "source area" in his seminal article, "Folk Housing: Key to Diffusion" (560). Zelinsky uses both "culture hearth" and "hearth area," but also describes, "the colonial hearth areas, that is, the nodal zones along the Atlantic Seaboard that proved to be the incubators for the national cultural pattern" (20).

7. Indiana planemakers actually had to compete with planes from Columbus, Ohio, where convict labor was also used by the Ohio Tool Company. There were also factories producing planes in 1850 in New England and upstate New York. In 1810, a few planemakers were included in the Census of Manufacturers. Three planemakers in Philadelphia and Pittsburgh sold planes for about 57 cents each at a time when there was competition only from English planes.

References Cited

Bjerkoe, Ethel Hall, *The Cabinetmakers of America.* Doubleday & Company, New York (1957).

Bridenbaugh, Carl, *The Colonial Craftsman.* New York University Press, New York (1950).

Ewing, Charles J., Early Plane Makers and Dealers of Louisville, Kentucky. *The Fine Tool Journal* 30: 69–72 (1985).

Glassie, Henry, *Pattern in the Material Folk Culture of the Eastern United States.* University of Pennsylvania Press, Philadelphia, Pennsylvania (1968).

Heisey, John W., *A Checklist of American Coverlet Weavers.* The Colonial Williamsburg Foundation, Williamsburg, Virginia (1978).

Kerfoot, J. B., *American Pewter.* Reprinted by Bonanza Books, New York (1924).

Kniffen, Fred B., "Folk Housing: Key to Diffusion," *Annals of the Association of American Geographers* 55:549–77 (1965).

Montgomery, Pauline, *Indiana Coverlet Weavers and Their Coverlets.* Hoosier Heritage Press, Indianapolis, Indiana (1974).

Peattie, Donald Culross, *A Natural History of Trees of Eastern and Central North America,* 2nd ed. Houghton, Mifflin Co., New York (1966).

Pollak, Emil and Martyl, *A Guide to American Wooden Planes and Their Makers.* The Astragal Press, Morristown, New Jersey (1983).

Roberts, Kenneth D. *Wooden Planes in Nineteenth Century America.* Ken Roberts Publishing Co., Fitzwilliam, New Hampshire (1975).

Roberts, Warren E., "Turpin Chairs and the Turpin Family: Chairmaking in Southern Indiana," *Midwestern Journal of Language and Folklore* 7:55–106 (1981).

———. "Ananias Hensel and His Furniture: Cabinetmaking in Southern Indiana," *Midwestern Journal of Language and Folklore* 9:67–122 (1983).

———. *Some Notes on Early Indiana Planemakers and Dealers.* The Early American Industries Association, Levittown, New York (in press).

Rooney, John F., Zelinsky, Wilbur, and Louder, Dean R., *This Remarkable Continent: An Atlas of United States and Canadian Society and Cultures.* Published for the Society of the North American Cultural Survey by Texas A & M University Press, College Station, Texas (1982).

Smith, Edward C. Letter. *The Fine Tool Journal* 30:33 (1985).

Walters, Betty Lawson, *Furniture Makers of Indiana, 1793 to 1850.* Indiana Historical Society, Indianapolis, Indiana (1972).

Zelinsky, Wilbur, *The Cultural Geography of the United States.* Prentice-Hall, Inc., Englewood Cliffs, New Jersey (1973).

Overlooked Aspects of Folk Architecture

16

Function in Folk Architecture

This is the first article I wrote that dealt specifically with the subject of function and its relationship to traditional buildings. I have maintained from the first that it is important to understand functional considerations that include topics such as use of the building, the materials available to build it, the tools available to the builder and the ways in which those tools could be used, and the ways in which the building was heated, lighted, and ventilated. Once these factors are considered, one can turn to other possible influences such as aesthetics and diffusion for explanations of building design.

* * *

In the amount of time that is available to us, I can't hope to deal with any subject in any great detail. My announced topic is "Function in Folk Architecture," and I want to preface my remarks on folk architecture with a few generalizations concerning function in folklife studies. I'm afraid that relatively little attention has been paid to functional consideration by folklorists and folklife researchers in this country despite the example given us by anthropologists and others. There are probably a number of reasons why this is so. Collectors in the past, for example, have tended to concentrate on a single genre and have made no attempt to relate their collections to other aspects of the culture. In a large number of instances, too, folklorists have found that the items they are interested in are no longer functioning in a total context. That is, they have encouraged informants to dredge up from their memories items which they no longer use. An informant may, for example, describe a custom which has died out and the collector has no opportunity to observe its relationships with other aspects of the culture. I would suggest, however, that partly as an end in itself, partly as a basis for further research, more attention should be devoted to function in folklife studies.

This article is a revision of a paper originally delivered and later published as conference proceedings in *Folklore Forum,* Bibliographic and Special Series, No. 8 (1971): 10–14.

Historical reconstruction and diffusion studies, which have occupied most researchers in the past, are of great significance, but they need to be supplemented with functional studies. In examining an artifact, for example, one needs to know how old it is and whether it's found over a wide area or restricted to a small one. But one should also know, among other things, how it was used, how it was made, and why it was made of certain materials if one is to understand its true significance. It seems to me, too, that functional considerations are relevant not only to the study of folklife, but these same functional considerations can help in understanding a number of problems in contemporary urban American society.

In keeping with the theme of our conference, "Applied Folklore," I would like to suggest that functional considerations are far more relevant in this area than are historical studies and distributional studies. If we can see how a traditional item, be it of material or non-material culture, actually works in context and how it is related to the culture as a whole, we can probably find practical applications for this knowledge. It seems that some attempts to make practical applications of folklore in the past have been less than successful because many functional considerations were ignored. I think of attempts to introduce crafts programs which have been unsuccessful because the directors of the programs have ignored the ways in which the close relationship between the craftsman and his customer in the past influenced the craftsman's designs, his choice of materials, and his attitude towards his work.

One area of folklife research where there is a great opportunity for functional studies is folk architecture. Indeed, one of the outstanding features of folk architecture which helps to set it apart from fine architecture or academic architecture is its functional quality. Not only does the function of a building dictate its size, its shape, its location, and the number, size, and nature of the openings in it, but the ways in which it is built and the materials used in it are determined by a number of functional considerations such as availability of materials, durability of materials, ease with which materials can be worked, and so on.

On the other hand, in fine architecture, the appearance of the building, the effect the building will have on the beholder often seems to have been of greater importance than the use to which the building would be put. How else would we explain a railroad terminal built to resemble a Roman temple or a Gothic cathedral, a building with vast areas of useless space, and a building which was impossible to keep clean and soon became coated with soot and pigeon droppings. Or consider mansions built in the second half of the nineteenth century with towers sprouting from the roof, and buildings covered with ornate gingerbread trappings which were easily broken and hard to paint and keep clean. Surely the architects in these instances emphasized appearance rather than practical function.

Twentieth-century architects, too, have often ignored practical functional considerations. The National Trust for Historic Preservation recently acquired and moved a house in northern Virginia which had been designed by Frank Lloyd Wright. Wright had emphasized the horizontal elements in the house design to the point of insisting that all the wood screws exposed in the house should have the slot in the head perfectly horizontal. When the house was moved, though, it was found that it was full of termites and large amounts of infested material have had to be replaced with new material. Here's an obvious case where no detail affecting the appearance of the house was too small to escape the architect's notice, but he overlooked an important practical and functional detail—termite-proofing.

To return to the question of studying function in folk architecture, let me further note that there are still extant many examples of folk architecture. Indeed, folk architecture is still being built today. There are many knowledgeable people still living who can tell the student how a building was used and why it was built as it was. As an example, let me mention a personal experience.

For some time, I was aware that many traditional houses had windows and doors on the front and back but none in the gable ends. I was unable to understand the reason why this is so. Finally, though, it struck me that where I had seen dilapidated houses with windows in the gable ends, the wall beneath these windows was usually badly rotted from rain water which had run down the wall and leaked in around the window. On the back and front sides of a house, though, the overhanging eaves keep a great deal of water from running down the walls. I now feel that this is primarily the reason why gable end walls usually do not have windows in them.

Let me deal now with a few concrete examples of different aspects of function in folk architecture. One concerns changes in function and their effects on buildings. Large barns with rectangular floor plans are a common feature of the rural landscape in many parts of this country. Their main function is very apparent. Animals are stabled on the ground floor, and vast quantities of bulk hay are stored in the hayloft above to be fed to the animals during the winter. In many parts of southern Indiana changes in agricultural patterns have taken place which have rendered these barns obsolete, as many farmers have told me. One of the earliest changes was the introduction of hay balers which greatly reduced the bulk of the hay and made the huge hayloft unnecessary.

A complicated series of developments led to abandoning dairy cows and concentrating on beef cattle. Because southern Indiana is hilly, arable fields are often small, of irregular shape, and separated from one another by ridges, patches of trees, and creeks. Hence, large scale mechanized farming with huge tractors and combines is impractical in this area. Farms tend to be small, and the farm owner often works at a fulltime job in town so that he has only evenings and weekends to devote to the farm. Most farm produce cannot be raised in any quantity under such circumstances but beef cattle can be. Farmers tell me that while dairy cattle need shelter in a barn during the winters, beef cattle do not. They are left out in the field year 'round and bales of hay are hauled to them from stacks built on the ground and covered with plastic. I asked one young farmer if beef cattle wouldn't be better off in the barn during particularly cold weather, and it does get cold on occasion in southern Indiana. He said they would be, but said that if cattle were kept in the barn manure would accumulate which he would then have to pay to have hauled off to a dump.

Perhaps no clearer example of changing agricultural patterns and attitudes can be given than this. The big barns, therefore, are not used. They're not well adapted to storing equipment. Therefore, they are not maintained and many are disappearing rapidly. Most of those that remain in southern Indiana must be considered as functionless relics, not long for the scene.

Another aspect of function in architecture concerns the connections between building patterns and ways of life. For some reason I've been recently noticing a clear pattern concerning the large front porches on houses. I've not worked on this pattern in detail, but it seems to me that most houses built in towns, between about 1875 and say 1925, had large front porches—porches large enough so that the family could sit on the front porch in the evening in pleasant weather. Moreover, front porches were often added to older houses during this period. Special kinds of furniture were made during this period, too. A furniture factory in Martinsville, Indiana—Old Hickory Furniture—is about 20 miles north of Bloomington. The factory specialized in front porch furniture. It was common for families to sit on the front porch and visit with neighbors and passersby. Since World War II, however, the pattern has changed. A quick drive through residential districts which have sprung up in recent years will confirm the fact that most modern residences do not have large front porches. Instead, the patio at the rear of the house is more common.

I can only suggest a few reasons for this change. I suspect when the automobile was frequently used that it became less pleasant to sit out on the front porches because of fumes and dust and the impracticality of talking to a person who drove by in an automobile. Another factor would be the prevalence of radios first, and now television sets. I suppose many families would rather sit inside and watch television than sit outside on a front porch. In a broader way, though, it seems to me that contemporary families are more concerned with privacy than with being neighborly. Hence the front porch is no longer built, though of course, many still exist from earlier decades.

One final functional pattern may be discerned in traditional building practices, practices which most modern builders ignore. Examples can be drawn from New Harmony, Indiana, where a religious group with close ties with the Pittsburgh area founded a town in the early nineteenth century. The houses which they built there are a combination, it seems to me, of German and Anglo-American folk architecture in folk building pattern and folk building techniques. Fortunately for the student of function in folk architecture, a writer has lived in New Harmony for many years. His name is Don Blair, and while he doesn't consider himself a student of folk architecture, he nonetheless is a close student of the buildings in New Harmony, and since he lived there over a period of many years, he's been able to observe these houses over a long period of time. (See Don Blair, *Harmonist Construction,* Indiana Historical Society, 1962.) He's been able to see some of them torn down and re-erected, to see some of them moved, and so on, and as a result has gained a number of insights into the practical reasons why the houses were designed and built in the way they were.

He mentions some of the advantages of these houses. He says: "Here were built livable houses, economical to maintain, well insulated, centrally heated, functional and pleasing in design, and fire resistant, weather and storm-proof, termite-proof, and with many other advantages."

I'll cite only three of the points which he discussed. The frames of these houses were so well designed that, he says, it has been possible for some of the houses to have been moved as many as four times without any damage to them. These moves have been made without benefit of modern house-moving equipment. In some instances the houses were moved with rough, uneven rollers shaped from logs. As a rule, timbers were laid on the ground to make a rude track and to prevent the rollers from settling into the ground. The power for pulling the house forward would be supplied by a stump puller which would be anchored to trees along the route the house was taken. A house's ability to withstand such treatment very eloquently attests to the effectiveness of its planning and subsequent execution, he says.

A second point concerns the plastering of the houses. Blair says many of the houses have never been replastered, and the walls are in good condition and the bond between the bricks and the plaster is still solid. Because of their choice of materials and their use of certain sound principles of design, even the large areas of the living room ceilings are still smooth and show no tendency toward cracking.

The final point which I shall mention concerns the exterior of the houses. Blair says: "Visitors to Harmony reported that many of the frame houses were not painted, and the silver-gray of the unpainted wood was outstanding." One of the houses that was razed in 1945, that is 130 years after it was built, had never had a coat of paint. The weather-boarding and the exposed members of the frame were in such good condition that they were used in rebuilding other houses. The houses were designed so that the rain ran off before the boards were water-soaked and damaged.

Well, it seems to me in this area that contemporary builders and contemporary architects could learn a great deal from studying and observing the functional, practical features of folk architecture. Unfortunately, as many of us who have lived in houses that have been built in recent times can testify, the builders have ignored many of these old traditional practices, and as a result the houses do not last anywhere near as well as those built in New Harmony lasted, and can't be expected to last anywhere near that long.

17

Folk Architecture in Context:
The Folk Museum

My overriding concern for many years was to establish a folk museum at Indiana University and I had moved a number of buildings to the proposed site. This dream has never been realized, but it affected my approach to the study and understanding of buildings as demonstrated in this essay.

*　　*　　*

Since, I gather, I am presenting the views of the folklorist in this symposium on "The Reconstruction of Pioneer America," I feel that I should begin with a statement concerning current attitudes toward folklore among American folklorists. Although it somewhat oversimplifies the situation, I feel safe in saying that there are basically two strains of folklorists in the United States today. One strain descends directly from British folklorists of the late nineteenth and early twentieth centuries. Folklorists of this persuasion maintain that folklore is "oral literature," that is, mainly folksongs and folktales. Thanks to the British Empire of the nineteenth century, the British folklorists of that period likewise insisted that oral literature wherever found in the world was part of their area of interest. Their contemporary American followers at least pay lip service to this idea and insist that the American folklorist can profitably study myths and legends collected in remote parts of the world.[1]

A second strain of American folklorists is most directly derived from Scandinavian and German folklife research. They insist that all aspects of a culture, material as well as spiritual, should be studied together, but that the culture studied should be close at hand, leaving remote peoples to the anthropologist. Specifically, many folklorists of this persuasion feel that they

This article is a revision of a paper originally delivered at a meeting of the Pioneer America Society, and later published in the *Proceedings of the Pioneer America Society* 1 (1972): 34–50.

should concentrate on the traditional culture of western Europe and its New World derivatives, both its past history and its current status.[2]

In some respects, therefore, the second strain of folklorists is broader in its approach than the first, but in other respects it is more restricted. I number myself as one of this second group, but I must caution you that the group is relatively small and certainly in the minority among American folklorists as a whole. Hence the views I present are not those of all American folklorists by any means. I might mention that there is a growing tendency in the United States to use the term "folklore and folklife" to refer to holistic studies of traditional culture, but I prefer to call myself a folklorist because the phrase "folklore and folklife researcher" hardly rolls trippingly from the tongue.

Folk Architecture

When one examines the research which has been done in the United States which most closely approximates the work done in northern European countries by folklife students, he sees at once that folk architecture has been the most frequent subject. Scholars from several academic areas have made significant contributions. Geographers, led by Fred B. Kniffen of Louisiana State University, have probably made the largest number of contributions; but folklorists such as Henry Glassie of Indiana University, and architectural historians such as John Fichten have also been active. If one may judge by past issues of the professional journal *Pioneer America,* contributors have been much devoted to this subject. Indeed, the Pioneer America Society's goal of extensive recordings of early buildings has dedicated its membership to the most ambitious project in American folk architectural study that I know of. Published research on folk architecture mostly falls under one of three categories. The first, and by far the most common, may be labeled "descriptive and historic," for most publications describe specific structures in greater or lesser detail and record whatever historic data are available about them. A second category is "typological" wherein an attempt is made to establish the existence of a specific folk architectural type and to describe its characteristic features. The third category is "distributional" which sketches the geographical diffusion of architectural types and patterns or seeks the European sources of some building type or construction feature. Needless to say, any given study may fall under all three categories because the writer deals with a variety of subjects.

There are two closely related topics which have been virtually ignored by writers on folk architecture in this country. These are function in folk architecture and folk architecture in context. On the subject of function in folk architecture I have elsewhere made some preliminary observations,[3] but in dealing with the context of folk architecture, function can hardly be ignored. I shall, however, for the purposes of this paper consider function as simply one aspect of the entire cultural context of folk architecture.

Cultural Context

The importance of studying folk architecture in its cultural context can hardly be overemphasized. Descriptive, typological, and diffusion studies are of basic importance, it is true, but they barely scratch the surface of the subject. It seems to me that, to use Pope's phrase in a way he didn't intend it to be used, "The proper study of mankind is man," and that the proper study of the folk architecture specialist should likewise be man. He should view architecture as an index to human culture or a tool to aid in understanding human culture. In addition to describing buildings and plotting their diffusion, the student should be raising and investigating such questions as: "Why were these buildings built as they were?" "What do they tell us about people and the way in which they lived?"

Because the context of folk architecture is folklife in its entirety, it would seem logical that students of folklife can make a real contribution to the study of folk architecture. A famous American folk architecture scholar once stated that folk architecture is "so distinctly geographical in character, this would seem to be an area of enquiry that we [geographers] must keep as our own."[4] I will not make such a claim for folklife researchers, but I would beseech geographers and architectural historians to broaden their approach to folk architecture. Talk to the people who live in the buildings you study, for example, and seek their views on why the buildings were built the way they were, how they were used over the years, and how they have been maintained over the years. Examine agricultural patterns and food patterns to see their connections with architecture and do not overlook customs. I might even suggest that attitudes toward nakedness and sex relations have to be considered if we are to understand how an entire family could live in a house consisting of one room and a sleeping loft.

Not only is the holistic approach important for future research, but also it should be used in re-evaluating past work which has been done. To cite only one example, probably the most extensive study of diffusion in American folk architecture deals with methods of corner notching in log or horizontal timber construction.[5] Three main types of corner notching, namely, V-notching, dovetail notching, and saddle notching, are emphasized and their distribution over most of the eastern half of the United States is mapped. Conclusions are drawn concerning the coincidences between migration patterns and the diffusion of corner notching. Yet no attention is given to the fact that corner notching is only part of a much bigger question concerning the ways in which logs are handled by the craftsmen who built the structures.

In the amount of space available to me here, I can only touch on a few aspects of the larger question. V-notching and dovetail notching are closely associated with hewn logs, that is, logs whose inner and outer faces are hewn away so that the wall, when it is built, is only six or seven inches thick. Hewing flourishes in areas where hardwood logs are used. Saddle notching, on the other hand, is used mainly with logs that are left in the round, and round logs are found mainly where softwood logs are used. Hence a map of the distribution of corner notching is not of much use unless it takes into account the question of where hardwood and softwood forests predominate.

Had the authors considered another point that can readily be observed about log buildings they might have come to other general conclusions. Had they noticed that log buildings sit up on stone pillars at the corners so air can circulate freely under them in damp, warm areas of the country where termites flourish, while in colder, drier areas the buildings are closer to the ground with foundations completely around the outside perimeter, they might have concluded that the craftsmen who built log structures were aware of certain basic facts about construction and built the best and most durable buildings they could. Migration patterns are not enough to explain every feature of folk architecture. The knowledge and skills of the craftsmen who build and the tools and materials available to them are some of the factors that also must be taken into account.

In order to give some insight into both the possibilities and the complexities of the holistic approach to problems in folk architecture, I would like to deal at some length with a comparison between the types of fireplaces and chimneys common in American and Norwegian log buildings. I would like to emphasize at the outset that I fully realize that I cannot cover all the ramifications of the subject for I know that I have overlooked many and, at the same time, I cannot document many of my assertions, for I base them upon personal observation which may well be faulty. Nonetheless, I hope that the attempt may prove useful as an example at least.

Fireplaces and Chimneys

In most of the southeastern United States, log houses commonly have fireplaces and chimneys on the outside gable-end wall or walls of the house. If it is a one-room house, as many are, the chimney will be on one of the gable-end walls while if it is a house with two rooms, there will usually be two chimneys on the two outside gable-end walls. I cannot give figures for other states, but for southern Indiana at least 95 percent of the log houses I have seen conform to this pattern. These piles of masonry are usually built almost completely outside the house. There is an opening made in logs of the wall, and the masonry only extends into the house far enough so that the face of the fireplace is flush with the inside surface of the wall. The chimney rises completely outside the wall with several inches of space between the inner surface of the chimney and the outer surface of the wall. There are undoubtedly many reasons why this is so and it would be rash to say which of the reasons is most important.

The folklorist would probably first consider the power of tradition, for it is true that this pattern developed in England and was brought to this country with the immigrants, so that this was one of the patterns with which the builders were familiar. But I feel strongly that tradition in folk architecture does not operate in a haphazard way. Tradition perpetuates functional and practical patterns and practices which take into account such factors as the availability of building materials, the special qualities of these materials, the ease of maintaining a structure and its durability, the tools available for shaping and handling the materials, and the like. Hence I feel it necessary to look a bit beyond the tradition to see if we can isolate some factors which account for the reasons why this particular pattern developed in the first place and why it was perpetuated.

In the case of the log buildings I have been able to observe, I can offer the following suggestions. The pile of masonry making up the chimney and fireplace is, of course, tremendously heavy. Hence it may settle into the ground more than the house. Should this happen, it would have very little affect upon the house for it would be necessary only to add a little more clay around the fireplace opening. It is also true that the likelihood of the house catching fire if mortar should fall out from between the stones or bricks of the chimney is materially lessened if the chimney is several inches from the house. With other types of chimneys there is a problem with roof construction where the chimney passes through the roof. Prior to the time when sheet metal became generally available, it was hard to make a completely water-tight seal where the chimney passed through the roof. The chimney type I have been describing, however, simplifies roof construction, for the chimney does not pass through the roof at all. In every type of fireplace, of course, the masonry absorbs a great deal of heat from the fire and radiates it in all directions. In the houses I have been describing, almost all the cooking was done year round in the fireplace. Apple butter may have been cooked and laundry boiled outside over an open fire, to keep large quantities of steam outside the house, but most of the cooking was done day-to-day at the inside fireplace. In warm weather, much of the heat from the cooking fire was radiated to the outside by the masonry outside the house. In cold weather, of course, the loss of heat was a distinct disadvantage, but one cannot have it both ways. I assume, by the way, that the prevalence of chimneys in the center of the house in the northern United States may be accounted for in part by the necessity of using every bit of available heat in cold weather.

In Norway a very common fireplace in log buildings is built in the corner of a room (fig. 17.1). In comparison to the American fireplaces described above, the Norwegian fireplace has a much larger opening into the room, and the fire, one might say, is exposed on two sides instead of one. We have here, then, quite a different tradition of fireplace and chimney construction. A fireplace of this type radiates more heat into the room, a decided advantage in the colder Norwegian winters. Since the chimney must pass through a sloping surface of the roof, the Norwegian builder was faced with quite a different problem in roof construction than the American builder. The Norwegian builder, however, generally covered his roof with a different material than the American builder. The casual observer looks at old Norwegian log buildings in the countryside or in folk museums and admires the picturesque layer of sod on the roof with green grass and perhaps flowers in the summer. This layer of sod, however, covers a layer of birch bark and the sod's main function is to hold the birch bark in place, though it also provides good insulation. It was possible for the Norwegian builder to bring the layer of birch bark on the roof up around the chimney in much the same way that a modern builder uses metal flashing. With the birch bark and sod roof, therefore, it was possible to construct a roof which did not leak around a chimney which passed through a lower corner of the roof. The American builder, using wooden shingles, preferred to keep his chimney completely outside his roof or to pass it through the peak of the roof so that rain water would not run down the roof and get caught in the trough between the slope of the roof and the chimney.

Fireplaces and Cooking

There are certainly other factors, though, to consider about a fireplace besides its effectiveness in heating and its relationship to roof construction, for a fireplace was used for cooking as well as for heating. In examining log houses in southern Indiana I have found that the vast majority have only a simple fireplace of the familiar type used for both cooking and heating. I have never seen a fireplace with a bake oven built to one side in a log house, and separate summer kitchens with their own fireplaces are very rare and, when found, occur only with large, elaborate houses. Hence I am left with the conclusion that most Indiana housewives in earlier times did almost all

Figure 17.1.   Detail of Log House from Eastern Norway in the
Norwegian Forestry Museum, Elverum
The position of the chimney indicates that the fire-
place is in the corner of one of the rooms. Note the
sod and birchbark roof.
(Photography by author)

their cooking at an open fireplace. Most fireplaces probably had a crane device built into them so that a pot could be suspended over the fire, though the cranes have been removed from most fireplaces in modern times. Some cooking might have been done outside over an open fire, but day-in and day-out, most meals were probably prepared at the fireplace. When one considers the types of cooking it is possible to carry out at an open fireplace with the simple utensils available at an earlier day, it is clear that stewed and fried foods must have been common, whereas baked foods must have been uncommon. The only means of baking must have been to use a so-called "Dutch oven," a heavy utensil with a lid with a rim around it. This utensil could be placed in the coals with coals heaped on the lid. Fried pork with occasional fried chicken must have been the main meat eaten, and the popularity of stewed beans, hominy, and other vegetables is well attested.

Some form of bread, however, has always been a staple in the diet, but the loaf of wheat bread so familiar today could not have been baked with the fireplace and utensils I have described. Cornbread and biscuits, probably prepared fresh each day or for each meal, must have been the common bread types. A further discussion of common foods would lead us into such topics as the types of grain grown, the fact that hogs can forage for themselves in forests of oak, beech, and other nut-bearing trees while cattle prefer cleared pasture lands, and the smokehouse as a distinct architectural type, but perhaps this is enough to give some indication of the connections between the type of fireplace used and other aspects of the culture.

With the Scandinavian corner fireplace, boiling and frying would likewise be possible, but facilities for baking are just as limited as with the southern American fireplace. A common feature of Scandinavian farms, however, was a separate bakehouse, and here an entirely different type of bread, flatbread, was commonly prepared in earlier times. The bakehouse featured a large, flat stone under which a fire was made and large, thin loaves of bread, something like two feet in diameter and a quarter of an inch thick, were baked on the heated stone. Large quantities of this bread were baked a few times a year and stored in a separate storehouse for long periods of time. This type of bread could be made with the grains such as oats and rye which could grow in the Norwegian climate. Wheat, an essential ingredient of raised bread types, did not flourish in most parts of Norway. Moreover, the common Norwegian type of watermill needed a substantial flow of water and could not operate in the coldest parts of the winter or the drier summer months, hence the need for a type of bread which could be baked when freshly ground flour was available and could be stored for long periods.

A comparison of two types of fireplaces, then, leads inevitably into other considerations, for one architectural feature can hardly be isolated from its cultural context.

So far I have restricted myself to comments on the study of folk architecture in context and have said little about the reconstruction of pioneer America. I feel strongly that preservation projects of all types must be carried on if we are to begin to understand the past. It is surely valuable, for instance, to be able to see a building that has been lived in for a long period of time, to see how a succession of owners has modified it and adapted it to their own needs and desires, and to be able to perceive changes in the ways of life of people over a long period of time, including changes in building techniques and crafts. Certainly it would be unwise to feel that preservation should always entail restoration of a structure to its supposed original condition. In order to understand the past, however, there is a definite need for some restoration projects that present authentic examples of folk architecture in context. The ideal way to fill this need is the folk museum.

Folk Museums

The folk museum movement started in Scandinavia in the late nineteenth century when Skansen, outside Stockholm, opened in 1891, thanks to the labors of Artur Hazelius. Folk museums have since been founded in other European countries, but the United States has lagged far behind in this respect. A folk museum tries to display all aspects of old traditional ways of life. In a national or regional museum, for example, typical old buildings of various kinds are moved to one area and reconstructed, as far as possible, in their natural context. They are furnished with appropriate articles and, as far as possible, the activities associated with the given time and place are carried on. Home crafts, for example, like spinning and weaving, are done and small fields are cultivated near the buildings.

In the national or regional museum, buildings of various kinds and of various periods are brought in from the different parts of the country or region. In the museum as a whole there will be farmhouses and other farm buildings, village dwellings, craft shops, schools, churches, water and wind mills, and many kinds of construction will be represented, such as log, frame, brick, and stone. Where appropriate, a determined effort is made to screen buildings from one another by utilizing the terrain and landscaping with trees and shrubs.

The crucial question in deciding what building, what artifact, and what activity will go into a folk museum is: "What is typical for the time and place?" If a folk museum is to represent the way in which large numbers of people lived over a long period of time, it has to represent the typical rather than the atypical or the unusual. It is in this respect that the folk museum would seem to differ from other kinds of museums. An art museum, for example, stresses the finest rather than the typical, be it oil paintings or eighteenth-century furniture. An art museum is forced to display most items divorced from their context. Historical museums, especially house museums, can sometimes resemble folk museums, but in a historical museum the guiding principle must always be historical association. A house is chosen for display because a certain famous person lived there, for instance, and the question as to whether or not the house is typical for the time and place can hardly be considered.

In most European countries, especially Scandinavia, the national folk museums are intimately connected with education and research. The faculty in folklife research at a nearby university is usually part of the museum staff and university classes often meet at the museum. The research of the faculty and students is used to guide the museum in its program of acquisition and display. It is the task of research to determine what was typical of the old traditional way of life and to study the interrelations between the various aspects of the old society. Research guides the museum in every aspect of its operation and, at the same time, the museum sponsors and inspires the research of faculty and students alike. Hence the relationship is mutually beneficial. It is probably safe to assert that a folk museum is only as good as the research that supports it, for if the museum misinterprets or misrepresents what it has or overlooks important aspects of the old ways of life, its educational function, its most important one, must suffer.

It would seem clear that in the reconstruction of pioneer America, folk museums could play a very important role, for they could present different aspects of earlier ways of life in context. If special folk cultural regions could be identified in the United States, regional folk museums could be developed on the Scandinavian pattern if, of course, funds were available. A fine folk museum for the Pennsylvania Dutch region, for example, would be a great cultural and educational asset for the entire nation.

Notes

1. The July-September 1972 issue of the *Journal of American Folklore* (Vol. 85, no. 337) contains six articles of interest. One by William B. Gibbon, "Asiatic Parallels in North American Star Lore: Milky Way, Pleiades, Orion," deals mainly with the North American Indians. Another article by Harold Scheub, "Fixed and Nonfixed Symbols in Xhosa and Zula Oral Narrative Traditions," stresses this theme of remoteness.

2. See Don Yoder, "The Folklife Studies Movement," *Pennsylvania Folklife* 13, no. 3 (July 1963): 43–56, for a clear statement of this approach.

3. See "Function in Folk Architecture," *Folklore Forum,* Bibliographic and Special Studies, No. 8 (1971): 10–14. The papers reproduced in this issue were presented and discussed at a symposium on applied folklore held at Pittsburgh, Pennsylvania, May 22–23, 1971.

4. Fred Kniffen, "Folk Housing: Key to Diffusion," Association of American Geographers *Annals* 55 (1965): 552.

5. Fred Kniffen and Henry Glassie, "Building in Wood in the Eastern United States: A Time-Place Perspective," *The Geographical Review* 56 (1966): 58–65.

18

The Whitaker-Waggoner Log House
from Morgan County, Indiana

This, my only detailed description of a single log house, was presented at a conference held in Logan, Utah, in 1968. It was not printed, however, until 1976. Here again I have used the functional approach in trying to explain such features as the use of exterior siding over the log walls. I believe I was one of the first to defy the accepted wisdom of historians and architectural historians that log houses were never sided when originally built but that siding was only applied much later.

*   *   *

From early in the nineteenth century until the fall of 1966, a large six-room log house stood west of the town of Paragon in Morgan County, Indiana. While it is true that its very size alone would keep it from being termed a "typical" southern Indiana log house, still it shares a number of features with many other log houses in this area. This fact, plus the fact that it was torn down to be reassembled as one of the buildings in the projected Indiana University Outdoor Museum of Folk Life, warrants a detailed description of the house. The study of log buildings in the United States must be said to be very little developed. We have available at the present time a rather small amount of information for comparative purposes. What is needed is a series of articles and monographs describing log buildings in detail. This article may be viewed as a contribution toward this goal. It will be essentially descriptive rather than comparative; that is, it will describe the building but will not make many comparisons between it and other buildings either in Indiana or elsewhere in the United States. Comparisons are best made in the context of a broad survey, and that survey will be made at another time.

This article originally appeared in *American Folklife,* edited by Don Yoder (Austin: University of Texas Press, 1976), pp. 185–207. Reprinted by permission of the publisher.

According to local tradition and a family history in the possession of a descendant,[1] the house was built in the 1820s by Grafton B. Whitaker. He was born in Kentucky in 1799 and moved to Indiana as a young man. He was a prominent person in the area, a trustee of the Samaria Baptist Church, organized in 1829, and a school trustee. He was also an officer of the Forty-fifth Regiment of the State Militia of Indiana, a captain in 1828 and a colonel in 1833. The house and land passed through a number of hands in the nineteenth and twentieth centuries. The present owner, Roscoe Waggoner, bought the farm in the 1930s. He repaired the log house, which had been vacant for some time, and lived in it until the 1950s when he built a modern frame house nearby, using some materials from the log house. The log house stood vacant for several years until it was purchased by Dr. and Mrs. James Farr of Bloomington, Indiana, who, in turn, donated it to the Indiana University Foundation. It was disassembled in the fall of 1966 and hauled to Bloomington, where it is, as of this writing, stored on a tract of land adjoining the university campus, the proposed site of the Outdoor Museum.

The house consists of two parts, which probably were constructed at different times since the logs in the two sections have corner notches of two different kinds (fig. 18.1). The main and, presumably, earliest part of the house has V-notched logs. It is thirty-six feet in width and eighteen feet six inches in depth, with two rooms of approximately equal size on the ground floor and two matching rooms above; a log partition separates the rooms (fig. 18.2). While this part of the house is not a full two stories in height, neither can it be called a one-and-a-half-story structure. The walls on the second floor are about four feet in height along the eaves; that is, above the floor level are two and a half logs plus the plate before the roof starts. There is no hallway of any kind in the house and, as is common with log, frame, and masonry houses that do not have central hallways, there are two front doors, one for each room.[2] The staircase, which is enclosed, rises directly from one room and has a storage cupboard underneath it. Each downstairs room has a fireplace so that there is a stone chimney stack at each end of the house.

The rear wing, or ell, is part frame and part log, using single dovetail corner notches. It has nearly the same dimensions as the main part of the house, thirty-six by seventeen feet, but is only one story in height (fig. 18.3). The log portion of the wing is placed farthest from the main part of the house and is connected to it by the frame portion, since it is difficult to join two separate log structures directly to each other. Large sills and plates, however, run the entire thirty-six feet. A central chimney in the wing has two fireplaces, one opening into each room.

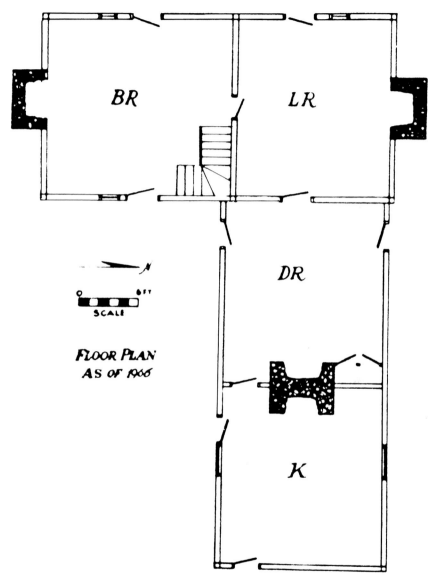

BR

LR

DR

K

N

6 FT

SCALE

FLOOR PLAN
AS OF 1966

Figure 18.1.   Floor Plan of the Whitaker-Waggoner Log House as of 1966
(Drawings in this chapter courtesy of Thomas Kirkman)

Figure 18.2. Whitaker-Waggoner Log House, Front View

Figure 18.3.   Whitaker-Waggoner Log House, Rear Wing, or Ell
Dimensions: 36 by 17 feet.

A description of the construction features of the house can logically begin with a discussion of the foundation and the masonry work. In general it may be said that the masonry work is of very high quality. Limestone in the form of naturally occurring field stone was used throughout. I might mention that the house stood in an area where much stone was available, for the surrounding countryside is honeycombed with caves and sinkholes. Porter's Cave, for example, is a large and well-known cave not more than one-half mile from the house. The clay that was used for mortar is particularly noteworthy, for it clung with remarkable tenacity to the stones when the chimneys were taken down; indeed, it seemed that it was harder to remove from the stones than conventional modern mortar would be. The clay was probably found in the vicinity of the house. Only above the roof line, where rain had gradually washed out the clay mortar, had it been found necessary to replace or patch the clay mortar with modern mortar.

The foundations of the house and the chimney stacks went only a short distance below the level of the ground, but they had supported the great weight over the years so that the house and chimneys showed no signs of sagging or uneven settling. At the time the house was disassembled, the stone foundation went around the entire outside perimeter, and I am inclined to believe that this perimeter foundation was original in that large stones at the corners were tied in with the rest of the foundation (fig. 18.4). Much more common in southern Indiana is the corner type of foundation, wherein a building is supported only at the four corners. When this corner type of foundation is used, however, people often fill in with stones between the corners at a later date to keep out small animals from underneath the house. Hence, it is difficult to determine whether the original foundation of a log building was of the perimeter or the corner type. This question, however, is of considerable importance, for the type of foundation that is used has a decisive influence on the general structure of a log building.

Because of the lack of detailed information on log buildings in the United States, it is impossible to speak with any degree of certainty, but I would like to suggest—and this suggestion of course must be tested in the light of further evidence—that the perimeter foundation represents a general northern building type while the corner foundation represents a southern type. In the southern United States, dampness and warmth dictated a corner foundation, for a free circulation of air under the house was necessary to prevent decay, while the general mildness of the winters did not cause too much discomfort from cold floors. In the northern parts of the country, however, a perimeter foundation was necessary in order to keep the house comfortable during the cold winters. Indeed, it was customary in New England, at least, to "bank" houses in the fall by piling

Figure 18.4. Whitaker-Waggoner Log House, Sketch of Foundation
at Southwest Corner
Sill, floor joist, and cross section of front wall. Note
that the stones in the foundation indicate that the entire perimeter was laid at one time. The large stone in
the second course at the corner is tied to the rest of
the wall. The large sill projects inward beyond the log
wall so that the ends of the floor joists can rest on it
rather than on the foundation.

leaves, straw, and the like around the foundations to prevent cold air from blowing under the house. At the same time, the climate was dry enough, generally speaking, so that decay was no great problem. When a true corner foundation is used, the house must be built in such a way that the weight of the structure is transferred to the corners. Huge sills, for example, are needed to support the weight of the floor without sagging and to carry this weight to the corners. When the perimeter foundation is used, however, the sills need not be so large, for the weight of the floor is carried by the foundation, which supports the sills along their entire length. Moreover, when the corner foundation is used, huge plates are required to support the weight of the roof and transfer this weight to the corners. The majority of the nearly three hundred log houses that I have examined in southern Indiana have this combination of corner foundation, large sills, and large plates. The Whitaker-Waggoner house, however, is unusual in that it has a perimeter foundation, large sills, and large plates. This combination points once more to the fact that southern Indiana is a transitional area with both northern and southern traits.

The shape and general construction of the chimneys and fireplaces can be seen in figures 18.5 and 18.6. The fireplaces had been boarded up in recent years, and when the kitchen fireplace was opened the original iron crane was found to be still in place. The interstices between the logs in the house were filled with flat stones plastered over with clay, unlike most log buildings, which use pieces of wood covered with clay "chinking."

On the stone foundation are laid, first, two large sills, hewn on all four sides, ten by fourteen inches and thirty-six feet in length. These sills are about eight inches wider than the rest of the wall so that the floor joists can sit on the part that projects inside the walls (see fig. 18.4). The floor joists are small logs, roughly eight to ten inches in diameter, with the tops and two adjacent surfaces hewn flat (fig. 18.7). The ends of the joists are likewise hewn so they can rest evenly on the sills. The flooring on the ground floor of the main house is one-and-a-quarter-inch-thick tongue-and-grooved ash, while the second floor has poplar flooring of similar dimensions, also tongue and grooved.

The walls of the house are, of course, made of what are conventionally called "logs," but the inadequacy of this term is at once apparent when we examine the actual timbers. They are logs that have been hewn on two sides to a reasonably uniform thickness of about six inches. The upper and lower surfaces have, however, been left with the natural curvature of the log; indeed, in most instances the bark has not even been removed from these surfaces. As a result, there are interstices between the timbers, or logs, varying from a fraction of an inch to as much as six inches. Larger interstices

Figure 18.5. Fireplace in Front Section of the House

Figure 18.6.   Exterior View of Chimney Construction

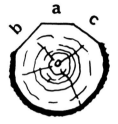

Figure 18.7.
Cross Section of a Typical Floor Joist on the Ground Floors
Hewn surfaces shown at *a, b,* and *c;* bark is on the remainder
of the log.

are rare because straight logs were chosen and, as previously noted, the
interstices are filled with flat stones covered with clay.

The logs naturally vary in width but average about sixteen inches. The
majority of them are beech, but other woods are found as well. One large
log in the rear wing, for example, is of mulberry wood. The corners on the
main part of the house employ so-called V-notches. Where the log partition
joins the outside walls the joists are halved together (fig. 18.8). The logs in
the walls are, therefore, only about eighteen feet in length; it is the
thirty-six-foot-long sills and plates that tie the whole structure together. The
logs rise only as high as the eaves; the gable ends between the top logs and
the rafters are filled in with hewn studs. The joists that carry the second
floor in the main part of the house sit in notches cut completely through the
logs in the wall. These joists were sawed, probably at a water-driven sawmill
that is known to have once existed in the locality. The fact that the joists are
carefully planed and the bottom corners are decorated with a bead molding
indicates that they were exposed to view from the ground floor when the
house was built.

Where doors and windows occur, the logs have been sawed out. An oak
timber approximately two by six inches in cross section, which has been
rived from a log, is placed flush against the sawed ends of the logs, and
oaken pins one inch in diameter have been driven through the timber and
into the ends of the logs. Over these riven timbers, of course, the more
finished door and window casings have been fitted.

Figure 18.8.   Detail of Log Construction
            This shows the junction of the log partition
            with the outside walls.

The plates are timbers hewn on all four sides about ten by fourteen inches by thirty-six feet in length. On them the rafters rest, and they and the plates overhang the wall by about eight inches. The plate's function is, as explained previously, to carry the weight of the roof to the corners of the house where the logs in the wall rest solidly on each other. The top log on the gable end, which supports the plates, extends out to each side so that the plate can overhang the wall. A small four-square hewn timber, which crosses the gable end of the house, sits on top of the plate. An oaken pin, or trunnel (treenail), two inches in diameter and a foot in length passes through this timber, through the plate, and into the log beneath it (fig. 18.9). At the point where the log partition passes through the house, another timber spans from one plate to the other and is dovetailed into the top side of the plate and pinned. This transverse timber ensures that the outward thrust of the roof cannot bow the plate out of line.

The rafters are hewn and approximately three by five inches in cross section. There is no ridgepole; instead, the rafters are notched and pinned together at the peak. Every other pair of rafters has a tie brace passing between them, forming the shape of a squatty letter *A*. These tie braces are notched and pinned to the rafters. The roof decking is of wide, rough-sawed boards whose edges have not been trued in any way; they show the contour of the log from which they were sawed. Sawed red cedar shingles covered the roof in 1966. They undoubtedly replaced earlier shingles that had been rived from native lumber.

In 1966 the outside of the walls was covered with clapboards of yellow poplar (*Liriodendron tulipifera*). It seems to be taken more or less for granted in the United States that, when a log building is covered with siding of any sort, the siding is not original but a late, indeed fairly recent, addition. Hence, whenever a log building is restored, rebuilt, or moved and re-erected either by an individual, historical groups, or museums, it is stripped of its siding so that the logs and the clay "chinking" are exposed to the weather (the clay is usually replaced with modern mortar). Moreover, illustrations in books and articles usually depict hewn-log structures without any siding. The serious student of folk architecture, however, can hardly afford to take for granted notions of this sort. I feel, therefore, that I must dwell at some length on this point.

When the Whitaker-Waggoner house was disassembled, it became clear that the clapboard siding had been put on at the time the house was built because, in the first place, on the gable ends the clapboards extended across behind the chimney and could only have been put in place before the chimney was built and, in the second place, wherever the siding was still in good condition, the surfaces of the logs underneath the siding showed no signs of ever having been exposed to the weather.

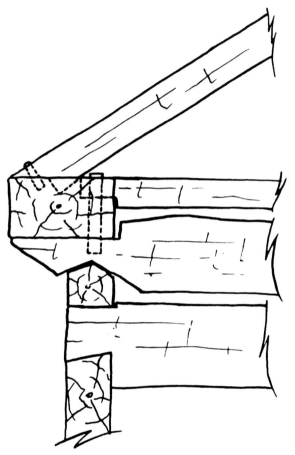

Figure 18.9.   Sketch of Southeast Corner of Rear Wing Showing Logs in Wall
This diagram shows log holding up plate; plate;
square timber dovetailed into top of plate;
trunnel driven through square timber, plate,
and log beneath; rafter notched into plate; and
trunnel driven through rafter into plate.

The Whitaker-Waggoner house is not an isolated example. Under normal circumstances, however, only when a log house is being disassembled is it possible to investigate this point. I have been able to examine several other hewn-log houses that were being torn down; after the siding was removed, it was clear that the outer surfaces of the logs had never been exposed to the weather. I have even found one house near Trevlac, Indiana, that, underneath the siding, had no chinking in the walls—clear proof that the siding had been applied at the time the house was built. I have also seen a number of hewn-log houses standing on their original sites that had no siding. Investigation has nearly always revealed, however, that siding had been on the buildings at one time. On the basis of the evidence now at hand, I am persuaded that, in nineteenth-century southern Indiana when a substantial hewn-log house was built as a permanent home, it was customary practice to cover the outside with siding of some sort, usually clapboards. This generalization, of course, is not meant to apply to other types of log buildings, especially those built with round logs.

Why were hewn-log houses covered with siding? Was it only for the sake of appearance, to make a log house look like a frame house? Actually, studying folk architecture has led me to conclude that it is severely practical and functional and very little given to ornamentation purely for the sake of ornamentation. The fact of the matter is that the exterior surfaces of hewn-log buildings are subject to severe deterioration when exposed to the weather. As a case in point, I can cite hewn-log houses at Spring Mill State Park, Indiana. In this instance old log houses were moved into the park in the 1930s and reassembled in an artificial "pioneer village" environment. Although the houses had been covered with siding previously and were in good condition after the passage of some one hundred years, after standing in the park without siding for about thirty years, the outside surfaces of the hewn logs have in many cases deteriorated very seriously to the point where many of the logs have been replaced (fig.18.10).

Leaving hewn logs exposed to the weather creates at least three major problems. First of all, the logs develop cracks of various sizes as they season and water gets into these cracks and causes decay. There was in the past no practical way either to prevent these cracks or to fill them. If the cracks are filled with mortar, it soon works loose as detailed below. Modern wood preservative, of course, can be used with success, but they were not available in the past. In the second place, the "chinking" can never remain watertight for very long. No matter how well seasoned it may be, wood will continue to expand and contract with changes in humidity. When the weather is dry, wood contracts, and when it is damp, wood expands. This expansion and contraction occurs primarily across the grain; in the direction of the grain it is very slight. The amount of expansion and

Figure 18.10. Deterioration of Outside Surfaces of Hewn Logs without Siding

contraction, of course, depends upon many factors: the type of wood, the amount of humidity, and so on. A log two feet in width (and logs of this size are not uncommon in southern Indiana log houses) would expand and contract at least a quarter of an inch over the course of a year with extremes of humidity. What effect this "working" of the wood has upon the joint between the log and the chinking should be apparent at once. The space between the curved surfaces of the log and the clay or mortar makes a natural channel for water to enter and cause decay, and this situation is aggravated when the bark is left on the upper and lower surfaces of the log, as is often the case (see fig. 18.11). The third problem concerns the door and window openings. It is very difficult to make a watertight seal where the casings of doors and windows meet the logs because of the uneven surfaces of the logs and the chinking. Water can get behind the trim and cause rotting. In abandoned log houses that have fallen into disrepair, one nearly always finds that the logs under windows and the sills under doors have rotted badly. It seems to me, by the way, that this is one reason why log buildings have few windows on the gable ends but usually have the doors and windows on the front and back: the overhanging eaves on the front and back of the house help to keep rain water from running down the walls and getting behind the door and window trim. When siding is used on a house and kept in good repair, on the other hand, it is possible to make a watertight seal around the doors and windows. Frame houses that are covered with clapboards, for example, have stood for centuries without any rotting of the frame under the doors and window.

To return now to the details of the Whitaker-Waggoner house, the main structural features have been dealt with, but some remarks on other features are in order. When the house was built, two separate small porches, each six feet ten inches in width and extending six feet seven inches out from the house, covered the front doors. The outlines of these porches were still clearly visible on the siding of the house, and probing in the ground established their foundations. The plate at the front of the house was boxed in, and dentil moldings made of pieces of lath were nailed on to create an interesting neoclassic detail.

The most noteworthy features of the interior are the doors, the mantelpieces, and the built-in cupboards. It is obvious that a carpenter of unusual ability designed and built these features. The doors in the back part of the house are of simple "board-and-batten" design. They consist of vertical boards with tongue-and-groove joints and decorative bead moldings on each edge and two battens four inches wide and one inch thick with wide beveled edges nailed horizontally on the backs. The doors in the front of the house, however, are of an unusual eight-panel design (fig. 18.12). The mantelpieces, and three of the four are preserved, show clear neoclassic

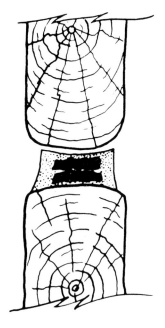

Figure 18.11.
Cross Section of Two Logs with Chinking
The chinking consists of flat stones and clay. The
gap where the clay has pulled away from the upper
log is exaggerated here for purposes of illustration.

influences (see fig. 18.5). All three are basically alike though, of course, of
different dimensions. A large built-in cupboard occupied the niche between
the fireplace and the wall in the dining room (see fig. 18.1).

A detailed description of the other buildings and the site is not
advisable, for several of the buildings have been constructed in recent years
by the present owner. While it is true that the student of folklife cannot be
guided by antiquarian principles, accepting only what is old and discarding
what is new even if traditional, nonetheless a detailed description of the
other buildings on the site and their relative ages would occupy too much
space and deserves separate treatment. A few noteworthy features concerning the site may, however, be mentioned. About 150 yards north of the
house stands a large log barn enclosed on all four sides by attached frame
sheds (fig. 18.13). The barn is of the two-crib type; that is, two sets of logs
are separated at the ground level by an open runway. Above the runway,
however, two logs and a large plate span the entire structure and tie it
together.[3] The logs in the barn are hewn on two surfaces and joined at the
corners with single dovetail notches as are those in the rear wing, or ell, of
the house. The logs in the main part of the house, it will be recalled, are

Figure 18.12.   Front Door
One of two front doors, this is of an unusual
eight-panel design.

Figure 18.13.   Log Barn on the Whitaker-Waggoner Farm

joined at the corners with V-notches. Between the house and the barn is a small ravine with a spring. Building sites for old farmhouses in southern Indiana, I might add, seem to have been chosen because of the proximity of springs. At least, practically every old log farmhouse I have visited has been located near a spring.

It is axiomatic that written records, whenever available, should be used in attempting to date a building. Unfortunately, in this instance, as is so often the case, the written records are inadequate. Land deeds tell us when the land was entered and a family history tells us when the supposed builder or, at least, the first owner came to Indiana from Kentucky. They do not, however, establish beyond doubt that the existing house and barn were built at this time; it is always possible that other buildings that have since disappeared were the original structures and that the existing buildings are later replacements. Indeed, in this case, since the existing structures are so large and must have taken considerable time to build, there is a strong likelihood that Grafton B. Whitaker erected some smaller, less-permanent house to live in while he cleared his land and later built, or had built, these structures.

The student of folklife, of course, is always aware of oral traditions. While it would be unwise to raise here the familiar question of oral tradition as "authentic" history, it is clear that, in attempting to establish a date at which a house was built, oral traditions must be treated with caution. There seems to be a general tendency for oral tradition either to exaggerate the age of a building or to be content with the too-vague phrase "It's over a hundred years old." In this case, oral tradition reports that the rear wing of the house was added at a later date and that the logs in the rear wing came from another old building. Since the corner notches of the logs in the main part of the house and in the rear wing are of two different types, this tradition seems plausible. It is, however, also possible that the relatively small log portion of the rear wing embodies logs from the original house that was built on the site. Oral tradition also maintains that a huge stone foundation extended ten feet into the ground under each chimney stack and that all the logs in the walls were held together at the corners by hidden pins or trunnels. The fact that the chimney stacks, which are massive piles of stone, were in perfect condition in 1966, and had neither sagged nor settled over the years must have given rise to the tradition concerning the foundations. Excavation revealed that the foundations extended no more than a foot or two below ground level. The fact that large trunnels are visible in the attic where they penetrate the plate and hold it to the logs probably gave rise to the tradition concerning the trunnels in the corners of the logs in the wall. When the logs were taken down, no trunnels of this sort were found; indeed, the corner notches commonly employed in hewn-log buildings are designed to hold the logs tightly in place at the corners and make any other type of fastening unnecessary.

In attempting to fix dates for the construction of a building, a detailed examination of the fabric of the structure itself is essential and must be used to supplement and counterbalance the information gleaned from written records and oral sources. Unfortunately, determination of dates on the basis of such an examination is also fraught with difficulties. In the first place, it is often only when a building is being disassembled that it is possible to find enough evidence to reach meaningful conclusions; if a building is in good condition, the really important evidence may be covered by relatively modern additions. In the present case, the most indicative feature, to be mentioned below, could only have been discovered when the house was being disassembled. In the second place, any house that has been lived in over a period of years has undergone many changes and additions. Doors and windows, for example, are added and removed, new floors are laid over old, rooms are remodeled, and so on. Moreover, some portions of a building, especially the roofing, are naturally subject to wear and have to be replaced from time to time. In the third place, it was much more common in the past than it is today to use materials salvaged from other buildings either in the original construction of a building or in later repair and remodeling. Hence, it is possible to find materials much older than the building itself incorporated into it. House logs, especially, can easily be used over and over again since it is mainly the corner notches and their own weight that hold them together. Time after time I have been told that log buildings, or parts of them, have been taken down, moved, and reassembled or added to other structures, and I have no doubt that these reports are substantially correct.

To deal point by point with the various features of the Whitaker-Waggoner house from the standpoint of dating would be fruitless. Most features of the construction could have been used at almost any time in the nineteenth century, not to mention the early part of the twentieth century, or even the eighteenth century, although the history of Indiana largely precludes this last possibility. One of the reasons for this state of affairs is that which attracts the folklorist to folk architecture: tradition exerts a powerful sway in the choice of building materials and in building techniques, and tradition in this case is buttressed and reinforced by functional considerations. For example, hewn logs were used in the construction of this house, we might say, because this was a traditional way of building. But we must also add that the materials were readily available for this type of construction, that the builder was familiar with the required building techniques and had the necessary tools, and that the finished building was staunch, commodious, and pleasing to the eye, required a minimum of upkeep, and was superbly insulated against both the cold of

Indiana winters and the heat of Indiana summers. Other types of construction were theoretically possible. Grafton Whitaker might have built a stone house. The materials for a stone house were at hand and superb masonry skills were also at hand; witness the stone fireplaces and chimneys. The materials for a frame house were also at hand, and the skills needed, while of a slightly different order, are no more demanding than those required for a log house of this sort. In the last analysis, the folklorist must probably fall back upon the comfortably vague word *tradition.* Whitaker probably built the kind of house he did because it was the kind he was familiar with. He knew that type of house and he knew its very obvious virtues. He wanted a house that was substantial and enduring and chose not to experiment with unfamiliar types—a wise choice, I might add, in the light of hindsight.

But to return to the features of the house that might help in dating it, most of the features cannot allow one to be very exact. Many features tell us at once that we are dealing with early rather than contemporary construction: the logs, sills, plates, rafters, and studs are hewn rather than sawed; hand-molding planes, rather than material from a planing mill, were used for decorating the interior; and clay was used in the masonry rather than modern mortar. As it happens, however, it is the hardware to which we must turn for more exact evidence, to be more specific, the door hinges and the wood screws that hold them on. The paneled doors in the front of the house, I assume, are original. They are handmade of yellow poplar with through-mortice-and-tenon joints pinned with wooden trunnels, and they harmonize with the rest of the interior woodwork. I believe they were made by the same carpenter who made the mantelpieces, for instance. The hinges appear to be original, for they exactly fit the only mortices on the door and door frames. If hinges have been replaced on a door, it is very rare to find them fitting the mortices exactly. The hinges in question are butt hinges of cast iron and obviously of an early type in that the pin was an integral part of the casting rather than a separate part as in modern, so-called loose-pin hinges. The cast-iron butt door hinge was patented in England in 1775 and rapidly replaced other types of hinges.[4] The hinges were held to the doors and frames with flat-headed, blunt-ended wood screws. Henry Mercer tells us that the wood screw in use in the early nineteenth century was "invariably blunt-ended," that a machine to point the ends of wood screws was patented in New York in 1846, and that the pointed variety of screw "universally superseded the pointless screw."[5] The hinges and their screws show that the house was probably built after 1775 and before 1846. The history of settlement in Indiana allows us to be more precise: after 1820 and before 1846. Greater precision than this we probably cannot obtain. The rest of the hardware in the house would agree in a general way with these dates. No eighteenth-century handmade nails were found, for instance, but there were great quantities of machine-made cut nails of the type manufactured after 1820.[6] Although many of the original door latches had been replaced by modern knobs, several cast-iron latches of an early-nineteenth-century type were on the doors.

A brief summary of the history of the house may close this discussion. The main part was built probably in the late 1820s and the rear wing shortly thereafter. The rear wing used partly logs from some other building. At the time the house was built, or very soon thereafter, it was covered with clapboard siding. Although a number of minor changes and additions were made over the course of the years, the only significant one was the removal of two small front porches, until the fall of 1966 when the house was disassembled to be rebuilt eventually in the Outdoor Museum of Folk Life at Indiana University.

Notes

1. Mr. J. B. Whitaker of Paragon, Indiana.

2. See Henry J. Kauffman, "The Riddle of Two Front Doors," *Dutchman* 6:3 (Winter 1954–55): 27.

3. This type of barn has been discussed in Henry Glassie, "The Pennsylvania Barn in the South," *Pennsylvania Folklife* 15, no. 2 (Winter 1965–66): 12–16.

4. Henry C. Mercer, *Ancient Carpenters' Tools,* p. 259.

5. Ibid., p. 256.

6. Ibid., p. 246. Mercer errs in stating that the machine-pressed wire nail "revolutionized the nail industry by driving the cut nail out of the North American market, about 1890" (p. 238). The cut nail is presently available at any Indiana lumberyard, for it is still widely used for nailing hard woods, such as oak flooring. Being brittle, it will not bend in such applications as will a wire nail. It has other practical advantages, too. Being rectangular in cross section, if it is driven into the wood with its long axis parallel to the grain it is less likely to split the wood than would a round nail of comparable size. Moreover, since it tapers on two surfaces from the head to the point, it can more easily be removed from wood than can the wire nail.

Bibliography

Erixon, Sigurd. "Är den nordamerikanska timringstekniken överförd från Sverige?" *Folkliv* 19 (1955): 56–68.

Glassie, Henry. *Pattern in the Material Folk Culture of the Eastern United States.* University of Pennsylvania Monographs in Folklore and Folklife, no. 1. Philadelphia: University of Pennsylvania Press, 1968.

———. "The Pennsylvania Barn in the South." *Pennsylvania Folklife* 15, no. 2 (Winter 1965–66): 8–19; 15, no. 4 (Summer 1966): 12–25.

————. "The Types of the Southern Mountain Cabin." In *The Study of American Folklore: An Introduction,* edited by Jan H. Brunvand, pp. 338–70. New York: W. W. Norton, 1968.

Fife, Austin, Alta Fife, and Henry Glassie, eds. *Forms upon the Frontier: Folklife and Folk Arts in the United States.* Monograph Series, 16, no. 2. Logan: Utah State University Press, 1969.

Kauffman, Henry J. "Literature on Log Architecture: A Survey." *Pennsylvania Dutchman* 7, no. 2 (1955): 30–34.

————. "The Riddle of Two Front Doors." *Dutchman* 6, no. 3 (Winter 1954–55): 27.

Kniffen, Fred. "Folk Housing: Key to Diffusion." *Annals of the Association of American Geographers* 58 (1965): 549–77.

Kniffen, Fred and Henry Glassie. "Building in Wood in the Eastern United States: A Time-Place Perspective." *Geographical Review* 56 (1966): 40–66.

Mercer, Henry C. *Ancient Carpenters' Tools.* 3d ed. Doylestown, Pa.: Bucks County Historical Society, 1960.

Roberts, Warren E. "Folk Architecture." In *Folklore and Folklife: An Introduction,* edited by Richard M. Dorson, pp. 281–93. Chicago: University of Chicago Press, 1972.

Shurtleff, Harold R. *The Log Cabin Myth: A Study of the Early Dwellings of the English Colonists in North America.* Cambridge: Harvard University Press, 1939.

Wacker, Peter O., and Roger T. Trindell. "The Log House in New Jersey: Origins and Diffusion." *Keystone Folklore Quarterly* 13, no. 4 (Winter 1968): 248–68.

Weslager, Clinton A. *The Log Cabin in America from Pioneer Days to the Present.* New Brunswick, N.J.: Rutgers University Press, 1969.

————. "Log Houses in Pennsylvania during the Seventeenth Century." *Pennsylvania History* 22 (1955): 256–66.

————. "Log Structures in New Sweden during the Seventeenth Century." *Delaware History* 5, no. 2 (September 1952): 77–95.

19

Some Comments on Log Construction in Scandinavia and the United States

Knowing that it was a strongly-held belief among architectural historians that log construction was introduced to colonial America by the Swedes who settled in Delaware, I went to Scandinavia expecting to find many similarities between the log buildings there and those I had been examining in Indiana. I was surprised to find far more differences than similarities, so surprised as to decide that American log construction could not have been introduced here by the Swedes. This decision is all explained in this essay.

*　　*　　*

At the very outset it is necessary that qualifications be made to the title of this article. "Log construction" refers to the use in buildings of horizontal timbers interlocked at the corners. The reasons that "log" is an unsatisfactory term will be discussed below, but it is the only term for this type of construction that seems to be in wide use currently in the United States. In studying horizontal timber construction, there is at present no satisfactory substitute for fieldwork, for actually examining existing structures. While much has been written on this subject, detailed descriptions of all aspects of the construction of individual buildings in the United States are relatively rare.[1] It is, therefore, necessary to examine actual structures rather than to use written sources. In Scandinavia I have examined buildings mostly in Norway and there chiefly buildings which have been moved into folk museums. In addition to sampling the rich published material for Norway, I have benefitted from consultation with Hilmar Stigum, chief curator of the Norwegian Folk Museum and professor of ethnology at the University of Oslo. I feel that while some of the details which I will treat concern Norway only, much of what I will say also holds true for Sweden. Consequently, I

This article originally appeared in *Folklore Today: A Festschrift for Richard Dorson*, edited by Linda Dégh, Felix Oinas, and Henry Glassie (Bloomington: Indiana University Press, 1976), pp. 437–50. Reprinted by permission of the publisher.

feel justified in speaking broadly, though somewhat loosely, of Scandinavia. In the United States my fieldwork has been restricted almost exclusively to southern Indiana where I have actually examined about 400 log buildings. The published literature and some short field trips elsewhere in the United States have led me to conclude that much of what I will say may hold true for other areas in this country where the British-American building tradition flourished.[2] Those who have a personal acquaintance with log buildings elsewhere in the United States, however, will have to determine how applicable the following points are outside Indiana.

Now that these preliminary qualifications are disposed of, the valid question, "Why compare horizontal timber construction in Norway and Indiana?" may be raised. In 1922, Kimball proposed the idea that Swedes introduced log construction into America and that gradually this form of building was adopted by other Americans.[3] In 1938, Shurtleff gave this theory such impetus that it now seems to be widely accepted among architectural historians and others who have dealt with log buildings.[4] A comparison between Scandinavian and American horizontal timber construction may, therefore, be useful.

Horizontal timber construction has a long history in Norway where a number of such buildings from the Middle Ages still exist, so that it is possible to trace changes in construction methods over the centuries. In southern Indiana, however, existing log buildings date mostly from the nineteenth and early twentieth centuries and conform quite closely to one main type with certain easily understood exceptions. It is quite likely that the earliest settlers, in desperate need of shelter, hastily erected crude shelters of round logs, but none of these have survived to my knowledge. Since the 1930s, many log houses have been constructed as vacation homes and for other purposes also. Most of these have either been built with old logs salvaged from houses and barns or with smaller, round logs. It is only the main type of horizontal timber construction of the nineteenth and early twentieth centuries that will be considered in this paper. Both the very early and the late use of round logs will be ignored.

Let us begin our consideration with the timbers used to form the walls of buildings of many kinds: houses, barns, storehouses, and so on. In the very earliest buildings from the Middle Ages in Norway, the logs were left almost entirely in the round, but for centuries later the logs were carefully shaped before being built into the wall. The inside and outside surfaces were gently rounded, the top was flattened, and the bottom had a concave groove to allow the timber to fit snugly over the one below it (see fig. 19.1). In this way no chinking was needed between the timbers to produce a weathertight wall. Pine or other softwood was customarily used because, of course, it was readily available, and the timber was given its final shaping

Figure 19.1.
Cross Section of Two Typical Wall Logs in a Norwegian Log House
Also known as horizontal timbers, these logs are carefully shaped so that they fit so tightly upon one another that no chinking is needed between the logs.

with drawknives of various kinds. The timbers were shaped in this way for a variety of reasons. The gently rounded shape was decorative and the shaped timbers did not protrude on the inside of the walls as the round log would. In the process of shaping, most of the outside sapwood which decays most readily was removed and the harder heartwood which resists decay remained. As it comes from the tree, a log is, of course, bigger at the butt end than it is at the top, and the process of shaping, most of the timber straightened it so that it was more nearly the same size for its entire length. In relatively late work after sawmills came into use, logs were sometimes sawed square at the mill and used in buildings.

In southern Indiana, logs were nearly always hewn on two surfaces to a reasonably uniform thickness of about seven inches. Hardwoods were invariably used because throughout most of this area conifers of a size suitable for building purposes did not grow. The tulip tree, or yellow poplar, was most commonly used, because, among other reasons, the wood is relatively light in weight, easily worked, and resistant to decay. Oak, beech and other woods were sometimes used, probably because long straight logs of these species were readily available. The tool used to hew the logs was primarily the broadaxe. Hewing with the broadaxe is mostly a process of splitting away pieces of wood of various size. It is a process well adapted to hardwoods, while the Norwegian drawknife technique wherein wood is always cut away is best used with softwoods. The hewing technique which produces a usable timber from the log is also basically the same as that used in hewing the heavy timbers for sills, corner posts, and the like used in buildings of frame construction. While the sides of the timbers in southern Indiana were hewn, the tops and bottoms were left with the natural curvature of the log (see fig. 19.2). Most frequently the bark was not even removed from the top and bottom surfaces. This fact insured that when the logs were placed in the wall the natural curvature of the logs plus the taper from the butt end to the top left gaps or interstices of varying widths between the logs. These interstices were filled or chinked. First, pieces of wood or flat stones were laid between the logs and then clay was plastered on, both from the inside and the outside. This technique is reminiscent of some forms of half timber construction wherein a frame of heavy timbers is constructed. Between the timbers sticks are inserted which are then plastered with clay. An even closer resemblance is found in a type of frame construction occurring in New England, and, perhaps, elsewhere in the United States. After the frame of heavy timbers is constructed, vertical planks are used to fill in between the timbers of the frame and the walls are then covered with clapboards. J. F. Kelly, in *The Early Domestic Architecture of Connecticut,* describes one building by saying, "The planking of the Norton house is placed so that spaces of about two inches width occur between the planks. These spaces were plugged with a mixture of clay and cut straw" (p. 41). This sounds very much like the chinking between horizontal timbers.

Various ways of joining the timbers at the corners are used in Scandinavia. They nearly always have one common characteristic in that the ends of the logs protrude for some distance past the corners. Great care was taken to insure that the joints fitted tightly and smoothly and often there are complex locking devices such as keys or wedges that are hidden inside the joints.[5] In some early work in Sweden full or double dovetail joints were used at the corners, but it was not until timbers sawed square at mills came into wide use that the dovetail joint became common.

In southern Indiana the so-called single dovetail joint was used most commonly to lock the timbers together at the corners. I have found only one building using the full dovetail joint, and that is a house built in New Harmony by the Rappites, a religious group from Germany who spent ten years in Pennsylvania before coming to Indiana in 1814. The V-notch was also used, though far less commonly. Whichever type of joint was used, the joint was always fitted very carefully. With joints of this type, too, the ends of the logs do not protrude past the corners.

In most parts of Norway the walls of horizontal timber buildings were never covered with boards on the outside. The horizontal timbers were treated with pine tar and other preservatives, and seem to be unaffected by weathering and decay to any noticeable extent. In western Norway, where the climate is far damper than elsewhere in the country, weatherboarding is

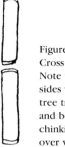

Figure 19.2.
Cross Section of Two Typical Wall Logs in an American Log House
Note that the logs have been hewn to a uniform thickness on their
sides while the top and bottom retain the natural curvature of the
tree trunk from which they are hewn. The bark remains on the top
and bottom surfaces. The gap between the logs would be filled with
chinking consisting of chunks of wood or pieces of stone daubed
over with clay.

used on the exterior walls. That is, horizontal boards whose edges overlap
are nailed or pegged on so as to cover the walls. In southern Indiana where
the hewed timbers usually develop seasoning cracks into which rainwater
could penetrate and cause decay and where driving rains would wash away
the clay used for chinking, it was customary practice to cover the outside
walls of horizontal timber houses with clapboards as soon as they were built
or shortly thereafter.[6] This is, of course, the same exterior siding as is used
on frame houses. A log house covered with clapboards in good condition
can hardly be distinguished from a frame house by the casual observer.

As long as the four walls are of even height, the horizontal timbers are,
of course, locked together at the corners. When the gable ends of the walls
are to be filled in from the line of the eaves to the ridge, however, a special
problem presents itself because no longer are there corners to interlock. In
most Norwegian construction the gable walls are built of short horizontal
logs held together with pins or trunnels. The construction of the gable end
walls in this instance cannot be separated from a consideration of the roof
construction for where the gable ends are built of logs, long timbers
comparable to purlins, called *åsen* in Norwegian, run lengthwise from one
gable end to the other. These timbers both brace the gable ends and hold up
the roof (see fig. 19.3). Sometimes, however, *åsen* are used which are lower
than the roof and serve only to brace the gable end. At any rate, the roof is
not primarily supported by rafters which run from the ridge to the eaves.
The most common roof covering in Norway, and by far the most
picturesque, is birch bark covered with sod. The birch bark turns the water

Figure 19.3.   Sketch of a Typical Roof Framing System for a Norwegian Log House

The gable end wall is built up of progressively shorter logs or horizontal timbers (1). Purlins, or *åsen*, run parallel to the long walls, their ends resting on the gable and walls (2). These purlins not only support the roof but brace the short logs in the gable end walls and help hold them in position.

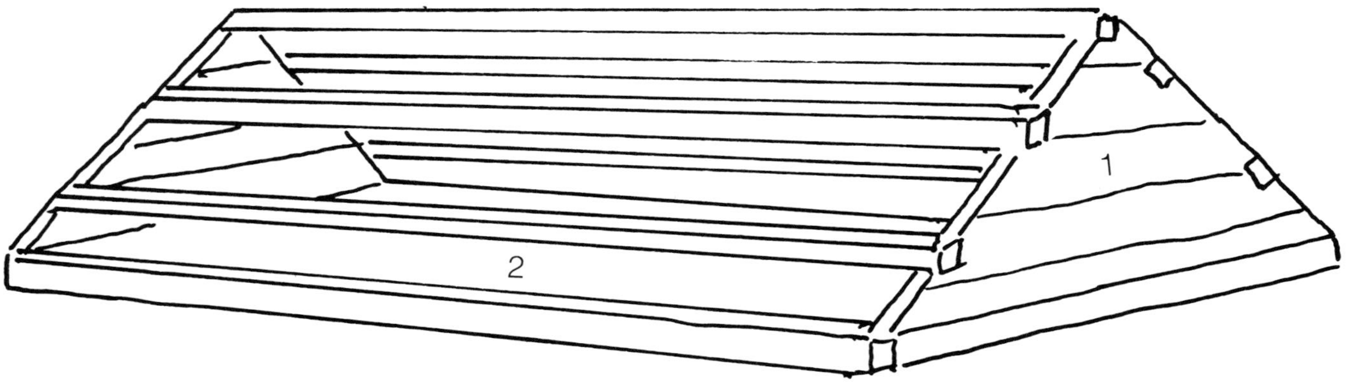

and the layer of sod holds the birch bark in place. Other roof coverings are used, however, including wooden shingles, but the wooden shingles I examined were unlike American shingles, being thin and narrow, perhaps three inches in width.

In Indiana the upper gable ends of walls are almost never built of logs or horizontal timbers. Instead, the space between the rafters and the last log which can interlock with a matching log on the side wall is filled in with studs which run vertically (see fig. 19.4). This studding is normally covered on the outside with horizontal clapboards. Rafters made of hewn timbers, wider at the base and tapering towards the peak, or made of poles hewn flat on one side, are fastened together at the peak with an open mortise and tenon joint and pinned. In later work, sawed rafters are used, generally with a ridgepole to which they are nailed. Even sawed rafters sometimes taper, being broader at the base. The roof covering was always wooden shingles, though of course, in recent times metal or asphalt roofing has often been used to replace shingle roofs. Older men with whom I have talked recall that around the turn of the twentieth century roofs were frequently covered with long wooden shingles about three feet in length which were split or "rove" out of oak blocks with a froe. I have found only a few long neglected buildings which still have these large shingles on the roofs, pretty well rotted away, but in a few buildings I have found these large shingles tucked away in attics or shoved between logs and forgotten. During most of the twentieth century a shorter shingle usually fifteen or sixteen inches long was used. These shorter shingles were also rove out by hand but more usually were cut by a shingle machine or, more recently, sawed. It should be emphasized that the construction of the gable parts of the walls and the construction of the roofs of horizontal timber buildings in Indiana is, in all respects, identical with that of buildings of frame construction in the same area.

Wherever the horizontal timbers are cut out for door and window openings, some provision must be made to hold the ends of those timbers which are cut completely through. Various ways are used in Norway, but in one common method a pole is fixed into holes in the top and bottom timbers which span the opening and the shorter timbers at the sides are notched around this pole. Only one method seems to have been used in Indiana for holding the cut ends of the timbers at openings. A plank, either hewn or sawed to the right dimensions, is placed flush against the cut ends of the timbers. In early work a hole is then drilled through the plank and into the ends of the timbers and a wooden pin or trunnel is driven into the hole or, in later work, nails are simply driven through the plank and into the ends of the timbers. The doors themselves used in Norwegian buildings are of many types while windows which open are usually of the casement type

Figure 19.4. Sketch of a Typical Roof Framing System for an American Log House
The horizontal plate (1) rests upon the top log in the gable end wall (2). The coupled rafters (3) are jointed at the peak. Their bottom ends rest on the plate. Studs (4) are fitted between the top log and the end rafter.

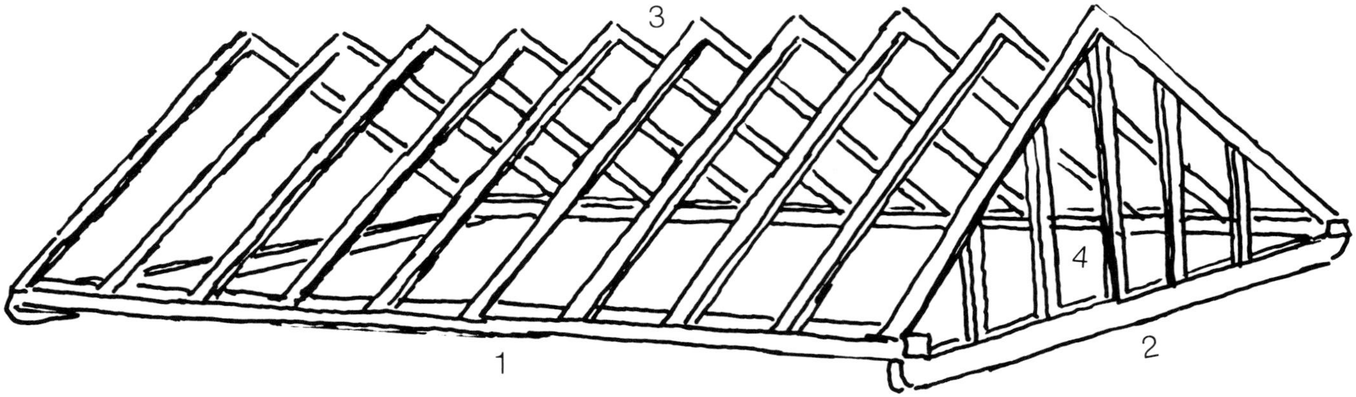

which swing out on hinges. Doors in Indiana are of two types. The most common is of board and batten construction wherein vertical boards are held together by two or three horizontal battens which are nailed across the back of the boards. The battens are chamfered on all four outer edges. Doors of panel construction are used, though less commonly. Indeed, the same house may have doors of both types. Windows which open are always of the sliding sash type in which the upper sash is fixed while the bottom sash may be raised and lowered. The doors and windows used in horizontal timber houses in Indiana, therefore, are identical to those used in frame and masonry houses in the same area.

The design and construction of chimneys and fireplaces and their location in a building are influenced by a number of factors such as whether the fireplace is used for heating alone or for both heating and cooking and what kinds of cooking and baking are done at the fireplace. The development of Norwegian fireplaces and the types used in various parts of the country are subjects far too complicated to explore here. In general, however, it may be said that baking was done in a separate small building with its own fireplace and chimney, and that, in recent times at least, fireplaces in houses are usually built inside the walls of the house, frequently in a corner, and that they are usually open on two sides. In Indiana, fireplace and chimney construction is remarkably consistent. It is true that some horizontal timber houses have no fireplaces because they were built at a time when stoves were available and a fireplace was no longer essential. Most houses, however, do have a fireplace and it is placed almost invariably so that it is centered in the gable end wall. Almost invariably, too, the fireplaces may be said to be partly inside and partly outside the house; that is, a large hole is cut in the wall and the fireplace built so that its inside surface is flush with the inside surface of the wall. The back part of the fireplace is, therefore, outside the wall and the chimney rises completely outside the wall. Fireplaces and chimneys of this type seem to be unknown in Norway, while Norwegian types are not found in Indiana. On the other hand, fireplaces and chimneys of the type found in horizontal timber houses are used in houses of frame construction in Indiana. Indeed, E. Estyn Evans considers chimneys of this type to be distinctively English.[7]

The oldest houses of horizontal timber construction in Norway were basically one-story, because fireplaces and chimneys were not used in early times. Instead, a fire was built on the floor in the middle of the main room and the smoke escaped through a smokehole in the roof above the fire. Obviously, a second story was impossible with such an arrangement. In later centuries two-story houses were built, but the construction of such houses is so widely varied that it is unwise to attempt to describe them here. In Indiana, two-story houses of horizontal timber are not uncommon and the construction is relatively simple. The walls are carried up to an appropriate height by adding more timbers locked at the corners just as are those at a lower level. At an appropriate level, joists to support the second floor are added. These run parallel to the gable ends of the house and rest on timbers in the side wall, notches usually being cut in the timbers to receive the ends of the joists. A single layer of floor boards is nailed to the joists running at right angles to them. The same system is used in other log houses to provide a ceiling for the first story and a floor for the sleeping loft, only in this case the side walls are not so high and the joists are fixed in the side wall only a few feet below the eaves. I have never found a horizontal timber house in Indiana which could be called a true one-story house. They are always either one-and-a-half stories or two stories. It can be seen that the method of building the ceiling for the first floor which also serves as the floor for the sleeping loft or the second floor is essentially the same in horizontal timber houses as it is in frame houses.

One final point concerns the general floor plan and layout of houses. Again, horizontal timber houses in Norway show a great variety in this regard, varying not only from one part of the country to another but from century to century. Perhaps only one generalization need be made: usually there is more than one room on the first floor. Indiana horizontal timber houses, on the other hand, show a remarkable uniformity as to floor plan. By far the most common is a single room, rectangular in shape, measuring roughly twenty-four by eighteen feet with the shorter walls being the gable ends. There are, of course, variations on this basic plan, but several of the variations consist of simply another room of the same dimensions and identical construction built as a separate structure and not directly connected to the first, but connected by means of some sort of frame construction. Such are the so-called dog-trot and saddle-bags types.[8] What might be called "horizontal timber mansions" do exist in Indiana, wherein timbers up to thirty-six feet in length are used to make a house with several rooms on each floor, but even these, while of greater length, tend to be only eighteen or twenty feet in width. It may be said that horizontal timber houses in Indiana, therefore, differ markedly as to floor plan from horizontal timber houses in Norway. They actually resemble in floor plan, however, frame houses in Indiana and elsewhere in the United States. Indeed, the construction of the floors and the roof are probably the factors which dictate the rectangular shape and general dimensions both of horizontal timber and of frame houses.

This comparative survey has, of necessity, been rather sketchy and incomplete. I hope, however, that I have succeeded in establishing two points. The first is that there is very little resemblance between Scandinavian and American horizontal timber construction. The only resemblance is in the use of the horizontal timbers themselves. Since horizontal timber construction is found in many other parts of northern Europe—though not in Great Britain—one can say that American horizontal timber construction resembles that of other countries at least as much as that of the Scandinavian lands. As a matter of fact, at least in Poland and Switzerland, interstices are left lengthwise between timbers and filled in with clay or mortar, as in American construction. The main evidence adduced to support the theory that American horizontal timber construction is derived from Swedish sources is the fact that Swedes were building horizontal timber houses in the new world during the seventeenth century,[9] but so were the French-Canadians,[10] and perhaps other peoples as well. On the basis of the present evidence, I believe that it is only safe to say that horizontal timber construction was not invented in the New World but is a European importation. More specific statements should be postponed until further research, especially fieldwork, is done, for premature generalizations are more likely to retard scholarship than to advance it.

The second point that I hope this survey has established is the fact that there is a marked resemblance between horizontal timber construction in America and frame construction in America which is undoubtedly of British derivation. Everything about an American horizontal timber house resembles frame construction except the walls themselves, and even here there is some resemblance to British half-timber work. I feel it is a mistake to assert that most American horizontal timber construction is a derivative from Swedish or German sources. It would be more realistic to consider it as growing out of British-American frame construction.

Appendix A: Early Horizontal Timber Buildings in the United States and Canada

As an extended footnote to the discussion above, I would like to cite some references to early examples of horizontal log construction arranged by the national origin of the builders. I have not included references to Swedish examples, since they have been thoroughly treated by Shurtleff and by C. A. Weslager, *The Log Cabin in America* (New Brunswick, N.J., 1969), nor have I included German examples. Most early references are, unfortunately, tantalizingly inconclusive.

French

1. Professor Luc Lacourcière has shown me photographs of a French-Canadian house built about 1640 near Quebec. The walls are of squared timbers joined at the corners with full dovetail corner notching with no interstices between the logs. The exterior of the walls has always been covered with siding.

2.   H. C. Mercer, "The Origin of Log Houses in the United States," *Old-Time New England* 18 (July 1927): 5, cites a reference which he translates as follow: [In Three Rivers] "The first parish church built in 1664 was in round wood dovetailed at the corners." He also cites an ambiguous reference from 1635 and other later ones. Kniffen and Glassie dismiss the 1664 reference as "an isolated freak," p. 50, n. 28.

British

1.   "In the *Description of the Province of New Albion* which Sir Edmund Plowden published in 1648 as a promotional pamphlet for the colony he had been trying to establish in New Jersey since 1634, six distinct building types are listed which, he says, were commonly used by new settlers in all the English colonies . . . [One type is] 'a log house of young trees, 30. foot square notched at the corners.'" Cited by Alan Gowans, *Images of American Living* (Philadelphia, 1964), p. 12.

2.   Garrison houses in New England: It has long been recognized that garrison houses, which are large buildings constructed primarily for defense, were built with horizontal timber walls at an early date in New England. Those who have stressed Swedish and German sources of log construction in America have denied that garrison houses could have influenced dwelling houses in America. Kniffen and Glassie state that garrison houses used horizontal timbers morticed into corner posts (p. 51). However, a number of published photographs clearly show garrison houses with horizontal timbers locked at the corners with full dovetail joints and without interstices between the timbers. Such are Mercer's figures 2 through 10 showing Maine and New Hampshire garrison houses dating as early as 1640 and figures in George Francis Dow, *Every Day Life in the Massachusetts Bay Colony* (Boston, 1935; reprint, New York, 1967), plates 11 and 12. The structure described by J. Frederick Kelly in "A Seventeenth Century Connecticut Log House," *Old-Time New England* 31, no. 2 (October 1940): 28–41; is undoubtedly another garrison house dating from 1670. It uses horizontal timbers with square corner notches and has no interstices between the timbers.

The Indiana log house is, as I have shown above, closely related to frame houses of British derivation, the only difference being in the horizontal timbers themselves used to construct the walls. These timber walls, moreover, were normally covered over with clapboards on the exterior and plaster or wainscoting on the interior. It is, therefore, illogical to reject garrison houses as a possible source for horizontal timber walls on the grounds that garrison houses were not dwelling houses. If Anglo-American settlers borrowed only horizontal log walls from Pennsylvania Germans, and did not borrow any other construction details, is it not equally possible that they learned how to use horizontal log walls from garrison houses without copying other construction details?

3. Log houses in New England: Mercer (figs. 11 and 12) shows two Massachusetts buildings with horizontal timber walls which are too small to be garrison houses. One dates "according to tradition" from 1638. These houses are covered with siding so that the corner construction cannot be seen.

4. Log Houses in Other Colonies: C. A. Weslager, *The Log Cabin in America* (New Brunswick, N. J., 1969), pp. 111; 142–43; 147 n. 22, cites a number of references to log houses in Maryland from 1658 ff. and South Carolina from 1690 ff. He also cites references to log houses owned by Englishmen in Pennsylvania from 1685 ff. (page 210).

5. Log houses in Nova Scotia: "When Gargas . . . visited Port Royal in 1687, he reported that all the houses were low, made of rough pieces of wood, one on top of another, and roofed with thatch." The Rev. James MacGregor, a Presbyterian missionary, arrived in Pictou in 1786. He found "how the majority of the Scots lived in log huts with moss stuffed in the chinks and roofs formed of the bark of trees." Cited by George E. G. MacLaren, *Antique Furniture by Nova Scotian Craftsmen* (Toronto, 1961), pp. 2–3; 20. An advertisement in the *Royal American Gazette,* 13 January 1785, Shelburne, Nova Scotia, lists, "the lot . . . with a log house thereon, one story, and a half high, and a good cellar under it," Cited in *Antiques,* June 1968, p. 768. These eighteenth-century references are, of course, late, but they tend to reinforce the 1687 reference by showing that a tradition of log construction flourished in Nova Scotia.

It must at once be admitted that not all these citations refer unequivocally to the use of horizontal timbers notched together at the corners. Enough of the citations, however, are adequately clear to demonstrate that French and British settlers were building dwellings using such construction in the seventeenth century in the New World. I would not be rash enough to claim that this fact proves that American horizontal timber construction is either of French or British origin. It does seem safe to state, however, that while this form of construction is of European derivation, neither Sweden nor Germany can be said to be the sole source. It is possible that future research will show that there is a major primary source, but multiple sources must also be considered.

After the above was written, Charles F. Gritzner's article, "Log Housing in New Mexico," was printed in *Pioneer America* 3 (1971): 54–62. Gritzner presents convincing evidence to show that there is a tradition of building with logs of horizontal timbers locked together at the corners in New Mexico and Mexico which cannot be due to Anglo-American influence and can best be explained as of Spanish origin. It is, of course, unlikely that this Spanish-American building tradition affected horizontal timber construction in the eastern United States. The fact that this form of construction was known in Spain, however, reinforces my contention that there is no single source in Europe for American horizontal timber construction and that the possibility of a number of European sources must be considered.

Appendix B: The Horizontal Timber Buildings of Norwegian Immigrants to the United States

While there can be no adequate substitute for detailed field recordings, the following notes are presented in the hope that they will prove of some interest in connection with the foregoing discussion.

1.   *Norwegian-American log house now in the Norwegian Folk Museum in Oslo.* I have personally examined this particular building which was moved from Wisconsin and rebuilt in Oslo. The walls are constructed of timbers hewn flat on two sides and interlocked at the corners with half-dovetail joints. There are large interstices between the timbers which are filled with mortar. These, plus various other construction features, show that the house fits the British-American pattern in every detail. I was unable to discover a single feature which I could say was of Norwegian derivation.

2.   *The first Norwegian Lutheran Church in Manitowac County, Wisconsin.* A small drawing of this church, built soon after the arrival of the first settlers in October 1850, is reproduced in Rigmore Frimannslund, "Blant Norsk-Amerikanere i Wisconsin," *By og Bygd* 14 (1960): 14. Although it is true that most of the construction features cannot be determined from the drawing, it is clear that the walls are built of hewn logs with half-dovetail corners and with large interstices between the logs.

3.   *The Egge Cabin in the open air museum at Luther College, Decorah, Iowa, built by Norwegian immigrants before 1853.* A photograph of this building is given by Frimannslund, p. 3. The walls are of the same construction as the previous two examples and, as far as can be determined from the photograph, all other details conform to the British-American pattern.

4. *The Carl Knudsen house in Vermont, Wisconsin.* A photograph of this building is given by Frimannslund, p. 5. It was built in two sections. The newest part is of log but covered with clapboards while the oldest section has the logs in the wall exposed to the weather, As far as one can tell from the photograph, the oldest section conforms in all details to the British-American pattern.

5. *The John Bergen house in Norway Township, Racine County, Wisconsin.* Photographs of this building are given by Richard W. E. Perrin, *Historic Wisconsin Buildings,* Milwaukee Public Museum Publications in History, no. 4 (1962), p. 9. As far as one can tell from the photographs, this house does embody a number of Norwegian characteristics. The gable ends are built completely of logs, for instance, and purlins or *åsen* are used in the roof.

What can we conclude from this very superficial and imperfect survey? It would only be safe to state that some—perhaps many—Norwegians who came to this country either built or had others build for them horizontal timber houses of the British-American type showing no discernible Norwegian characteristics. One explanation for this fact is that in Norway the building of horizontal timber houses was done by craftsmen who attained a high degree of skill through long training. These craftsmen must have been relatively rare. Most Norwegian immigrants had neither the skill nor the tools required to build in the Norwegian style, but were capable, probably with the help of their neighbors, of building a comparatively simple British-American type of house. Only occasionally, as in the case of the John Bergen house, did an immigrant have the skill and the tools to build in the style of his homeland. This fact emphasizes, at least, the marked difference between the Norwegian and the British-American types of horizontal timber construction.

Notes

1. For noteworthy examples of detailed descriptions, see Henry Glassie, "The Double-Crib Barn in South Central Pennsylvania," *Pioneer America* 1 (1969): 9–16, and other articles by the same author. I have also written a detailed description of one house which is to be published in a collection of essays on American folklife edited by Don Yoder. There has recently been published a fine description of horizontal timber buildings, "The Log Architecture of Ohio," by Donald and Jean Hutslar, in *Ohio History* 80 (1971): 172–272.

2. Because I lack detailed information I will not attempt to deal with German-American, French-American, or Finnish-American log construction nor will I consider the obviously

important log buildings constructed at an early date by the Swedes in Delaware; I have been unable to personally examine any of these buildings.

3. Fiske Kimball, *Domestic Architecture of the American Colonies* (New York, 1922), pp. 6–8.

4. H.R. Shurtleff, *The Log Cabin Myth* (Cambridge, Mass., 1939). Sigurd Erixon in "Är den nordamerikanska timringstekniken överförd från Sverige?" *Folk-Liv* 19 (1955): 56–68, discusses one aspect of the problem, namely, the corner joints used in Sweden and the United States. Because he lacked adequate data from the United States, however, his discussion is inconclusive. Fred Kniffen and Henry Glassie have recently asserted that "The horizontal log construction with true corner timbering that came to characterize the American frontier . . . was introduced by the Pennsylvania Germans ," in "Building in Wood in the Eastern United States: A Time-Place Perspectives," *The Geographical Review* 56 (1966): 65.

5. See Sigurd Erixon, "The North-European Technique of Corner Timbering," *Folk-Liv* 1 (1937): 13–60. One of Erixon's figures is reproduced in Kniffen and Glassie's article, fig. 18 [see n. 4, above].

6. I have discussed the evidence which has led me to this conclusion in "The Waggoner Log House," article mentioned in note 1, above.

7. "The Scotch-Irish: Their Cultural Adaptation and Heritage in the American Old West," in *Essays in Scotch-Irish History,* ed. E. R. R. Green (London: Routledge and Kegan Paul, 1969), p. 79.

8. For photographs of houses of this type, see Fred Kniffen, "Folk Housing: Key to Diffusion," *Annals of the Association of American Geographers* 55 (1965), figs. 14, 15.

9. See Shurtleff.

10. Prof. Luc Lacourcière has shown me photographs of a seventeenth-century French-Canadian house with square horizontal timbers and dovetailed corner joints. Since this house has been covered with siding since it was built, it is possible that other French-Canadian houses have horizontal timbers hidden within their walls.

20

German-American Log Buildings
of Dubois County, Indiana

One of the concerns in the past of American folklife researchers has been with the immigrant experience in the United States. Hence the identification and study of the buildings of immigrant groups, understood to be groups other than British-Americans, has always been important, and German-American buildings especially so, thanks to the outstanding research done among the Pennsylvania Germans. This essay attempts to deal with the vexing question as to whether German immigrants brought with them a knowledge of how to build with logs or whether they learned in this country from their British-American neighbors. The paper was presented at a conference on German-American architecture held at Winterthur.

*   *   *

If it were possible to make a truly satisfying assessment of any ethnic architecture in the United States, at least four types of information would be required. We would need, first, a detailed, accurate description of the buildings, including form, construction, and use. We would need, next, information about the building tradition of the land from which the immigrants came and as it was at the time they came. We would need, third, information about the building tradition of those who had come earlier to the section of the United States being studied so we could recognize the building tradition with which the immigrants came into contact. Finally, we would need to know the nature of the relationships between the inhabitants who had arrived earlier and the newcomers.

In the course of the following treatment of the German-American log buildings of the Dubois County region of Indiana, each of these types of information will be at least mentioned; however, it is necessary to recognize that on certain points only limited information is available. It is most logical

This article originally appeared in the *Winterthur Portfolio* 21, no. 4 (Winter 1986): 265–74. Reprinted by permission of The University of Chicago Press.

to begin with some information on the German settlement in the area partly to show in a general way what the contacts were like between the Germans and the British-Americans who were living in the area at the time the Germans arrived.

When German immigrants came to the midwestern United States in the 1830s and 1840s, large numbers of them moved to southern Indiana. One region in which many of them settled is Dubois County and portions of surrounding counties. The county lies approximately 150 miles south and a bit west of Indianapolis and about 50 miles east of Evansville. The county seat is Jasper.

The place names of Dubois County, as is often the case, reflect some aspects of the settlement history of the county. Dubois is obviously not a German name nor is Jasper, nor, for that matter, is Huntingburg, another town in the county nearly the size of Jasper. These names tell us that the first settlers who named the county and laid out the first towns were not Germans. The first person of European ancestry to acquire land in what is now Dubois County in 1807 was Capt. Toussiant Dubois of Vincennes, a French town on the Wabash River.[1] Despite this first purchase of land by a man of French origin, there appears to have been no further meaningful French influence on the county.

The people who began moving into the area after 1807 were those who laid out towns with names like Jasper and Huntingburg—people of British ancestry who had been living in Kentucky, Tennessee, and states farther to the east such as Virginia, North Carolina, and Pennsylvania. By 1840, just before the main wave of German immigrants began arriving, about 5,000 people of British ancestry lived in the county.[2]

A further look at the place names shows that after 1840 some of the newcomers laid out and named their own towns which demonstrates that there was land left for the Germans to buy. It was, of course, this farmland available at low cost that attracted the German people to southern Indiana. Indeed, there was land available in quantities beyond the wildest dreams of those who remained behind in Germany.[3]

Another group of names—the "saints," such as St. Henry, St. Anthony, and St. Marks—tells us something else important about the newcomers: many of the German immigrants were Roman Catholics from southern Germany. Indeed, the Roman Catholic church played an important role in attracting German people to Dubois County. It is, therefore, not surprising that today a large convent, the Convent of the Immaculate Conception, is located on the edge of the Dubois County town of Ferdinand while Saint Meinrad's Archabbey and Seminary is just south of the county line.

German Immigrants and Earlier Settlers

What can we discover today about the relationships between the British-Americans and the newcomers? Information is scanty and difficult to obtain. One source of information is interviews. For example, in 1975 I talked with an eighty-year-old man whose grandmother had died in 1922. She had come to Indiana from Germany as a young wife around 1850. In response to my questions, my informant told me that his grandmother had never recalled encountering anything but friendliness from the British-Americans living in Indiana.

Another possible source of information would be letters, diaries, and similar documents. While I know of none from Dubois County that are available for study, there is evidence from Missouri, a nearby state with a parallel developmental pattern. There many German immigrants settled among British-Americans whose background was remarkably similar to that of the British-Americans in Dubois County—that is, they had come from the same regions in the eastern United States and were in the same social and economic classes. Letters written home by the German immigrants in Missouri have been preserved, and they testify that these strangers and foreigners were accorded a friendly reception. Charles van Ravenswaay, having analyzed many of these letters and the reminiscences written later in life by German-Americans, concludes: "Without the friendly aid of these American neighbors, it is unlikely that many German settlements could have survived, or that they could have succeeded as well and relatively quickly. In their memoirs German immigrants in Missouri speak with respect and admiration of the Americans they met, particularly in the country, and of their hospitality and friendly acceptance of immigrants whose language and customs differed so greatly. The skill of the American frontiersmen with their limited tools, and also their complete honesty, impressed the writers." Immigrant Gustavus Wulfing wrote, "One wood chopper can chop as much wood with an American ax as four strong fellows accomplish in the same time in Germany." Nicholas Hesse "felt grateful to [British-Americans] for their never-failing willingness to help build a house or aid the newcomer in other ways." According to van Ravenswaay, "Several immigrants wrote of spending a day felling a tree and attempting to split rails before an American neighbor showed them how it could be done in a few minutes.... Many German commentators spoke of their admiration for American farm women.... Without exception the newcomers lauded the immaculate housekeeping of these women, despite the difficulties of living in a log cabin crowded with furniture, other household articles, and family."[4] It is probably safe to assume, therefore, that the British-Americans in Dubois County gave a warm reception to the German newcomers, treating them in very much the same way that they would have treated British-Americans. It is probably safe to assume, too, that the British-Americans helped the German settlers to construct buildings, for house raising and barn raising were common community events wherein neighbors turned out to help one another.

Another type of evidence on a related topic can be gleaned from census records. These show that when the Germans began arriving they moved in among British-Americans. It is important to emphasize that the British-Americans did not live in clustered groups in one part of the county, nor did the Germans live in other separate clusters. The former had taken farms scattered rather widely throughout the county, following the practice of other midwestern settlers, and there was no major threat from Indians to cause them to form protective small settlements behind fortifications. The land has been purchased from the Indians who had, in the late 1700s and early 1800s, no settlements in the area and who had withdrawn northward before the European-Americans came. The German immigrants, for the most part, bought farmland and built their homes between the farms and homes of the British-Americans.

This picture of the intermingling of the two ethnic groups is made clearer when we look at some figures. In 1850 there were six townships in Dubois County. In one of these the German-Americans accounted for 10 percent of the population, in four they accounted for between 20 percent and 30 percent, and in one township only, Ferdinand, did their population rise to 50 percent. For the county as a whole, the German-Americans constituted 26 percent of the population.[5] Fortunately, we can turn to the census records for further elaboration on this point. The census takers went along each road in an area, stopping at each farmhouse in turn; of course, the entries in the census reflect this process so that we can tell from the sequence who lived next to whom.

Taking a page at random from the 1850 census which lists people living in the countryside, we find the place of birth of the "head of household" listed in the following sequence: Virginia, Indiana, North Carolina, North Carolina, Germany, Germany, Kentucky, North Carolina, Pennsylvania, Germany, Kentucky, Indiana. While it is true that the men who lived in the countryside may in some cases have been expert craftsmen, they almost invariably told the census takers that they were farmers. Living in the town of Jasper, which at the time had about 800 inhabitants, were a few men who told the 1850 census taker that they were carpenters. One such carpenter was from New Jersey and had living with him two eighteen-year-old apprentices, both born in Indiana. Two other carpenters in the town were born in Germany. This data also demonstrates the possibility of an inter-mingling of German and British-American building traditions and practices.

Finally, many of the people of German ancestry who arrived in Dubois County did not come directly from Germany; some had previously lived elsewhere in the United States.[6] So, of course, they could well have seen British-American architecture and might possibly have lived in British-American buildings. The same man I spoke of earlier reported that his grandfather emigrated from Germany to Maryland and worked on the canals there in 1834. After a few years he was able to send home for his fiancée to join him. He grew unhappy living among Irish-Americans and moved to Cincinnati where he found work. City life was not to his taste either, so he bought 80 acres of land near the town of Ferdinand, Indiana, from a man he had met in Cincinnati. He traveled down the Ohio River to Troy, Indiana, and walked the 18 miles overland to his acreage with a wife, six months pregnant, and two small children.

To sum up, then, the German-Americans were not isolated in enclaves, but settled among the British-Americans and frequently had British-American neighbors. The latter welcomed the new arrivals and helped them in many ways including, probably, helping to construct buildings. Thus there were many ways in which German-Americans could have learned about and could have felt the influence of British-American building traditions.

Log Houses

My description of the log buildings of the Dubois County region will concentrate on two types only, the predominant house type and the most common barn type. The following description of the log houses is based on two sorts of data. Twenty-eight houses were photographed and observed. Eight of these were measured, and floor plans were made for them. When measurements are given, therefore, they are the average for the eight. When descriptions are provided, they pertain to the entire number observed.

Twenty-six of the log houses belong to a single type, meaning that they are very similar to one another in basic design even though there may be some variations in details. The basic design may be described as a log, one-and-a-half-story, two-room house with a frame lean-to across the rear and with a special front porch under the overhanging roof line.

The main log portions of the eight measured houses (that is, the part without the frame lean-to or the front porch) averaged 33 feet 6 inches by 18 feet 6 inches. The two rooms, in a side-by-side configuration, are not of the same size, one being about 2 feet wider than the other. Thirteen of the houses have two front doors, and these are not symmetrically placed in the facade because of the difference in room sizes. When there is a single front door, it likewise is not symmetrically placed. Only two of the houses ever had a fireplace (fig. 20.1); the remainder must have been heated with stoves right from the time they were built. There is usually a boxed-in staircase in one corner of a room leading to the sleeping loft overhead. This loft, which is only usable over the two main rooms of the house because of the headroom, is separated into two rooms corresponding in size to the rooms below (fig. 20.2).

The most striking detail of these Dubois County log houses is a construction feature normally hidden. When the siding is removed from one of these log houses it is possible to see that a log extends from each end wall and from the center wall beyond both the front and the rear walls (fig. 20.3). The log projecting to the front supports a roof for the front porch. The average front extension is 5 feet. The log protruding to the rear supports the roof for the rooms of frame construction. The average rear extension is 8 feet. Usually it is a single log that extends at the front and the rear as shown in figure 20.4, but sometimes one log extends to the front while another extends to the rear.

These projecting logs, or cantilevers, demonstrate clearly that the two rooms of frame construction built as a lean-to across the rear of the house (usually a kitchen and pantry) were part of the original construction as was the front porch. The word *addition* so often applied to such rooms is clearly a misnomer here, for this type of lean-to was part of the *original* design and construction.

A comparison of this German-American house with log houses of British Americans in southern Indiana shows that the differences are many (see appendix). The German-American house is considerably larger than the most common British-American house. Of 296 British-American log houses measured in several counties of southern Indiana, 65 percent were one-and-a-half-story houses with a single room on the ground floor, while 15.5 percent were one-and-a-half-story houses with two rooms on the ground floor.[7] The typical one-and-a-half-story, one-room British-American log house has 376 square feet on the ground floor. The typical Dubois County German-American log house has 888 square feet on the ground floor if the two original rooms across the rear are included but the front porch is excluded.

In two-room, one-and-a-half story British-American log houses, the two rooms are nearly always the same size. In the German-American log houses, one room is slightly larger than the other. The British-American log houses usually have two front doors symmetrically spaced, while the German-American Dubois County houses usually have one front door which is not centered in the facade. Most "Yankee" log houses have a

Figure 20.1.   German-American Log House, Dubois County, Indiana

This house had a two-room floor plan, an asymmetrically positioned door, and a porch overhang supported by projecting logs; weatherboards protected the gable end. Abandoned long ago, it was used for storage for many years, and the frame addition at the rear was removed. The house burned down in 1975.

(Photographs and drawings in this chapter by author)

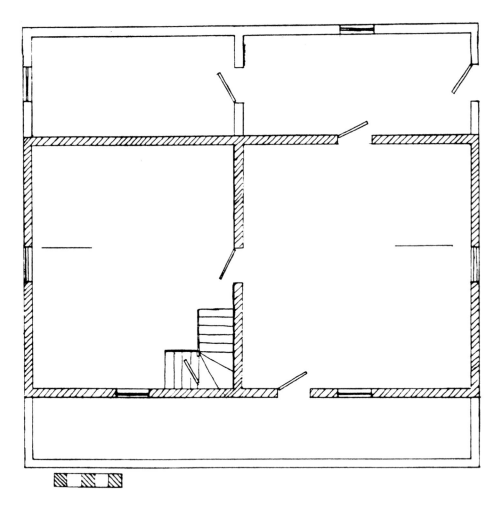

Figure 20.2.　Floor Plan of a Typical German-American Log House,
Dubois County
Walls built entirely of logs are indicated by diagonal hatching.

Figure 20.3.   Overhang of a German-American Log House, Dubois County
This view shows a cantilever.

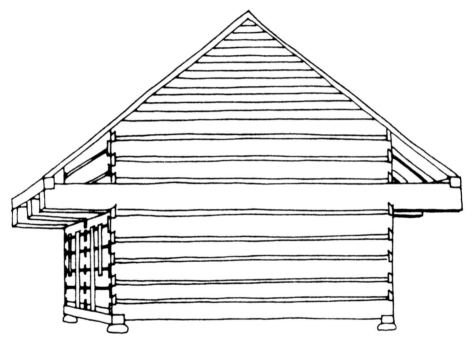

Figure 20.4. Side Elevation of a Typical German-American Log House,
             Dubois County
             This view shows the log portions. The top part of the end
             wall is covered with siding.

fireplace in every room. Only two of the German-American log houses had a fireplace, and that only in one of the two rooms. (It seems likely that the German people who came to Dubois County in the 1840s and 1850s had become accustomed to stoves in their homeland. Although stoves were expensive and difficult to obtain in Indiana, these people were not ready to do without them.) Finally, the use of protruding logs to support a porch roof and the roof for additional rear rooms has been found in southern Indiana in only German-American houses.[8]

Log Barns

Fifteen log barns have been measured in the Dubois County area. All are of the double-pen type; that is, on the ground level there are two log pens separated by a driveway (fig. 20.5). At a height of about 12 feet, there are two or more logs that run the entire length of the structure, starting in one log pen, spanning the driveway, and continuing over the second log pen (fig. 20.6). In the largest barn visited, these logs were 62 feet long.

In many of the barns, animals were stabled in one of the pens, while the other was used for storing grain. A few of the barns had driveways with heavy wooden floors, which according to their owners had been used for threshing grain. Overhead the entire loft could be used to store hay.

These barns share an important feature with the houses. On every barn except one, one log in each side wall of each pen extended forward to support an overhang, or "porch" roof, that stretched across the front of the barn (fig. 20.7, 20.8). (There are four side walls, two in each pen, so there are four projecting logs.) The average depth of the front extension was 6 feet.

Most of the barns also had logs extending from the same side walls to support a roof at the rear for a shedlike lean-to. The walls of this shed were of simple frame construction. As in the houses, in some of the barns the same log that extended from the front of the barn also extended at the rear, while in others one log protruded at the front while the log below it protruded at the back. The average rear extension measured 12 feet in depth. The overall size of the average barn, including both the front and the rear extensions, was 50 feet by 42 feet. The actual log pens and driveway at floor level covered an area 50 feet by 24 feet.

In most respects these Dubois County German-American log barns resemble log barns elsewhere in southern Indiana. Thirty-five British-American double-pen log barns have been found. Their average dimensions are almost the same as those of the German-American barns.[9] The only notable difference is that the German-American barns used cantilevers while the British-American barns did not.

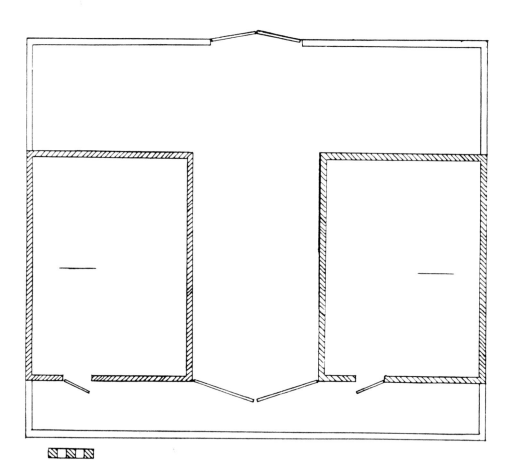

Figure 20.5.   Floor Plan of Typical German-American Log Barn, Dubois County
Walls built entirely of logs are indicated by diagonal hatching.

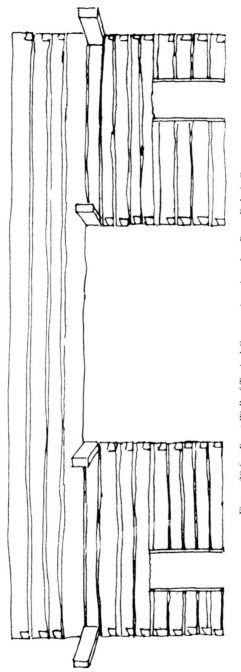

Figure 20.6.   Front Wall of Typical German-American Log Barn, Dubois County

Figure 20.7. Overhang of a German-American Log Barn,
Dubois County
This view shows a cantilever.

Figure 20.8.   German-American Log Barn, Dubois County
This example has a central driveway and two pens. A frame addition has created a
fourth bay at the left end of the barn; the lean-to at the right end is also a later addition.

Log Construction Techniques

For houses and barns in Dubois County, the logs themselves were worked in the same way. Each log in a wall was hewn to a uniform thickness of 7 inches so that two sides are flat. The top and the bottom of the log, however, were not worked and retain the natural curvature of the log. Since the tops and bottoms are unshaped, the logs are never truly straight in the vertical plane. The builders chose reasonably straight tree trunks to begin with, but the slight bends in the trunks and the natural taper from butt end to crown inevitably led to lengthwise gaps between the logs. In houses these gaps are filled with small chips of wood over which clay is smeared. In the barns, circulation of air is desirable, so the gaps are not filled. For both structures, half-dovetail notches are used at the corners (fig. 20.9).

Both in houses and in barns the logs are protected from the weather. For houses, because the sides of the logs were hewn flat and the corner joints produced a flush corner, exterior siding could be applied immediately. Every log house examined had clapboards, or weatherboards as they are called in southern Indiana, on exterior walls, and all evidence supports the conclusion that they had been installed when the houses were built.[10] On eleven houses the part of the front wall that is protected by the porch roof was not covered with siding; instead, the exposed logs had been whitewashed many times. In barns the front is protected by the overhanging roof, and the rear is protected by the attached shed. The side walls are covered with vertical board-and-strip siding which, appropriately, is usually called barn siding in southern Indiana. The boards are frequently rough-sawn oak, and the joints between the boards are covered with vertical strips in a board-and-batten fashion.

The use of siding over logs was a pragmatic decision. Logs left unprotected from the weather are subject to decay. Rainwater can get into cracks in the logs and into small gaps between the logs and the chinking. In hot, humid weather decay develops quickly in such environments. It appears that the individual features in the log construction technique work together to form a functional complex. As logs of hardwood season, they will surely develop cracks; thus, to protect the cracks from rain, the logs need to be covered with siding. Hewing the sides of the logs flat and joining the logs to form a flush or box corner make it possible to install siding at the time of construction. In other words, if one is going to build with logs from deciduous trees, one must recognize their unavoidable tendency to develop cracks and make provisions to compensate for it.

The foregoing discussion allows us to make three generalizations. First, we are dealing with a tradition of craftsmanship. As with all craft traditions, we can observe skill, knowledge, the benefit of experience, and an

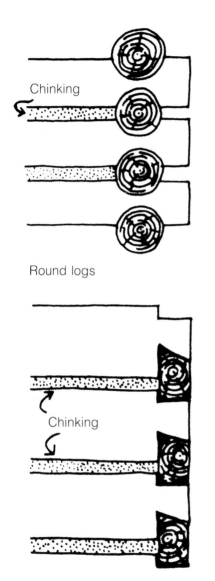

Chinking

Round logs

Chinking

Hewn logs

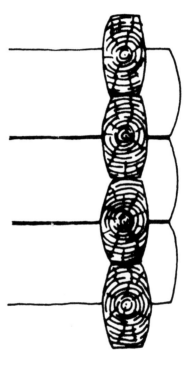

Shaped logs

Figure 20.9. Three Types of Log Construction

understanding of the characteristics of the raw materials. These buildings were not haphazardly thrown together by inexperienced amateurs looking for hasty shelter to be abandoned when time was available to build something better. These buildings were carefully built by men who had the benefit of both past experience and forethought.

Second, this way of building contradicts the generally accepted notion that all log dwellings are "log cabins" hastily thrown together by the pioneer who owned an ax but no other woodworking tools, who cut down trees and piled the round logs thus obtained atop one another with crude notches at the corners in which ends of the logs protrude a foot or more. Some such crude and temporary cabins may indeed have been constructed. That none have survived to the present is not surprising, for they were not intended to last. But if such cabins were built in Dubois County, they represented only a passing, insignificant phase. It is the carefully built and commodious structures that are significant, for they represent an important aspect of the county's architecture.

A third generalization is, simply put, that this way of building with logs is exactly the same as the British-American way but markedly different from the European-German way of building with logs. That the British-American and the German-American way are the same in Dubois County is abundantly clear. The hewing of the sides of the logs but not the tops and bottoms, the use of chinking, the half-dovetail corner notching, and the use of siding are identical. On the other hand, these same features set the German-American way apart from the European-German way. In Germany log buildings have shaped logs (see fig. 20.9). The outer side surfaces of the logs are carefully shaped and smoothed. The tops and bottoms of the logs are likewise carefully shaped so that the logs fit tightly down on one another, so tightly that no chinking is needed. The corners are joined in many ways but never with a half-dovetail joint (a full-dovetail corner joint may be used, but never the half-dovetail). Siding is not normally used over the logs. Moreover, there is actually very little log construction in Germany, and that is confined to a few small areas in the extreme south.[11] The conclusion, therefore, is inescapable. The German immigrants to Dubois County learned how to build with logs from British-Americans.

Origins

Are the Dubois County log buildings German or American? Do these examples of ethnic architecture copy Old World prototypes, or do they follow British-American models? No simple answers can be given.

First, there is a major unknown. We do not know if there is a European-German prototype for the Dubois County log house. So consistent are these houses in their form, size, and layout that we would expect them to be a copy of some common German house. No such common German house has been located. It is probably true that students of German folk architecture have not dealt with houses from the 1830–40 era. They have instead preferred to deal with earlier buildings. It is also puzzling that Germans who came to the United States at about the same time as the Dubois Countians but settled in other parts of the country such as Missouri appear *not* to have built houses of the same form, size, and layout.

After one has examined carefully log houses and barns in Dubois County, it is only possible to say the following: First, in form, size, and layout the log houses do not resemble British-American log houses. They do not, on the other hand, resemble closely any known German prototypes. Second, the log barns closely resemble British-American log barns in areas surrounding Dubois County. They may also resemble European-German barns, but they are virtually identical in form, size, and shape to British-American barns. They do have one feature, a wide overhanging roof along the front, that is, on the one hand, shared with the log houses of the area and, on the other hand, not found in British-American barns. Against this one feature we must balance many others, and the overall resemblance to British-American barns is, therefore, remarkably strong. Third, in regard to the actual technique of shaping logs and fitting them together, the Dubois County structures are built in exactly the same way as British-American ones in surrounding areas. This method of working the logs is remarkably different from the European-German way.

In some important ways the German-American log houses and barns in the Dubois County region resemble British-American log houses and barns in surrounding areas. In other important ways they do not. We cannot say with certainty, however, that in these ways they resemble specific German prototypes. They probably do, but at this time we cannot be certain. To be forced to make these statements is unsatisfactory.

The Doctrine of First Effective Settlement

The foregoing generalizations raise the need to examine a concept of great importance to students of ethnic folk culture in the United States. This is Wilbur Zelinsky's "doctrine of first effective settlement," defined as follows:

> Whenever an empty territory undergoes settlement, or an earlier population is dislodged by invaders, the specific characteristics of the first group able to effect a viable, self-perpetuating society are of crucial significance for the later social and cultural geography of the area, no matter how tiny the initial band of settlers may have been.... Thus, in terms of lasting impact, the activities of a few hundred, or even a few score, initial colonizers can mean much more for the cultural geography of a place than the contributions of tens of thousands of new immigrants a few generations later.[12]

In the case of the Dubois County region, the "earlier population ... dislodged by invaders" would be the Native Americans. The "first group able to effect a viable, self perpetuating society" would be the British-American settlers. The "new immigrants" would, of course, be the German-Americans.

When Zelinsky described the doctrine of first effective settlement, he applied it specifically to the northeastern United States. Does it, however, apply to other regions in the United States? If so, one would be forced to conclude that in most parts of the United States there can be no ethnic folk cultures. That is to say, in most parts of the United States, British-American settlers were the pioneers who displaced the Native Americans and established "a viable, self-perpetuating society" even though these same British-Americans were inundated later by large numbers of new immigrants. These later immigrants, according to Zelinsky, would lose most, or perhaps all, of their Old World culture and conform to the preestablished folk culture of the British-Americans. Hence the doctrine would exclude the possibility of an ethnic folk culture, if we mean by "ethnic folk culture" a group of people retaining Old World elements of significance and in this way differing from the British-American culture.

This article is not the place to discuss all the many questions that the doctrine of first effective settlement raises for study of ethnic folk cultures in the United States. In respect to the log houses and barns of the Dubois County area, we can say that the doctrine explains why these log buildings resemble in significant ways the British-American log buildings in surrounding areas. We can assume that the British-American settlers who were living in the Dubois County area before the German immigrants arrived had built log houses and barns like those throughout southern Indiana. But for the differences that exist between the British-American and German-American log buildings, we must find some other explanation. In this instance therefore, we may say that the doctrine of first effective settlement holds sway only in part.

Appendix: Other Construction Features

To make the record complete, some other features of Dubois County German-American log houses and barns follow.

Foundations. All the log houses and barns investigated sat on cornerstones, usually roughly cubical chunks of local sandstone. The buildings had no cellars, and in this respect they resemble British-American log buildings. (Roberts, *Log Buildings,* pp. 55–57, fig. 4–1.)

Windows. Windows in the log houses that appear to have been installed when the houses were built were of the double-hung sash type; that is each had a fixed upper sash and a lower sash that could be raised. Each sash usually had six panes in a three-over-three configuration. In many houses, probably around 1900, the six-pane sash had been replaced by a sash with two panes side by side. In these respects the windows closely resemble those in British-American log houses. They differ markedly from European-German windows which are nearly always casement windows.

Doors. Most seemingly original doors were of the board-and-batten type; a few were of the panel type. The same may be said for doors in British-American log houses. (Roberts, *Log Buildings,* pp. 107–8, figs. 4–22, 4–23.)

Rafters. In both houses and barns rafters were of a simple paired type usually spiked together at the peak. Most were rough sawn and nearly square in cross section. They are the same as rafters in British-American log houses and barns of the period. (Roberts, *Log Buildings,* pp. 86–89.)

Plates. Most of the houses and barns have no plates in the sense of a special timber at the top of the wall designed especially to receive rafter ends. Instead, the rafters merely rested on the top log inasmuch as the rafters were extended past the log wall to form the roofs for the front porch and rear shed extension. Usually it was not one long timber that served as a rafter, running in one unbroken piece over the main log portion of the building as well as over the porch or shed extension, but a rafter spliced at the log wall. Most British-American log houses and barns have heavy plates rectangular in cross section that are cantilevered out over the wall so that the roof extends several inches out over the wall (Roberts, *Log Buildings,* pp. 71–72, fig. 4–5; see also pl. 11, p. 199.)

Apexes of gable-end walls. When building with logs, one reaches a point in the gable-end walls where it is no longer possible to lock a log at the corner with another log in the long wall. This point is reached where the roof begins. Were one to continue upward with logs in the gable end, some other means of holding those logs in place would be needed. In the Dubois County log houses and barns, however, logs are not used from this point upward; instead, studs, or vertical timbers, are fastened to the top log and to the end rafter. Exactly the same system is used in British-American log buildings. (Roberts, *Log Buildings,* pp. 85–86.)

Notes

1. Elfrieda Lang, "The Settlement of Dubois County," *Indiana Magazine of History* 41:3 (September 1945): 245.

2. Lang, "Settlement," p. 246.

3. An Indiana lady of German ancestry told me that her great-grandfather moved to the Indiana town of Lawrenceburg where he worked as a cooper. As he surveyed his front yard on a cramped city lot, he is reported to have said that if he had owned that much land in Germany he never would have left.

4. Charles van Ravenswaay, *The Arts and Architecture of German Settlements in Missouri* (Columbia: University of Missouri Press, 1977), pp. 14–15 passim. Hesse lived in Osage County, Mo., from 1835 to 1837. After he returned to Europe he wrote *Das westlicher Nordamericka, in besonderer Bezieung auf die deutschen Einwanderer in ihren landwirthschaftlichen, Handels und Gewerbverhältnissen* (Paderborn, 1838).

5. Lang, "Settlement," p. 249.

6. Lang provides data compiled from the 1850 and 1860 censuses. An analysis reveals that nearly 25 percent of the people of German ancestry who settled in Dubois County had previously lived in other states for some time. Elfrieda Lang, "Conditions of Travel Experienced by German Immigrants to Dubois County, Indiana," *Indiana Magazine of History* 41:4 (December 1945): 342–43.

7. Warren E. Roberts, *Log Buildings of Southern Indiana* (Bloomington: Trickster Press, 1984), pp. 115, 122.

8. Franklin County in southeastern Indiana is another area of heavy German settlement. For documented houses and barns there with the same type of cantilevers, see Gary Stanton, "Bought, Borrowed, or Brought: Folklore Sources and Utilization Patterns of the Material Culture of German Immigrants in Southeastern Indiana, 1833–1860" (Ph.D. diss., Indiana University, 1985), chap. 3. Henry Glassie showed me a log shed located in a German-American area near Harrisburg, Pa., which used the same type of cantilevers. For a barn in Darke County, Ohio, with the same cantilevers, although the author does not specify if the barn is in a German-American area, see Donald Hutslar, "The Log Architecture of Ohio," *Ohio History* 80, nos. 3/4 (Summer/Autumn 1971): 224. For illustrations of this construction feature in log buildings in German American areas in Missouri, see van Ravenswaay, *Arts and Architecture,* figs. 6–1, 6–11, 6–20.

9. Roberts, *Log Buildings,* pp. 133–35.

10. For a discussion of the types of evidence concerning the use of siding on log houses, see Roberts, *Log Buildings,* pp. 75–86.

11. For German shaped-log construction, see Roberts, *Log Buildings,* pp. 17–21, 37. Terry Jordan testifies to the marked differences between the European-German way of building with logs and the British-American way. He bases these conclusions on fieldwork in the Black Forest and Canton Bern. He says of the German methods: "Log shaping, corner timbering, spacing in walls, roof construction, and dwelling floorplans all differ in fundamental ways from American types and methods" (Terry G. Jordan, "Alpine, Alemannic, and American Log Architecture," *Annals of the Association of American Geographers* 70:1 [March 1980]: 165).

12. Wilbur Zelinsky, *The Cultural Geography of the United States* (Englewood Cliffs, N.J.: Prentice-Hall, 1973), pp. 13–14.

Afterword

In my introductory essay for this collection of papers I spoke mainly about folklife studies in the past. What about the present? I am happy to be able to say that folklife research is flourishing thanks to the abilities and efforts of a thriving number of younger scholars (younger than I, that is). I feel it is my greatest contribution to folklife studies, and certainly my proudest boast, that many of these scholars did their graduate studies at the Folklore Institute of Indiana University and that I was chair or co-chair for their Ph.D. committees. What I have written over the years is a small contribution compared to those made by my ex-students.

Folklife studies are presently in good hands, then, and much valuable research is being done. It is an especially happy circumstance that scholars in other fields such as history and architectural history are turning to the study of traditional material culture. The Vernacular Architecture Forum is a relatively new but thriving organization composed largely of young architectural historians and the interests of the forum members appear to be primarily in folk architecture. The Pioneer America Society, a meeting ground for scholars in many fields interested in traditional material culture, has recently passed through a changing of the guard and has emerged as strong as ever, a good sign for the present as well as the future.

And what of the future? I hope an ever-growing number of well-trained scholars will continue to swell the ranks of folklife researchers. I hope that more college classes and more museums will deal with folklife so that they can give a truer picture of life in the past, and, finally, I hope that folklife studies can help to present a clearer appreciation of the old traditional way of life so that the contributions made to American life by countless numbers of small farmers, by carpenters, and by other craftsmen may be appreciated and that this appreciation may provide an intellectual basis for democracy, a basis not anchored on the belief that all progress comes from a handful of elite geniuses but from great numbers of intelligent, hardworking people, both men and women, who work with their hands and their minds and constantly improve the things they make or grow and thus contribute to creating a better life for everyone.

Index